"A tribute to a courageous woman who worked to reduce suffering. Dorothy Brooke had to be both compassionate and brave to go to faraway places to help horses."
—TEMPLE GRANDIN, author of *Animals Make Us Human*

"The legacy of Dorothy Brooke is extraordinary. Her work was inspired in part by another wonderful woman, the founder of World Horse Welfare, Ada Cole. Together they inspired the transformation of the lives of so many animals for the better. This is a story that is truly worthy of being told."
—ROLY OWERS, chief executive of World Horse Welfare

"A story of deep connection, compassion, empathy, and love. Thanks to the author for making Dorothy Brooke visible, and for taking the time to tell us about a most amazing and compassionate woman."
—MARC BEKOFF, author of *The Animals' Agenda: Freedom, Compassion, and Coexistence in the Human Age*

"For more than six thousand years, horses have given their flesh, their strength, their patience, and above all their spirit to the human enterprise. But beyond facilities needed to further exploit these gifts, humans have given surprisingly little back. Grant Hayter-Menzies movingly recovers the life of a determined and resourceful woman who dedicated herself to the rescue of horses. . . . Dorothy Brooke paid a bit back, changing the lives of many thousands of worthy horses, donkeys, and mules then and since."
—DR. PAMELA KYLE CROSSLEY, coauthor of *The Earth and Its Peoples*

"This lovingly researched, evocative biography of Dorothy Brooke proves her a heroine not just to the battered and beaten old war horses she saved in 1930s Cairo but to those who continue her legacy today."
—SUSANNA FORREST, author of *The Age of the Horse*

THE
LOST WAR
HORSES OF
CAIRO

THE
LOST WAR
HORSES OF
CAIRO

The Passion of Dorothy Brooke

Grant Hayter-Menzies

Foreword by Monty Roberts
Introduction by Evelyn Webb-Carter

ALLEN&UNWIN

First published in the United States in 2017 by Potomac Books, an imprint of the University of Nebraska Press, under the title *Dorothy Brooke and the Fight to Save Cairo's Lost War Horses*

This paperback edition published in Great Britain in 2018 by Allen & Unwin

Allen & Unwin
c/o Atlantic Books
Ormond House
26–27 Boswell Street
London WC1N 3JZ

Phone: 020 7269 1610
Fax: 020 7430 0916
Email: UK@allenandunwin.com
Web: www.allenandunwin.com/uk

A CIP catalogue record for this book is available from the British Library.
Set in Garamond Premier Pro by John Klopping

Paperback ISBN 978 1 76063 144 4
E-Book ISBN 978 1 76063 881 8

Printed in Italy by 🦌 Grafica Veneta

10 9 8 7 6 5 4 3 2 1

In honor of Cupid and of all the horses, mules, and
donkeys whose heroism never faltered in battles
they did nothing to cause

> In defense of all the animals who still
> today find themselves caught in the
> unending crossfire of human discord

In memory of my parents

> To Rudi, with love

Forty percent of the author's royalties will be
donated to the Brooke Hospital for Animals

A Soldier's Kiss

Only a dying horse! Pull off the gear,
And slip the needless bit from frothing jaws,
Drag it aside there, leaving the roadway clear,
The battery thunders on with scarce a pause.

Prone by the shell-swept highway there it lies
With quivering limbs, as fast the life-tide fails,
Dark films are closing o'er the faithful eyes
That mutely plead for aid where none avails.

Onward the battery rolls, but one there speeds
Heedless of comrade's voice or bursting shell,
Back to the wounded friend who lonely bleeds
Beside the stony highway where he fell.

Only a dying horse! He swiftly kneels,
Lifts the limp head and hears the shivering sigh
Kisses his friend, while down his cheek there steals
Sweet pity's tear, "Goodbye old man, goodbye."

No honours wait him, medal, badge or star,
Though scarce could war a kindlier deed unfold;
He bears within his breast, more precious far
Beyond the gift of kings, a heart of gold.

—HENRY CHAPPELL

CONTENTS

ILLUSTRATIONS

FOREWORD

Anyone who knows my work with and love for equines also knows my core principle—to leave the world a better place, not only for animals but for people, too. Because without our care, the animals who delight us, who serve us, cannot be healthy or happy.

Yet too many working horses, mules, and donkeys around the world are neither. That's why I support the work of Brooke, as a Global Ambassador and as a man who loves horses.

I feel a synergy with Brooke, which works to ease the suffering of working equines through education of owners as well as through free expert veterinary care for animals.

I also feel a kinship with Mrs. Dorothy Brooke, the organization's founder. Mrs. Brooke saw suffering and did not look the other way. She rolled her sleeves up and got to work.

Brooke still does this, every day, in countries around the globe. As you read Grant Hayter-Menzies's moving account of how an English general's wife saved the lost war horses of Cairo, I know you will be as inspired as I am to follow her example and help make the world a kinder, healthier place for the animals who serve us and love us. As Mrs. Brooke well knew, compassion is the key.

Monty Roberts

PREFACE

When I was about seven years old, and out shopping with my mother, I convinced her to take me into a pet store located in a central California town near where we lived. Those were the days when we didn't know everything we do now about these happily named places of unhappy business.

I remember going into this particular store, holding my mother's hand, and walking down a corridor lined with wire boxes. Animals were living in them—a charitable word, *living*—and most seemed to be nervously eating or hiding or both. I stopped at one cage. In it was a fluffy ginger guinea pig. She was smaller than the others hopping and chortling around her. Her gaze seemed lusterless as she sat there, looking out from the cage; she seemed fragile as the larger, more vigorous guinea pigs raced around her. I asked my mother if I might have her. The store owner told me she was a bad choice because she was ill and wouldn't live long. That made me persist. And I began to cry. I knew the little ginger guinea pig was indeed what the man called "the runt of the litter." Her dim eyes didn't shine like those of the others. She seemed just to want to go to sleep and never wake up. But I couldn't bear to let that happen. I had to try to save her.

My mother gave in.

Making Rosie happy became the sole reason for my existence. I put her in a cage, for which my father had made her a little wooden house to hide in. I gave her special treats—lettuce, fortified biscuits we'd bought from the pet store, fresh water every day. I took her out and held her in the sunshine, which made her red fur look strangely pale. I was so sure that my love could help her get better that when I came home from school and saw the look on my mother's face, I refused to believe that Rosie was dead. "I found her that way this morning," my mother explained. We looked at the little ginger body lying still. I'd written "ROSIE" over the door of her house, but she had died outside it, as if she wanted death to come and claim her with the least amount of trouble. "At least she knew you loved her," said my mother.

I was touched, therefore, to find that Dorothy Brooke, whose rescue of elderly and abused former war horses and army mules forms the subject of this book, was also drawn to what her chief veterinarian Dr. Murad Raghib called "the destruction cases"—the animals purchased from their owners at Dorothy's Cairo hospital with the express purpose of giving them a few days of rest, feed, water, and treats, before sending them off to what Dorothy hoped was the leafy green meadow of equine heaven. She knew, to quote Anatole France, that "until one has loved an animal, a part of one's soul remains unawakened." And that until one has reached out to help an animal in need, the purpose of that love seems wasted.

Dorothy Brooke's soul was awakened one fall day in 1930 Cairo, when she first glimpsed sick and starving cab horses at the city's main train station, English horses with the arrow brand of the British Army still visible on their flanks. A woman of privileged background, who was only in Egypt because her officer husband was posted there, Dorothy looked at these animals' ravaged bodies and into their lifeless eyes, and she knew that something needed to be done, and that she was the one to do it. She would spend the next quarter-century of her life working to help ease the sufferings of these betrayed warriors. Once she had rescued all of the war horses that she could find, she turned to the sufferings of native horses, mules, and donkeys. And she developed a philosophy for their human owners, caught in the same wheel of pain as their working animals. Blame poverty, Dorothy said, not the men degraded by it. Strike the problem at its root—the need for education of owners in proper, regular care for their animals—and you will have improved the life not just of animals but of owners, of families, perhaps even of society as a whole.

The beauty of Dorothy Brooke's holistic vision is not just that it was put into practice long before such thinking was a normal ingredient for a healthy animal welfare program, or that it proved to be such a success, not merely for the animals and their owners but for the survival of Dorothy's hospital in Sayyida Zeinab district, where it remains busy today. It is that Dorothy's vision proved to have a life of its own.

Spawned by her hospital in Cairo, Brooke, one of the world's largest animal welfare charities, now works in eleven developing nations, addressing veterinary care and education for children and adults, which together have helped desperate animals in the thousands. And, I like to think, it has helped push humanity closer to an understanding of what we owe the animals who help us prosper, whom we love and who love us in return.

INTRODUCTION

When my mother died, I found a small, well-thumbed book by her bedside. The book was *For Love of Horses*, Glenda Spooner's compilation of the diaries of Dorothy Brooke, founder of the Brooke Hospital for Animals in Cairo, Egypt.

It was an early edition, and I just put it in my bookshelves and thought little more about it, until one day somebody mentioned the Brooke charity and the story that started it all, and I vaguely remembered I had seen a copy somewhere. In due course I found it and was fascinated by what I read.

Much of my leisure time has been spent in the company of horses, whether hunting, playing polo, or trekking along old military campaign routes in scattered parts of the world. I have been lucky, too, that in the course of my career I have been required to ride in several ceremonial parades, a particularly pleasant duty. So all in all, I owe a lot to my "long faced" friend.

Once my working days were over, an opportunity rose to be chairman of Brooke, and with great good fortune I caught the selector's eye. It is in that capacity that I write this introduction.

This book, beautifully written by Grant Hayter-Menzies, tells a story that has not been fully explained before, and it is good that those of us who admire the work of Dorothy Brooke will now know how the charity started and was able to develop to what it is today, a global charity that works in eleven countries around the world. Imagine how Dorothy would have felt seeing how her idea has developed since her death.

A few years ago I visited Dorothy's grave in Cairo, and it was this that went through my mind. Her legacy is with us today, and it is admirable that Grant Hayter-Menzies wishes to tell the story and does this so well. Dorothy would have been delighted.

Maj. Gen. Sir Evelyn Webb-Carter

THE
LOST WAR
HORSES OF
CAIRO

Prologue

Dorothy

Egypt, thou knew'st too well,
My heart was to thy rudder tied by the strings,
And thou shouldst tow me after.

—WILLIAM SHAKESPEARE

I f we were scanning the manifest for a particular ship sailing from England to Port Said, Egypt, in October 1930, we would notice nothing very much out of the ordinary.

Reading down the columns, scored in blue and red lines on paper of a pale official green, we would meet merchants and colonial officials on their way "out" east, teachers and remittance men and missionaries and what Max Rodenbeck terms "the Imperial Fishing Fleet . . . the flotilla of debutantes who set out from home each winter with the express aim of trauling for a husband in the British colonial service."[1]

They came from Belfast and Glasgow, Fareham and Portsmouth, London and Edinburgh, like a lot of other people sailing east that season. And among them we would see the names of a couple who by all available information were pretty much like most other people on that sailing. They were Geoffrey Brooke, a British cavalry officer, and his wife, Dorothy. Both were in their late forties.

The Brookes were en route to Cairo. Though Egypt had become a sovereign state in 1922, British forces after the close of the Great War had kept a foot in the door, protective of Egypt and of the Suez Canal as gateway, among other things, to India. As such, they had left behind small occupying forces like the British Cavalry Brigade, which Geoffrey Brooke was coming out to Egypt's capital city to command.

The Brookes were similar in appearance and personality, each tall, lanky, and lithe. Brought up riding ponies and horses since childhood, they seemed to take on equine characteristics themselves. With Geoffrey, a champion jumper in younger years, this was especially apparent; photographs of him on horseback give the impression of a man who was as much horse as human, so that it is difficult to see where one begins and the other ends. Despite being well into what was, in 1930, considered to be middle age, the couple shared a gracile stance characteristic of blooded horses, a relaxed ease often seen in upper-class people who amid privilege had been trained never to take anything for granted, to live a combined credo of the Golden Rule drilled into them in their nurseries, alongside unfailing noblesse oblige.

Had you seen them walking together on the deck of their ship, you might think the Brookes a pair who had been together for most of their lives—indeed, for so long that any individual idiosyncrasies long ago blended into equal halves of the same person. They were certainly soul mates who shared, among other things, a deep love of horses. But they had only been married four years earlier, after lives spent with others had broken up and sunk, like the old world of czars and sultans and country houses to which both had been bred, after the world-altering devastation of World War I.

We know that for Dorothy, it was love at first sight. And events were to bear evidence that, for Geoffrey, it was very much the same— love that kept its promise to stay firm through better or worse.

Both Brookes came from backgrounds deeply rooted in the British Isles.

Geoffrey Brooke, who could have been describing himself when he wrote, in his novel *Horse Lovers*, "he was decidedly slim in limb and body, punctiliously neat in dress," was born June 14, 1884, in Dublin into the Protestant Anglo-Irish landowning class. His family connections brought him within reach of Continental aristocracy—one of his cousins was the peppery, exuberant, and brave Daisy Princess of Pless, English-born consort of a Prussian aristocrat, who wrote of Brooke in her diaries. Brooke's trajectory took him farther afield than Central Europe, all the way to Russia, where in 1906 he was assigned to the British Embassy in St. Petersburg, serving with the Sixteenth Royal Lancers.[2]

Not long after he arrived, Brooke met a Russian noblewoman, Baroness Vera von Salza, a general's daughter born in Tsarskoye Selo who was fourteen years his senior, and they were married in London on October 14, 1908. Already married and divorced—as her English marriage license manages to fit into the small box provided for "Condition," she was "previously the wife of Stanislas Lucien Alfred Gabriel Mechin Baron Mechin to whom she was married in Russia and from whom she obtained a divorce in France"—Vera had grown up in wealth that was to be cancelled abruptly by the Russian Revolutions of 1917–18.[3] That future cataclysm was unimaginable to the young couple, as to most Russians, but the events that led to the demise of imperial Russia and a clutch of other kingdoms came quickly enough when the assassination of an Austrian archduke in Sarajevo suddenly jerked the seal ribbons of dozens of international treaties.

On that day, June 28, 1914, the world as everyone then knew it began to slip like a broad, deceptively placid river, moving ever faster toward the brink of a raging waterfall. Established realities changed forever that Sunday. Levers and gears set in place by the abuses of empires old and fading and young and foolhardy, and a general failure of diplomacy so criminally incompetent no punishment could compensate for the destruction it unleashed, clicked and began to function as a machine that created, with all the mechanical precision of the age, a comprehensive, all-destroying worldwide war. So began the toppling of thrones across Europe, the snuffing out of lights in ballrooms and boardrooms that people had assumed would burn forever, replaced by signal flares and exploding gunpowder and miles of war-torn desolation.

Poets like John Masefield, in his midthirties when the war broke out, already saw what was coming for "generations of dead men" when he wrote that first August of

The harvest not yet won, the empty bin,
The friendly horses taken from the stall,
The fallow on the hill not yet brought in,
The cracks unplastered on the leaking walls.

Whether in "the misery of the soaking trench" or "freezing in the rigging," these men would know only a puzzled despair in that moment of death, "when the blind soul is flung upon the air," dying for an idea "but dimly understood." Just as poignant is his image of "friendly horses" being taken from their familiar stalls and also, like the human soldiers, flung into a void.[4]

Geoffrey had played a significant role in the conflict, serving as lieutenant-captain and then staff captain of the Third Cavalry Brigade the year the war began. He became brigade-major of the Second Cavalry Brigade the next year and in 1918 served in that capacity with the Canadian Cavalry Brigade. In the war he rode two of his prize mounts: Alice, who was injured and taken home, and Combined Training, who was wounded but stayed with his master and was fit enough to win the King George V Gold Cup for Geoffrey for show jumping in 1921.[5]

It was in this final year of the war that Geoffrey, who had already been recognized for bravery (one of the first officers to be gazetted for the Military Cross, in 1915), took part in a battle that assigns him a place in history and connects him to one of the most savagely bloody sallies of the war. At the end of March 1918, as commander of the Sixteenth Lancers, Geoffrey led what is considered the last major cavalry charge of military history, in which nineteenth-century equine culture flung itself at twentieth-century firepower, in the form of German machine gunners from the Twenty-Third Saxon Division entrenched in Moreuil Wood southeast of Amiens. The cost to men and horses was enormous, but the Saxon Division was forced from the Wood (twice, since they regained it the next day), and with this battle the slow but steady disintegration of Germany's Spring Offensive began. For his part in the charge, Geoffrey was awarded the Distinguished Service Order, as well as the Croix de Guerre.[6]

Emerging intact from a war that had swallowed up so many other men, whole or in part, Geoffrey returned to England and passed Staff College in 1920. Between then and 1923, when he served as chief instructor of cavalry at Weedon in Northamptonshire, Geoffrey and his Russian wife (with whom he had had a son, Peter, in 1909) were divorced. As was often the case with couples who by some miracle had made it through the cataclysm together, the Brookes found themselves too changed to continue that bond after it was over. Geoffrey seems to be describing their marriage and Vera's intense personality in the wife of Archie Languid, characters in his 1927 novel *Horse Lovers*. Mrs. Languid "was an erratic, self-centred creature, incapable of deep affection, and a good many years his senior" who had a passion for gambling and disliked living in the country, "whereas Archie's chief interest in life lay in his estate and his horses. . . . A makeshift, peace-at-any-price domestic policy gradually developed into sullen warfare, and eventually resulted in the breaking of the nuptial ties." The break was perhaps not helped by the fact that Vera Brooke's family, and thus Vera herself, had lost everything they owned and the lives of several family members to the revolution. Vera's later life is not known, though she did leave Geoffrey with several Fabergé objects, mere remnants of her family's former Russian splendor.[7]

For his part, as a bachelor again Geoffrey began to pour his encyclopedic knowledge of horses into books in a literary stream that enlarged to a cataract. Starting in 1924 and continuing for another thirty years, Geoffrey would publish several volumes, nonfiction and fiction, on horse training, hunting with horses, riding and stablecraft, polo ponies, the foibles and virtues of the horse set, and everything in between. He wrote of horses with a sensitivity that stands out all the more, considering what he had witnessed them endure in battle. "The real lover of horses is a student of equine psychology," Geoffrey wrote in 1924, "and finds in the horse those qualities so beloved by man—courage, unselfishness, fidelity. What more does one ask for in a friend?"[8]

Geoffrey might well have continued in this course, focused on his stables, his writing, and his surviving comrades at arms as they reminisced every year on Remembrance Day. But he was to meet a woman who, while so similar to his own nature and interests, was just unique enough to change the course of his life completely.

Dorothy Evelyn Gibson-Craig was born in Melrose, Scotland, on June 1, 1884.[9]

She arrived a few days after the seventy-first birthday of Queen Victoria, whose Golden Jubilee marking her fiftieth year on the throne would be celebrated three years later. In a more than coincidental sense, Dorothy, whose nickname among family and friends was Dodo, was born with one foot in the twentieth century, the era of greater rights and freedoms for women, and the other in the nineteenth, when compassion for the rights of animals first took deepest root, alongside abolition of chattel slavery and child labor, as a social concern.

Young Dorothy, who was followed by siblings Cecilia (Cicely) Dulcibella, Eardley Charles William (later sixth/thirteenth baronet), and Marjorie Violet, was a daughter of Henry Vivian Gibson-Craig and wife, Emily Dulcibella Wilmot, and granddaughter of Sir William Gibson-Craig, second baronet. The family seat, Riccarton, was a massive gabled stone mansion in Edinburgh, much influenced by the Scottish Baroque style made de rigueur by the historical novels and histrionic tastes of Sir Walter Scott. The house was demolished in 1956, a year after Dorothy's death, and its grounds are now the location of Heriot-Watt University, but its cemetery remains the property of the Gibson-Craigs. Many of the family members interred there fought or died in the two world wars of the twentieth century—a link with soldiers and warfare that was to thread itself throughout Dorothy's future life and the work to which she devoted it.[10]

In 1905 Dorothy, who had grown up to be a willowy beauty, became the wife of Lt. Col. James Gerald Lamb Searight of the Royal Scots (Lothian Regiment). Born in 1878, Searight, whose family nickname was Gerry, was a thin, angular man who had served in the Boer War in South Africa (1899–1902). How they met we do not know, but Dorothy married Gerry in Great Kimble Church in

Buckinghamshire. Gerry suffered from an illness contracted in South Africa and was in many ways still an invalid when he married Dorothy. Her willingness to marry a man believed to be terminally ill has much about it that foreshadows her future work with sick and dying horses in Egypt. As it happened, Gerry did live on, dying in his eighties in 1959, and the Searights had three healthy children over the next several years: two sons, Rodney, born in 1909, and Philip, born in 1916, and daughter Pamela (Pinkie), born in 1915.[11]

Despite his long life, Gerry's health never completely righted itself. This, however, did not stop him from wishing to be of service at the outbreak of the Great War. Gerry served as lieutenant-colonel, commandant, in the Royal Defence Corps. This home-based unit was composed of garrison battalions formed in 1917 in which soldiers who, for reasons related to age or health, were not considered fit to take part in the fighting overseas but able enough to do their bit at home. This was a job that allowed Gerry to remain close to home yet play a significant role in defending the nation. He was judged by others to have carried it out extremely well: for his service, Gerry was awarded the Order of the British Empire.[12] Dorothy demonstrated bravery of her own by remaining in London with her children; her youngest, Philip, had an abiding early memory of having to dart under a table in his nursery when zeppelins floated, eerily clanking in the dark, over the city, a trial run for the Blitz of 1940.[13]

Dorothy and Geoffrey may have met some time shortly after the end of the war, perhaps as early as 1919. These were the years composing what Juliet Nicolson terms "the great silence"—when, between the deafening noise of war and the frantic music of the Jazz Age, the "English habit of maintaining difficult feelings was to suppress rather than discuss them, as if by remaining silent the feelings would disappear."[14] Under this thinnest of veneers applied for the most irrelevant of reasons boiled storms of bereavement, bitterness, passion. Whatever was happening between Gerry and Dorothy, it seems to have been well concealed, at least from those around them, and perhaps from each other, in the approved English way; yet storms of the heart are rarely containable. Geoffrey divorced Vera in 1922, and after Dorothy and Gerry were divorced, Geoffrey and Dorothy had a Registry Office marriage. They lived at Tidworth, Wilt-shire, where Geoffrey served as colonel of the Sixteenth Lancers until called up to take the Cavalry Brigade post in Cairo—which brings us to four years later, when their ship docked in Port Said and they disembarked in the autumn heat, so at variance from the damp cool of the English October they had left. They had a four-hour train journey ahead of them to Cairo.

Some of those 124 miles ran along the Suez Canal, tribute to the genius of human ingenuity and bone of contention in past and future wars. Dug in 1859 to link the Red Sea and the Mediterranean and obviate the lengthy and expensive sea journey around the horn of Africa, the canal, worked by the forced labor of thousands of Egyp-tians, was completed ten years later. It opened to great fanfare, with the khedive (viceroy) of Egypt, Isma'il, barging down the waterway with the Empress Eugénie of France beside him, their ship surely a wondrous sight to desert Bedouin who from a distance would have glimpsed sails and prow floating magically through desert dunes. Though plagued by cost overruns, the canal proved as great a boon to shipping as predicted, but, as mentioned, it was also and almost from the start a curse to peace. After helping the khedival government put down a native uprising in northern Egypt, Britain was recom-pensed with occupation of Egypt and Sudan, along with respon-sibility for protecting the canal (and reaping its benefits). Because Egypt was technically part of the Ottoman Empire, this set up ten-sion between the two imperial powers. When the Great War broke out and the Turks sided with Germany, seizing the canal became the aim of both the Sublime Porte (the Ottoman imperial court) and Berlin. Britain sent an army to defend the canal, which is why so many English horses had been brought, blinking, to the shim-mering deserts of Egypt, the Sinai, and Palestine in the Great War.

Not one to rhapsodize on scenery, Dorothy was more likely focused not on the sand-strewn topography rushing past her pas-senger car window but organizing her thoughts on what she would need to do to manage her new household in the Cairo suburb of Heliopolis, and on the busy social calendar that came with being the wife of the commander of the British Cavalry Brigade. According to Glenda Spooner, a close friend, from the very start "Dodo had social chains" that she could not break—she would have to field five hundred callers just in the first month and a half of taking residence in Cairo. As Florence Nightingale, to whom Dorothy would one day be compared, wrote in her mid-Victorian complaint against the narrowed roles expected of Victorian women, "Women have no means given them whereby they can resist the 'claims of social life,'" taught as they were that a woman wasn't a lady if she didn't happily permit herself "to be interrupted at all hours," regardless of her hopes, dreams, or plans. Claims on Dorothy's time would not be merely enacted within the Brooke villa; both Brookes faced obligations to dine out "three days a week, [give] dinner parties themselves on two nights as well as a lunch party every Sunday, followed by 'being at home' that day to about thirty people," wrote Spooner. Of these details Dorothy and Geoffrey were still mercifully less aware than they would be once their train reached Cairo, which itself was a setting rich with much that was, to them, at that moment utterly unknown, save for the geography classroom imagery and basic facts all people of their generation had at their fingertips, conveniently colored pink on maps of the British empire.[15]

By the time of the Brookes' arrival in October 1930, Cairo had passed through thousands of autumns and remained much the same as when it began, in legend, as the cosmic battleground of Set, god of war and upheaval, and Horus, god of sun and life. The very name of Egypt's capital, Cairo—*al-Qāhirah*—refers to victory in battle. The rival gods' wrestling match had been a stalemate, but afterward many other more mortal armies had conquered the city over its millennia of existence, establishing periods of light between periods of darkness, as well as darkness in periods of light, along with overlapping layers of cultural influences. Successive waves of dynasties followed the reigns of the pharaohs responsible for building the pyramids at Giza and the temples and tombs at Memphis, on the opposite side of the Nile. The British had been a force in Egypt since the last decades of the nineteenth century, having instituted what Wilfrid Blunt called a "veiled protectorate," but foreign influence, including successive waves of refugees from a variety of nations, had long been part of Cairo's makeup and often a source of as many vices as virtues. By the time the Brookes arrived in fall 1930, Cairo was less a garrison for Britain than a popular wintering place for wealthy foreigners, like the debutantes referenced by Max Rodenbeck, or prancing through Agatha Christie's *Death on the Nile*, the last line of which—"It is not the past that matters, but the future"— contains the seed of what was to end this colonialist fantasy world a quarter century later.[16]

Pathé newsreel cameras from the 1920s and 1930s offer us glimpses of what awaited Dorothy and Geoffrey Brooke on their arrival in the Egyptian capital. In the flickering frames, one sees elegantly garbed Europeans seated on the terrace at Shepheard's Hotel, with its arching sign on the roof, gazing down with a certain dismissive indifference at robed tourist guides being harangued by police, guides who would take some of these same tourists, clad in incongruous spats or silk frocks, on the backs of camels to the pyramids or through the plundered detritus of temples whose histories they made up as they went along, gesticulating under impassive smiles of stone kings. Or the newsreel lenses might shift from panoramas of the golden dusty city, glimpsing domes and minarets, bazaars crowded with men in *gelabiya*, selling a thousand and one things or services under awnings or in alleyways, to focus on the water carriers, each bent brown back bearing a shining darker brown goatskin bladder filled at the lip of the broad Nile, the life-giving and dangerous river whose flat surface was crowded with the billowing wings of felucca sails. Or they might observe one of the many demonstrations, usually by young people, that erupted on certain days when students, according to a British satirist, "having found their examination papers beyond their powers, . . . had downed their books and gone into the street yelling for 'Independence.'"[17] (If anything, these youths were as keen for independence from their parents' bourgeois aspirations to French culture as they were from British rule.)

From the terrace at Shepheard's, those foreigners just passing through might also observe the quieter processions of Muslim men holding aloft draped coffins en route to quick burial before sundown, weaving their dignified way among the spluttering motorcars already clogging every street in the city. And threading their way among them they would see horse-drawn trams (then in the process of being replaced by electric ones) or horses pulling cabs known as gharries, and mules with panniers filled with goods rocking on their backs or hitched to simple carts, their enormous wheels dwarfed by the combined loads of supplies and several human passengers. Even allowing for the jerkiness of old celluloid footage, it is obvious from the newsreels that the animals had to give a strained heave to gain forward momentum in pulling these overly heavy loads. Judging from their thin legs and visible ribs, they had little muscle with which to do so—today as then, working equines are often hired from stable owners whose lack of care of the animals the hirer is in no financial position to remedy, making the animals' situation worse. So off they struggle, the bony horses and mules of 1932. Like many working equines of the twenty-first century, they drag their burdens through crowds busied with more immediate matters, under the eyes of tourists focused not on present pain but on taking in a fantasy of past glories.

Dorothy was not a naive foreigner arriving in the Middle East blinkered to conditions existing there. According to her granddaughter, travel writer Sarah Searight, Dorothy had already heard enough about the sad circumstances of Egyptian equines to seek out evidence for this shortly after she arrived. And she had already been moved to action by the plight of horses suffering in her own country. In 1926, Dorothy had become a founding member of the International League for the Protection of Horses (ILPH), now World Horse Welfare, the brainchild of a Norfolk woman named Ada Cole. While living as a nun in Antwerp, Cole had witnessed sick, elderly English workhorses, most of them half-dead from a rough sailing across the Channel, being whipped down a gangplank and marched for miles to be butchered in a Belgian abattoir. Cole's efforts resulted in the banning in 1937 of exportation of live horses from Great Britain for slaughter (a practice still present in the United States and Canada) and formed the basis for the ILPH and its wider-reaching work to improve equine welfare around the world. There is little doubt that the organization that Dorothy would found in

Egypt derived a good part of its inspiration in Ada Cole's work for compassionate treatment and euthanization of working equines.[18]

But timing is everything. By 1930 the world's attention had turned away from the horrors, human and animal, of the Great War. The stock market crash in 1929 and subsequent worldwide economic depression had clamped down on partiers living high on a boom that could not last. If the frenzied celebration had been a way of forgetting the loss of a whole generation of young men a decade before, the despair of the downturn focused attention more on present-tense survival than past losses, which postcrash could no longer be contemplated through a haze of champagne. Nobody wanted to be reminded of a war that was, after all, meant to end them all, the cost of which was even then being weighed as draconian compared to the benefits attained. And so, as acts of heroism by British forces continued to loom large from the battlefields of memory, these were mostly confined to the stage of the European theatre of war—the fields of Flanders, the forests of the Argonne, from which had flowed so much blood and poetry. The battles in the eastern Mediterranean became a footnote to these European struggles. Aside from the writings of T. E. Lawrence, first made public in 1922, there was not much said or thought about the desert campaigns—in Egypt, Persia, Syria—of the Great War, which had taken place concurrently with action on the western front. Of those who did remember, their voices were not always welcome, their service considered more vacation than warfare compared to action in the French trenches—underscored by the opinion that the eastern front need never have been fought in the first place. The conversation and the controversy continue today. Journalist Khaled Diab has speculated that "had Turkey emerged victorious or not taken up arms, the Ottoman Empire would not have been partitioned, and the Sykes-Picot carve-up, which has given the Middle East some of its most troubled borders, would not have taken place—at least not then." But the Ottomans distrusted the British more than they disliked the Germans, and the Germans "were prepared to go to extraordinary lengths of mendacity in order to rouse the Mohammedan world," writes A. J. Barker, and there was no difficulty, in a nation that was to expunge anything not strictly Aryan from its pedigrees only a generation later, finding an alleged descent for the Hohenzollern family, to which the kaiser belonged, from a sister of the Arab Prophet Mohammed (peace be upon him).[19]

This, along with promises of a more material nature, proved heady stuff for the Turks. So the "sick man of Europe" looked to Germany as its last hope for resuscitation and for regaining its lost Egyptian province. A year after the outbreak of the European conflict the Turks, allying themselves with the kaiser at the last minute, attempted to seize the Suez Canal, Britain's most valuable route to India, which all nations coveted. Concerned with protecting its Berlin to Baghdad railway, which didn't stand much of a chance with England as effective suzerain of Egypt (regardless of the fact that it came under Ottoman rule), Germany needed Turkey's proximity as much as Turkey needed its firepower. To meet this threat, the Egyptian Expeditionary Force (EEF) was assembled by the British Army in March 1916, and what came to be called the Sinai and Palestine Campaign began.

The sacrifices made by men and women in the east were bitterly real. What we do not hear about as often as the sacrifices warrant are stories of the other soldiers—the "long-faced chums," as they would be described in later years—who fought in the sands of the east. Helping win the battles of Romani, Gaza, and Jerusalem, among many skirmishes that determined the course of the war, were horses, mules, and donkeys, most drawn from England, Canada, Australia, New Zealand, and the United States (starting in 1914, four years before human soldiers shipped out to the war). Many had originally been transported to the European front, where they had already seen service in the slimy, frigid death pits of trenches and shell craters before being shipped further to the heat, sand, and flies of the desert east. And it was to be there that those animals who survived combat, harsh conditions, exhaustion, and starvation were to be left behind like surplus equipment, falling under the control of a native population who, in general, held concepts of animal husbandry very different from where the animals had been born and bred. The animals' Egyptian owners were for the most part very poor people who had been kicked around by life, men who seldom had enough to feed their families and who could not spare patience or compassion for the beasts of burden they, and the British Army, had made of former war horses. Stories circulated about members of Yeomanry regiments riding their mounts into the desert and shooting them rather than have them fall into the hands of Egyptians, whose abuse of animals they had witnessed in certain instances and believed was widespread. Even if this did happen, it provided release for a comparative few. Most of those horses that lived on were worked till injury or other infirmities passed them down the chain to where even a poor man could afford to work an animal to death if he got a good day's labor from it, since, after all, he had paid very little to purchase it—the terrible arithmetic of market forces and the diminishing returns of hard labor. A poem, "The Remount Train," published in the *Brisbane Courier* in October 1918, spoke to these animals' collective fate:

> Wave the flag, and let them go
> Hats off to that wistful row
> Of lean heads of brown and bay
> Black and chestnut, roan and grey
> Here's good luck in lands afar
> Snow White streak, and blaze, and star
> May you find in those far lands
> Kindly hearts and horsemen's hands.

On the October afternoon in 1930 when she arrived with Geoffrey at Ramses Station in Cairo, Dorothy was likely still cogitating over organizing the life that lay ahead of them for the next few years in this hot, dusty, crowded, and strange city. They were waiting for their car when Dorothy happened to notice her own wistful row of lean heads brown and bay.

Several pairs of emaciated, ragged gharry (taxi) horses stood, heads bowed, their drivers bartering loudly for passengers. A gharry, derived from the Swahili word for *cart*, was a form of public transportation in Cairo, differing in size, shape, and comfort for passengers, well known to visitors throughout what foreigners called "the

East." Almost forty years earlier, one such visitor was to write of the "dozens of ramshackle vehicles drawn by animals for which it would be hard to find an English name that would convey an adequate idea of their shape and build," greeting him at the docks in Calcutta. It seemed incredible to him that the "lean and bony" cab horses of Calcutta could pull anything, but they did because, of course, they had to. The sight of underfed draft horses attempting to pull overweight gharries was, in Cairo, the least of what many foreigners in the city saw daily. Honor Baines, an Englishwoman who would later support Dorothy's charitable work, recalled arriving in Cairo with her parents around this time. Only six years old, she saw "ponies and donkeys, flies covering their eyes and noses and sores, the animals so thin that one could, as my father said, hang a hat on their withers. I can also remember seeing animals left to die in the sun."[20]

Though Dorothy and Geoffrey had been given some idea that they would find much to alarm them in the streets of Cairo, the gharry horses were even more mortifying because of an added trenchant detail. Dorothy immediately noticed the horses' size, which, even in their wasted condition, made them tower over native Arabs. Then she saw something else. Against the background of a wasted flank, still clearly visible, was the jaunty arrow-shaped brand of the British Army. These haggard nags standing in the hot sun were not only English horses; they were former war horses, animals whose efforts had helped win the Great War. "Although they were battered by Cairo traffic," wrote Sarah Searight, "as under-nourished as their owners, some reduced to skin and bones, [Dorothy] nevertheless could distinguish the magnificent frames of the Percherons and Walers that had carried cavalry regiments to war and kept them armed and fed. A Cairo gharry was a poor reward."[21]

This was only a glimpse. Then a shining car arrived, and Dorothy and Geoffrey were whisked away from the heat and dust of the station, from the silent misery of the abandoned war horses, to a pleasant villa in Heliopolis that would be their Egyptian home for the next several years, a place of parties and merriment.

But the sight of those horses had shaken Dorothy Brooke's life to its core.

At the same time, an idea began to take root that only grew stronger the more it was opposed, doubted, discouraged, even attacked. Dorothy needed to help these battered war horses. And she needed to find all the others rumor claimed were to be located within the city or in the quarries outside on its limits, still laboring despite age, illness, injuries, despair. The thin rumps and jutting spines of the gharry horses would prompt in Dorothy a shift in thinking not just about caring properly for working horses but why they *should* be cared for—to honor the right of a working animal to have a life free of pain, hunger, and thirst, and to get to the root cause of why their owners, for whom they were the sole source of income, would neglect and even abuse them in the first place.

As Dorothy would learn in time, too often these owners were themselves disenfranchised, judged low on the scale of worldly values. Evicted from work they and their ancestors had always known on farms that spread out from the Nile, these peasant farmers were victims of centralization of resources and of what Egypt scholar Alan Mikhail describes as "a dehumanization that affected *both* animals and humans."[22] Pushed out of their villages, men and their families ended up in the city; unskilled in any of the services demanded in urban life but acquainted with working animals, they found themselves in a Cairo awash with cheap war horses and army mules. So they put them to work and often worked them into the ground. Lao She's novel *Camel Xiangzi (Rickshaw Boy)* ends with lines that could describe the situation of many of these men and animals, laborers trapped on a treadmill that kept them just one step ahead of death. "Watching a skinny stray dog waiting by the sweet-potato vendor's carrying-pole for some peel and rootlets," Lao She writes of the impoverished rickshaw puller, "[Camel] knew that he was just like this dog, struggling for some scraps to eat. As long as he managed to keep alive, why think of anything else?"[23]

Dorothy did not know the problems to this depth or detail. Yet from this October day she would try to effect change in the lives of people who played a role in their animals' misery, to clarify to those looking on in horror from the heights of privilege or ignorance that it was poverty, not people, that was the enemy; compassion and education were the tools for combating it and the cruelty that trails in poverty's wake and makes the fight for survival justification for cruelty. Above all, Dorothy was moved most to see innocent animals that had fought wars they had not caused and that had been left behind through no fault of their own suffer a misery they did not deserve. She wanted to do something for them before it was too late. In so doing, the general's wife from England was to set in motion a concept of practical compassion that outlived her lifetime. "At its last gasp," writes Susanna Forrest of Dorothy's achievement, "the working horse had found an ally in womankind."[24]

In memory of those working horses, let us leave Dorothy and that hot October afternoon in 1930 Cairo. Let us rewind back in time— back through the frantically hedonist 1920s, when nobody wanted to remember anything before today; back to the Great War, the end of a brief age of innocence for both humans and animals, back to the whys and wherefores of how war horses like those harnessed to misery at Ramses Station ended up in Egypt in the first place. How the triumphs and tragedies they and their soldiers experienced in the war's last years are vividly highlighted in the story of one small mare, who served and survived in Europe, Egypt, and Palestine, and whose good luck ironically saved her from outliving the war itself.

1

Dawn Raiders

By the galloping horses, nostrils wide, panting,
Beating hooves sparking against the earth,
The dawn raiders stir up a storm of dust,
Attackers appearing suddenly amid the attacked.
Man is ungrateful to his Lord
And indeed, is witness to this.
Indeed, he is strong in his love of wealth.
But don't men know that, on the day when
what is in the graves is scattered,
And what is in man's breast is harvested,
Their Lord is the only one who knows them best?

—QURAN, CH. 100: *SURAT AL-'ĀDIYĀT* (THE COURSER)

1. Cupid

Concerning the war I say nothing—the only thing that wrings my heart & soul is the thought of the horses. . . . I walk round & round this room cursing God for allowing dumb brutes to be tortured—let Him kill his human beings but how CAN HE? Oh, my horses.

—EDWARD ELGAR[1]

The astonishing thing is that in the highly mechanized 1914–18 conflict, whether in Europe or the east, cavalry was even given a role to play. Indeed, British prime minister David Lloyd George would complain in 1934, the year Dorothy Brooke founded her equine charity, of the "ridiculous cavalry obsession" of British officers in the Great War.[2]

In an era of weaponry capable of blasting a unit to heaven from the other side of a valley, cavalry seemed to belong to an earlier age of the rapier and hand-to-hand combat. Geoffrey Brooke's famous charge on Moreuil Wood in 1918 was rather more an anomaly than the norm, and certainly the carnage it caused among men and horses was no recommendation for the use of equines in combat. "Cavalry lost much in popular esteem during the War," wrote Ernest Harold Baynes. "There was no field for cavalry's salient characteristics."[3] Yet those characteristics were to have a use, though not in the European theater where so much of the world's attention was focused. Thanks to these equine soldiers, the Great War "was won for the Allies beyond all question when the whirlwind campaigns in Palestine and Syria turned an enemy flank, and forced Turkey to capitulate," weakening Germany's foothold in the region.[4]

Philosophers fancied the world captured in a dewdrop; poets

have seen war's horror and life's hope in a soldier's tear. Even so, the huge, unknowable story of English horses in Egypt during and after the Great War is epitomized in the brief, brave life of Cupid, a bay mare born and bred in the meadows of Essex.

Foaled in 1909, Cupid had been given as a present to Vernon Laurie, fifteen-year-old son of City broker Ranald Laurie, in 1911. Shortly after the outbreak of hostilities in early August 1914, Cupid and three other Laurie horses—Flashlight, Nimrod, and Polly—were joined to "B" Battery 271st Brigade Royal Fleet Auxiliary (RFA); Ranald was commander of the local Territorial Field Artillery Brigade and was responsible for purchasing horses for it. After training in England, Cupid joined other horses selected for active service in a crowded sailing across the Channel to Le Havre, where they boarded a "filthy, damp and cold" train for St. Omer, then on to Lynde in the Nord-Pas-de-Calais region.

There, many of the horses had to be reshod since the glutinous, gluey mud had robbed them of their shoes, as with the boots of their human counterparts. It was here that Cupid, who had been exposed to gunfire in the training camp in England, first got to experience the real thing amid the rain and wind. She spent almost two months in northern France before being sent with Vernon to Marseilles, where she, Flashlight, Nimrod, and Polly boarded the SS *Andriana*. With them were a contingent of Australian Walers and troops and Bosche, a small yellow dog with a curly tail who had followed Vernon back from a café in Marseilles. They were all bound for Alexandria.

The voyage lasted four days. While the seas were generally calm, there was prolonged rolling that unsettled the horses, already agitated from the stifling heat down in the horse decks. The cramped conditions could be tragic. An officer of the Second Royal Irish Regiment, Maj. Patrick Butler, was to write about one such sailing in which he saw a horse "behaving like a mad thing, [who] threatened to smash his way out of his pen." Because of the close quarters in which all the animals were crammed, it was impracticable to use a bullet on the maddened horse, so the grooms bled him to death. "Poor beast," added Major Butler, thinking of what awaited all the horses, "his troubles were over early." During the sailing, the Lauries' Nimrod, who had failed to eat, weakened and then collapsed. This had already happened with several of the horses. Even though the conditions were crowded, they did not prevent the use of a gun: the "echoing crack from a .45 revolver was heard more than a few times," writes Martin Laurie. Nimrod could not be made to stand, though Vernon and the other men tried for an hour. So a shot rang out; Nimrod's lifeless body was dragged overboard, and Vernon watched the corpse as it floated away in the ship's wake, his face wet with tears.[5]

By February 12, 1915, a month after the Turkish army began its march toward the Suez Canal, and a few days before they were driven back toward Beersheba in the Negev Desert, horses and men had reached port in Egypt and entrained for Cairo, whence they headed for Mena Camp in the shadow of the pyramids at Giza. During their six weeks at Mena Camp, Cupid was ridden around the ancient tombs and learned hard lessons in less interesting novelties, such as the flies and sandstorms that tormented animals and men alike.

Bosche was not permitted in the camp (or was not well concealed enough to remain there). After some searching and asking around it was determined he could be looked after at the Cairo Society for the Prevention of Cruelty to Animals (SPCA) while the regiment was at Mena Camp. Vernon described the SPCA as having in its care hundreds of horses, mules, and donkeys, as well as camels, other dogs, and even a kangaroo that had been brought along as mascot of an Australian regiment. Concern for animals was by no means unique to just a few in the British forces and did not go unnoticed among the locals. Sapper H. P. Bonser wrote of a day visit to Cairo in 1916 during which, while other soldiers visited the red light district, he and a mate fed four starving cats with meat they had bought specially, an act that touched native Cairenes standing nearby. "This caused quite a stir," Bonser remembered. "The men made friendly noises, and a number of them offered sweetmeats." Afterward, he wrote, whenever he and his fellow soldiers were in the neighborhood, the locals remembered their act of kindness, dubbing them "The askaris [soldiers] who fed pussini."[6]

Cupid would spend April to July 1916 in the machinery-clogging sands near El Shatt (*Mina'ash Shatt*), later the site of an infamous World War II refugee camp, where the Suez Canal is linked to the Gulf of Suez. Despite the oppressive heat, she and the other mounts were well watered. This was thanks to the camels. Throughout the desert sorties, these animals steadily carried water and food for the horses—indeed, without them, "General Allenby himself admits that he could not have hoped either to take Beersheba or to press through Palestine after its capture."[7] On a reconnaissance mission in the desert, Cupid just missed the fate of ten horses and thirty-two camels unlucky enough to be with them. While they were gathered in one area being watered, a pair of German planes appeared without warning, spraying bullets over the terrified animals tethered to their watering troughs. A soldier was killed as well, but Cupid lived.

Six months later, the brigade marched from El Shatt north to Moascar near Ismailia and on to Kantara (*El-Qantarah el-Sharqiyya*) and El Gilban (*Sheikh Abu Gilbân*), and then in February 1917 they began their trek along the ancient caravan route into Palestine. Their menagerie now included not just Bosche but also a goose named Lordy, a friendly bird whom the men could not leave behind or even imagine wanting to eat, though few were not hungry. Lordy traveled on horseback or on mechanized transport and was fed bread scraps. No one, writes Martin Laurie, would ever have considered eating him. Nor did Bosche have to worry about keeping up; he hitched a ride with the ammunition column, "lying in the sun on top of one of the wagons and being spoilt rotten by the men who drove them."[8]

The Battle of Romani, fought on August 3–5, 1916, had proved to be a decisive step forward in both the defense of the Suez Canal and the decision taken afterward to send British forces deeper into Ottoman Palestine. Australians commanded by Gen. Harry Chauvel and Turkish forces under German general Friedrich Kress von Kressenstein, supported by the German Air Force, clashed in what Stuart Hadaway describes as "a First World War battle won principally by cavalry, albeit ones who used their horses to gain superior mobility before fighting on foot."[9] The fact that the horses were rarely engaged in direct combat did not keep them out of harm's way: many died from heat exhaustion. It is terribly easy to see why. "The load carried by a Mounted Rifleman's horse in the field is considerable," wrote Lt. A. Briscoe Moore of the New Zealand Mounted Rifles in late 1916. Aside from the rifleman himself and his heavy kit, haversack, food, and all manner of bags, sacks, and supplies for horse and man, each horse carried a weighty bandolier of ammunition around its neck.[10] Under this burden, in torrid heat, with constant shortage of water and seldom enough rest, a given desert campaign horse had more to worry about than shellfire. "Since leaving their quiet homes in south Essex some two and a half years before," writes Martin Laurie, "the horses and men had travelled some 3,800 miles through England, France and North Africa." These were not, he points out, animals whose normal day would have included anything much beyond a hunting excursion, delivering beer or milk, or ploughing a field. Yet as unfamiliar to her as her new war service was, Cupid held up under her duties without apparent difficulty.[11]

Conditions combining sandstorms and lack of water for bathing were barely endurable, even for hardened soldiers. Sapper Bonser described how "it was impossible to see a man twenty yards away" in one of these storms, and how the sand got absolutely everywhere: "all over our perspiring bodies, sand on every mouthful of food we ate, and a sip of tepid water left sand on our lips."[12] Hence the delight of arriving at El Arish on the Mediterranean, a town of largely mud brick dwellings; the outskirts of the town were surrounded by fruit plantations. There, after pitching tents under the date palms, men and horses were able to bathe in fresh, cool saltwater waves. The relief was brief; soon the brigade was on the road again toward the ancient city of Gaza, its white minarets and white walls sharply outlined against the distant Mediterranean Sea. This lovely vision was to be smashed to pieces during the First Battle of Gaza, fought on March 26. Vernon and Cupid could only watch, since the brigade was held in reserve and under cover, but both spent another of their nine lives as enemy fliers took note of their location and directed gunners to start firing toward them. When the brigade itself was called into action, Cupid again made it through safely. The EFF was defeated in this first battle with the Turks, as well as in their second attempt in April. Needing rest, Cupid's brigade was sent to a camp near Deir al Belah ("monastery of the date palm"), a former crusader stronghold southwest of Gaza, trying to survive the heat, the flies, and the lack of adequate water. Hot days, frigid nights, and sand "frequently as deep as their knees and hocks" made every step an ordeal.[13] The third and, for the British, successful Battle of Gaza began on October 27, aided by the Royal Navy's bombardment from the sea, and by November 7 the city was taken from the Turks. Sapper Bonser, riding through later with his cable team, remembered "an untidy dilapidated Gaza from which most men had fled. Here and there a dark face peeped stealthily from a doorway, but, apart from the troops hurrying through, it was a place of desolation."[14]

Taking the city had been excruciating for everyone. "Our horses are rather pulled down by excessive work," Vernon wrote on November 12. The animals were tasked with carrying ammunition, work that was hard on the horses in the humid heat. In what remained of the year, Martin Laurie writes, "There was very little rest for either man or beast" in the quest to pursue and capture the Turkish army.[15] As the brigade prepared attack for Mulebbis (Peta Tikvah, an Orthodox Jewish religious settlement dating from the nineteenth century) on December 26, Vernon's father wrote of a landscape soggy as a wet sponge, entirely lacking in roads, in which one lost all sense of direction and where, in the vacant sparseness, it was easy to look at the fact that men and animals were reduced to half their rations and wonder whether they would end up with nothing to eat at all in a countryside denuded by Turkish forces. Yet by January, the constant rains had abated and conditions improved to the point where the horses could be allowed to graze on fresh grass. "What a relief the green was, from the glare of the sand, and how greedily the horses cropped the sweet grass and young corn," wrote one soldier.[16] The Lauries wrote of witnessing friendly interaction between brigade members and people in one of the villages close by their camp. Commanders gave permission for horses from the brigade to be lent by day to farmers for their spring ploughing, the Turkish Army having taken all the villagers' able-bodied animals.[17] Army veterinarians did what they could for the animals, whose hooves had never been trimmed, whose unhealed pack sores from poorly fitting harnesses were never treated. Some of the men could not bear seeing these donkeys being overloaded, whipped and otherwise abused. Sapper Bonser related how one of his unit, a young soldier from Sheffield, described as "a rough handful," actively intervened when he saw Syrians goading their donkeys with sharp packing needles. On one occasion this soldier tussled with a Maronite priest who was about to jab his donkey with a needle. Taking the priest's clenched fist, he drove the needle into the man's own hand, prompting him to topple with a scream off the back of the donkey. "Our young driver walked off with the needle," Bonser wrote; it has to be wondered, however, whether this resulted in a needle-free life for the priest's animal.[18]

By March, little Bosche, who had survived so many near disasters and did not even allow the first two battles of Gaza to separate him from his soldiers, had disappeared, as had the goose Lordy, also never seen again. This depressing news was counterbalanced by Ranald Laurie's investiture in Tel Aviv with a medal awarded him for his service during the First Battle of Gaza. The ceremony took place at the Jewish Agricultural College, where the medal was presented by His Royal Highness the Duke of Connaught, the popular governor general of Canada and father of Princess "Pat," for whom the Princess Patricia Canadian Light Infantry was named. As Ranald pointed out later, the medal was "subsequently removed and handed back to do duty at another investiture of another Division another day & so on," lending the ceremony an unexpected surreality.[19]

By summer Vernon had been posted to command of the Division Ammunition Column (DAC), and with him Cupid reached Haifa in October and then Acre, en route to Beirut. "This part of the journey was to be very hard on the horses," says Martin Laurie, "and the men; the weather was excessively hot and they were plagued by torrential thunderstorms."[20] Faithful Cupid went wherever her master did, sometimes with him leading her, as Vernon did when, on the way to Sidon, troops had to crawl along paths cut into seaside cliffs, stretches of which were barely wide enough for a single horse. Vernon and Cupid arrived in Beirut on October 31 to find that the Turks had surrendered the previous day. No one knew what was coming next. Germany was still very much in the fight, and it was considered possible that the men and horses who had made it this far into the eastern Mediterranean might have to ship out again for France, where most of them had started almost four years earlier. Beirut was certainly a milestone for Cupid, as Martin Laurie writes. She had been at war for four years, two months and twenty-seven days, and she had obediently and bravely traveled over four thousand miles. Ranald Laurie was disturbed by the condition of the horses after this massive journey, their sides "thin as rakes" from lack of forage and supply. Nonetheless, Cupid and Polly, though in poor shape, served in their turn as Vernon rode back and forth from the docks, accompanying convoys of feed and supplies for animals and men. They were engaged in this daily exhausting shuttle when word came, with the ringing of bells, that Germany had signed the armistice on November 11 and that hostilities were to cease at 11 a.m.[21]

After the jubilant evening they woke up to a morning of sober reality. "What to do with all these animals at the end of the war was a major problem," wrote Sarah Searight. There is no evidence that the military apparatus had already totted up the theoretical expense of shipping all the horses back to where they had come from, but the decision to not bother to do so was heartlessly swift. The expense, of course, went beyond shipping the animals home. Thanks to their having been sent to places far from where they had started, all the surviving horses had to be assumed to be harboring incipient infections from the locales of battle that could never be brought home to England. The costs for quarantining them, as Sarah Searight points out, would have alone been astronomical. Though all of this was understood and, at least in theory, agreed to, nobody seemed to want to take responsibility for euthanizing the animals, which in itself threatened costs in organizational time and funds for disposal of the corpses that nobody had to offer.[22] Ranald Laurie wrote home that "they will not I am sure ship any of these horses home, if they get them to Egypt they'll turn them into hides and tallow, if we leave them here we shall have to shoot the lot. Well, my dear, so ends the Great War."[23] One Royal Yeomanry regiment held a quasi funeral at Gaza, in which "items of saddler and spurs, etc., were buried and a wooden memorial erected bearing the inscription (much abbreviated): 'Stranger pause and shed a tear—A regiment's heart is buried here.'"[24] For reasons not explained in the Laurie record, though some of the mounts were left in Beirut with occupying forces, rendering many of their departing handlers inconsolable, Cupid, Polly, Flashlight, and other horses made it aboard the ss *Huntsgreen* (originally the German *Derflinger*, seized and renamed at Port Said after the outbreak of war). All arrived safely in Cairo on December 14, 1918.

The brigade settled in at Helmieh, site of a rest camp that included hospital facilities in the flat deserts outside Cairo. At Helmieh those men who were not critically injured or gravely ill found relief from boredom or bad memories in classes and sporting events. And their horses were not forgotten: there were races, jumping, and other equine events to keep them busy. While there, Cupid's brigade groomed their mounts for the Armistice celebration in Cairo, which ended with a march past Gen. Sir Edmund Allenby in Opera House Square. In yet another passing brush with Great War greatness, Ranald rode Flashlight and Vernon rode Cupid under the galvanizing gaze of the Liberator of Jerusalem. The parade was a happy prelude to the Christmas party that followed back in Helmieh, yet sadly it was also the beginning of the end for Flashlight, Polly, Cupid, and the other equines stabled at the camp.[25]

Men began to leave for Kantara, where a camp had been established to repatriate and demobilize soldiers, and in January Vernon's time came to depart. Before he left, Martin Laurie writes, Vernon rode Cupid as often as he could and continued to discuss with his father what could be done about bringing her back home to England with him. By the time he had to leave, they had not formulated a plan, but Vernon, as ever, was optimistic. "I have had to leave my horses at Cairo," Vernon wrote in a letter before getting on his train, "but we have faint hopes that we may be able to get one home"—that one being Cupid. Ranald would give it all he could to make that happen, Vernon added.[26]

Then came news that defeated any further hopes. On February 16 Ranald wrote to Vernon that none of the horses were to be transported from Egypt. All their own animals, to the tune of fifteen, were slated either for destruction or to be handed over to the Army of Occupation, which meant they would remain in Egypt or farther afield.[27] Because of this order, "many [of the horses] were therefore taken to the local markets and sold to local farmers," writes Sarah Searight. So arose the stories of isolated cases that coalesced to become a legend, in which officers rode their mounts into the wastes of the desert and shot them rather than leave them in Egypt, a fate to which soldiers in France were no more willing to consign their mounts when the war was done.[28] Indeed, one Australian Imperial Force (AIF) officer, Maj. Oliver Hogue, also known as "Trooper Bluegum," wrote a poem encapsulating the dilemma as well as the prevailing stereotypical view of Egyptian horse handlers:

I don't think I could stand the thought of my old fancy hack
Just crawling round old Cairo with a 'Gippo on his back.
Perhaps some English out in Palestine may find
My broken-hearted waler with a wooden plough behind.
No, I think I'd better shoot him and tell a little lie:
"He floundered in a wombat hole and then lay down to die."
Maybe I'll get court-martialled but I'm damned if I'm inclined
To go back to Australia and leave my horse behind.[29]

The Australian government used a system of classification that, according to Jean Bou, did little more than delay the inevitable. Per age and physical condition, a given horse would be "passed on to imperial units, pooled in remount depots for later reissue or, failing that, sold. The older and unfit horses would be destroyed." The latter animals were given a sad send-off: "manes and tails were shorn (horse hair was valuable) and their shoes removed"; then the horses were taken out and shot under the eye of a veterinary officer.[30]

It was as if the horses and mules stabled in Helmieh somehow sensed their coming fate.

The night of February 20–21, 1919, a violent sand storm rattled the nerves of men and animals. Mules in general are not as skittish as horses, but something—a flapping piece of canvas or being struck by flying debris—made one of them go berserk. The mule broke free of its restraints and ran through the stable complex. Ranald Laurie would point out that Cupid, for all her docility, had a very short temper when confronted by other horses. When the mule ran toward her, Cupid either stood her ground or reared up in defense. The larger mule collided with her and knocked her to the ground. Ranald brought three veterinarians to look at the injured Cupid; all agreed that there was no way to save her. Crouching beside Cupid and speaking soothing words, Ranald brought out his pistol and ended her suffering. He then asked the veterinary sergeant to save one of Cupid's hooves. It was cleaned out and brought home to Essex, where, encased in brass, it still serves as a doorstop in the Laurie family's home. Ranald was done with war and death. It was this part of war and death, he wrote his wife, that he hated most.[31]

Cupid's war service and the story of how she died are only known to us through the fact that she remained with her owner throughout the war, and that her owner recorded her every adventure, including her final one. Her death was a blessing in disguise. Strong horses like Cupid, who had survived deserts, disease, unremitting hard work, and lack of food and water, might well have lived many years longer. Although some of the horses at Helmieh were given over to the Army of Occupation (and we don't know where these eventually ended up), many more, along with mules and donkeys, were sold in the Egyptian markets. Among these may have been the gharry war horses Dorothy Brooke saw on her first day in Cairo, eleven long years later. Perhaps the wounded and abused old warrior who was to capture Dorothy's heart and move her to dedicate her life to saving working equines like him had fought, like Cupid, in the deserts of Egypt and Palestine. Only he had had the bad luck to survive.[32]

2. Old Bill

Conquests on earth are written by the blood of horses.

—AMAL DONQOL

Wishing to help the gharry horses at Ramses Station and finding a way to realistically do so were, as Dorothy Brooke discovered, not quite the same thing.

Even the afternoons, said to be a lady's time to dispose of as she wished, were not Dorothy's own: they were taken up with polo matches—Geoffrey being a preeminent player—and by a variety of other events requiring her presence. Even had she found the perfect excuse, short of being at death's door, Dorothy's absence from any of the above would probably have been considered disturbing, if not an affront, to the dignity and esprit de corps of the small, socially interdependent British minority in Cairo—a city in which colonialism firmly held the upper hand until forcibly removed following the Suez Crisis in 1956. Right up to that ejection, British expatriates and British troops held on to this last tattered proof of the once great military power that had been the British Empire. Part of that colonial presence was to show up crisply on time, all the time, regardless of physical weariness and emotional disengagement.

Due to this life, in later years her friend Glenda Spooner would describe Dorothy as a woman who, in her first few months in Cairo and throughout a schedule of duties dictated by her role as the wife of a high-ranking British officer, had to learn to operate in two distinct worlds. To many in Cairo's foreign community Dorothy was a superb and engaged hostess, a pillar of expat British society, who gave excellent parties and had a genius for organization.

(This was a gift she would prove by writing a book, *Tribulations of a Well-Meaning Woman*, about how best to organize the lives of British military wives and their children abroad.)[1] To herself—for the moment at any rate—and to a few close friends, Dorothy was simply exercising the animal rights activism she had always devoted so much energy to in England. But in the very different atmosphere of Egypt, a culture about which she then knew next to nothing, she was flummoxed as to how to put an end to the suffering of these emaciated equine war veterans.

The taxi horses at the train station continued to haunt Dorothy throughout that fall and winter. Sometime in the first months of 1931 she began to make enquiries within her social circle in Heliopolis, asking friends and acquaintances, officials and servants, and old Cairo hands whether any of them had seen branded former war horses working anywhere in or outside the city. When people did respond, Dorothy was told that while a few former war horses—or *maybe* they were war horses; nobody could really be sure, could they?—had been glimpsed working here and there over the years, most were probably dead now; the ones Dorothy had seen would have been the very last survivors. And anyway, she was warned, it was dangerous for a foreigner to mix in these things—aside from the presumed physical dangers to a European woman in proximity to "native" men, there was the colonialist social rank factor to contend with. Stooping to involve herself in the affairs of Egyptian cabmen meant crossing the line established between conqueror and conquered. The facts of the matter are that nobody in Dorothy's circle appeared inclined to assist in what most probably saw as a hazardous caprice. It was also seen, claimed Glenda Spooner, as an unnecessary distraction with which many could not bring themselves to sympathize. "Nothing makes the average Englishman more uncomfortable than to be told about anything unpleasant," commented Spooner.[2]

But not all British people in Cairo had been willing to look away from unpleasantness of this nature. Since the 1890s, Cairo had had a branch of the Royal Society for the Prevention of Cruelty to Animals (called simply SPCA, to set it apart from the British RSPCA). Prior to this an army chaplain had tried to set up an organization to help animals and prosecute abusers, but he ruined his opportunity by taking a whip to a camel driver he had caught mistreating his animal—an all too common response of outraged foreigners. Charges were pressed, the chaplain was brought before the Consular Court that tried foreign cases, and the end result was that his rescue organization was closed and his fate a deterrent to any other foreigners who might wish to involve themselves in the same work and expose themselves to the same hazards. Later on, Sir Evelyn Baring, British consul general in Egypt between 1883 and 1907, showed interest in establishing an SPCA in the city, and in due course an animal hospital was constructed on Shari'a al-Sahel Street, in the Bulaq district bordering the Nile River. The SPCA took on all animal cases, but possibly because of its British origins and governance, and because of the sheer number of horses, it specialized in working equine cases from the streets of Cairo. From this location in Bulaq in 1906 alone, the SPCA oversaw in excess of five thousand convictions for various types of animal cruelty—the sort of good news that has a bad news sting, as it showed how much animal suffering there was in Cairo, and implied, given the potential numbers in such a large city, that there were probably many more thousands of abuse cases than were reported, problems the SPCA had to work all the harder to try to solve.[3]

It is certainly possible that foreign interest in these animals' fates made matters worse. John Chalcraft writes that there were probably many foreigners in Cairo whose support for the SPCA had as much or more to do with "colonial identity politics . . . in which the self-consciously 'civilized' emphasized their negative response to the brutal acts of barbarous 'natives' in order to reinforce their own putative superiority and claim to rule," as it did in the simple act of rescuing an animal from misery.[4] Alan Mikhail puts it more starkly. "In these colonial hierarchies," he says, "nonhumans often stood above certain kinds of (nearly always non-European) humans." Consciousness of this on the part of the animals' owners was not likely to translate to a kindness they may have felt was lacking toward themselves from their Egyptian overlords or from British colonial government officials.[5]

Spooner tells us that even people who admitted they knew that an SPCA branch existed in Cairo seemed unable to pinpoint for Dorothy exactly where it was—perhaps, as with the topic of surviving war horses, this was a form of gentle dissuasion to save Dorothy from descending into the dangers of direct contact with Egyptian natives. However, it is not likely many in Dorothy's social circle even had direct knowledge of the poorer areas of Cairo, where the SPCA was located. In the end, this location, not far from the main train station of Cairo, may have helped Dorothy find it: it was at the station that she had first seen the branded gharry horses, and the gharry drivers would have known all about the hospital, as there was a strong economic bond between the Cab Drivers' Union and the SPCA clinic.

However she did it, Dorothy did finally find herself at last at the gates of the Cairo Society for the Prevention of Cruelty to Animals. And as she would write in her diary of what would be, by any measure, the most important day of her life, it was both shock and inspiration together:

> I well remember that first visit. About fifty boxes [stalls] were surrounded by a large flower and vegetable garden. Beyond these a gate opened into two yards. Open sheds surrounded three sides of each of these. In one shed patients, recently admitted, were awaiting "maleening" . . . a test for glanders—the scourge of the country. Other open sheds contained animals already maleened but awaiting results—which takes twenty-four hours. The remainder of the space was occupied by rows of little donkeys, tied to their manger, and a sorry sight most of them were. Poor little starved, overworked drudges.[6]

Dorothy would have found many cabmen at the location, along with their horses. "The SPCA's facilities were well used by the local gharry drivers," writes Sarah Searight, "who had clubbed together to hire some thirty of the SPCA boxes for a small annual subscription, enabling their animals to be treated for well below the normal cost." It must have been a relief for Dorothy to discover that there were at least some gharry drivers in Cairo who recognized the benefit of caring for the health and well-being of their animals.[7]

It's useful to recall that Glenda Spooner often compared Dorothy to Florence Nightingale. Another well-born Englishwoman drawn to the east, Nightingale had received a call to do something extraordinarily unusual with her life: to devote it to a cause bigger than itself, well outside the sphere to which true ladies were meant to confine themselves.

Born in Italy in 1820, Nightingale, who died only twenty years before Dorothy's arrival in Cairo, had been an animal lover since childhood. "It was characteristic of Florence," wrote her biographer, "that her heart went out to the less favoured ones, those which owing to old age or infirmity were taken little notice of by the servants and farm-men." A slender, coldly elegant beauty in her youth, Nightingale shocked her family by announcing her desire to go into nursing, a profession considered out of bounds for a gentlewoman, for whom any profession at all was out of the question to begin with. She struggled between duty to family and social position and listening to what her heart told her she must do. And it was while on a visit to Egypt, while staying outside Cairo, that she wrote in her diary, "God called me in the morning and asked me would I do good for him alone without reputation." A career and immortality were hers for the seizing. At the outbreak of the Crimean War Nightingale would become famous as "the lady with the lamp" for British troops and a pioneer for the nursing profession and for women's autonomy.[8]

One of Nightingale's greatest contributions to the field of nursing was her application of statistics, the gathering of data from every possible angle to determine and meet specific needs. She was known to visit hospital wards armed with writing materials, making copious notes on best practices. Though Dorothy carried no notepaper with her that first day at the Cairo SPCA, the Nightingale simile was apt: also a person for whom organization was supreme and one who tried to learn as much as she could from a given situation, she filed many mental notes as she toured the premises. Though she knew very little about what it took to run an animal hospital, Dorothy would find that there were certain practices at the SPCA that she would have done differently, while there were others that she could build on for what would become her own future rescue work. But her first and most important discovery was made on a subsequent visit to the property. As with Nightingale, out of the blue she received her own "call from God" in the form of an elderly war horse of Cairo.

The English chestnut stood in one of the stalls lining one side of the SPCA paddock. "He was without exception," Dorothy wrote later, "the most dreadful looking horse I had ever seen in my life."[9]

When young, the English chestnut had developed a huge frame that, in Egypt, must have made him conspicuous next to the smaller donkeys and native horses working the streets of Cairo. Now his bones, jutting against his stretched flesh, stood out like details on an equine anatomy chart. Indeed, part of the horse's tragedy was that he was so large. In the care of the British Army he would have received feed necessary for his size. But in the hands of a poor Egyptian he would have only been given enough food to keep him alive. Thus he was at least as damaged through malnutrition as he was because of all his untreated physical injuries. The washboard ribs, swollen joints, legs that shook, and eyes lacking shine and depth were heartbreaking to see on an animal who still bore the broad arrow brand of the British Army across his left rear quarter. "Obviously he had been a good horse once," Dorothy recalled. "He had been happy and well fed as the other poor animals had never been. He had been born in England, had known our green fields, been groomed and cared for. He had moreover served in Palestine and suffered hardships in that campaign that few horses have endured in modern times. And then we had sold him to this." Dorothy could see that even had his elderly, overworked body been relatively sound, his spirit was already dead.[10]

Through her visits to the facility, Dorothy had come to know Dr. Ghazi, the SPCA hospital's veterinary surgeon. She asked him about the old English horse and was surprised to be told he was being kept in the hospital only for a few days. Dorothy was aghast at the idea that the horse would ever be well enough again to be released back to his owner and his work. She was no veterinarian, but she had no difficulty seeing that as the animal was also lame in his other three legs, he was unfit for any further work at all; that it would be cruel to subject him to further misery and that he should be put down at once. Dr. Ghazi explained that as the horse was technically only lame in his near foreleg, as soon as this healed the SPCA had no legal means by which to keep him. What he told Dorothy about the horse's owner explained a lot about the animal's condition. The man was very poor, said Dr. Ghazi, and also "very bad." This was not the first time his horse had been seized by police. Incredibly (to Dorothy if not to Dr. Ghazi), the SPCA board had always given this particular horse a pass to continue working. In order to be judged eligible for euthanasia, an animal had to be unable to do any work at all—in other words, had to be flat out and dying on the street— and the board had decided to err on the side of the owner's interests rather than the animal's. This horse's owner was too poor to obtain another horse to keep his livelihood going. Despite what a man had done to make this animal's life a hell, "we have to consider the men these animals belong to," Dr. Ghazi insisted.[11]

Dorothy asked how much it would cost for her to buy the horse from its owner. She expected to pay only a few shillings for an animal in such poor condition. Dr. Ghazi suggested £9, a sum that took Dorothy aback. To put this price in perspective, a pound in 1930 would be worth about £57 in inflated 2015 values. Multiply that by nine and you have a very large sum to shell out in the early years of the Great Depression. Dr. Ghazi told her that the purchase price was deliberately set at that rate to allow the owner to purchase another horse; otherwise he and his family would have no horsepower to haul or pull and thus no way to make a living. At this point, writes Spooner, Dorothy "was feeling so sick she did not argue further."[12] She paid over the money without further argument, only to discover that she would have to wait another forty-eight hours before she could take possession: the owner had to formally seal the bargain by accepting her money. And until he showed up at the SPCA, the horse remained his property. The owner couldn't be contacted as he was not meant to retrieve the horse for another two days. So Dorothy, maddeningly, had to wait to bring the animal's sufferings to an end. These two days were among the worst of Dorothy's life. Had she been free to do so, the moment she handed the cash over to Dr. Ghazi she would have led the animal to a quick euthanization. As there was nothing, legally, that she could do, Dorothy decided she must make the stallion's final hours as pleasant as possible. In what would become a Brooke Hospital tradition, she gave the horse a name. He was dubbed "Old Bill." In what would become another tradition, Dorothy lavished on him all the personal attention she could, an expenditure of time and effort that would gain her a reputation for eccentricity among many native Egyptians when introduced to her style for the first time, which, later, developed into a deep respect.

That first day and the next, Dorothy drove to the SPCA stables to visit Bill. She ensured he had all the feed and water he needed, and she caressed and soothed him and talked to him. One of the more wrenching experiences Dorothy was to have in her future rescues of war horses was the pricking up of battered old ears at the inflection of a voice speaking English, a language most of these animals had not heard since the war. "Every horse is endowed with a retentive memory," wrote Geoffrey Brooke in 1927, "though he is unable to reason for himself. He cannot understand why he has changed hands. . . . he will remember [his master] years after."[13] But nothing Dorothy said had any such effect on Old Bill. If he was deadened to a once familiar language, Dorothy still expected Bill to brighten at the sight of the unimaginably delicious treats she offered him, but all was in vain. Nothing mattered to him anymore. Even soft straw spread for him to lie down on seemed to mean nothing. Old Bill stood over the straw on his trembling legs, with Dorothy beside him, helpless to do anything.

In what would become another integral feature of her future work—what we might call a sort of forensic crime scene record—Dorothy had a photograph taken of Old Bill in front of the SPCA stables. People may still see the photograph today, one of the most famous images in the history of equine rescue. Bill's huge frame, imposing despite his emaciation, dwarfs the stable hand holding his bridle. All four legs are swollen; even the front left foreleg, which he seems to be favoring while the right hangs back tentatively, looks bent and misshapen. His coat is scarred, rough, and the ridge of his backbone can clearly be seen. His hooves have not been trimmed, and his eyes, as Dorothy noted, are lifeless. "He was past enjoyment," wrote Glenda Spooner about this photograph of Bill, "all he wanted was rest."[14]

Eventually the horse's owner did arrive and took the money without argument. Directly afterward, Dorothy went to Old Bill's box. She found him looking at her from the shadows. For the first time, he appeared alert, as if he knew that his waiting was over. Within minutes of the purchase, Dorothy had Old Bill put to sleep.

At the price of £9, Old Bill could have been considered Dorothy's good deed for the entire year. Even for a woman of means this was not an expenditure she could afford to make every week or even every month. Yet for her nine pounds, Dorothy had received so much more than just Old Bill's release from his damaged body. Through the process of his discovery, purchase, and humane end, Dorothy learned a lesson she would not forget. Old Bill had been trapped in a circle of pain that was not just his own, and in order to stop it, the human had to be addressed along with the animal.

Perhaps when the owner arrived to take Dorothy's money, she had been expecting a surly man, the stereotyped "cruel eastern foreigner" of the lowest class, but she had seen something in his eyes or demeanor that proved that even someone Dr. Ghazi described as a "bad owner" was human after all. A man whose scope of agency had been reduced to the point where he himself has no value in his own society might all too easily transfer that valuelessness onto beings even weaker than he. "Just as livestock, dogs, and elephants were stripped of their constructive social and economic functions in the early nineteenth century," writes Alan Mikhail, "so too were Egyptian peasants, the uneducated, the disabled, the poor, the sick, the criminal, and the itinerant cut out of the productive social and economic realms of Egypt later in the century."[15] Any constructive function this horse's owner may have had was stripped from him by a social and political system that ranked him low on the human totem pole. The irony, as in all societies, is that men like Old Bill's owner supported everything above him—the grander, more flamboyant parts of the totem—yet they were fixed in place; their job was to carry the load.

Men like these could be called cruel in the extreme—Old Bill could not have ended up in such desperate straits had there been a caring soul anywhere near him to put a stop to his suffering. Yet Bill's owner had no real existence in the eyes of society, and he knew it. He had likely not been shown compassion for his own plight and had grown not to seek it. In this black-and-white world, you were alive or dead, hungry or full, asleep or awake. The deadness in Bill's eyes, so obvious to Dorothy, would not have been so to his owner, whose own eyes were blind to such nuances because they were dead themselves.

It would have been easy for Dorothy to conclude that some sort of mandatory education system—pointing out errors and ensuring they were corrected—only need be put in place for all owners of working equines in Cairo to take better care of their animals, so that another Old Bill need never suffer again. But she found she possessed that rare form of compassion generous enough to embrace not just animal suffering but the human causing it, and the logic to see that until the latter's problems were addressed, the former would always be part of the endless cycle of pain.

Dr. Ghazi's comment—"We have to consider the men these animals belong to"—had shocked her at first, because all she could see was a horse that in England would never have been allowed to reach such a state of misery. It was now that Dorothy began to develop what for her time was a radical plan. If the owners of former war horses were to be induced to part with them, she reasoned, it had to be for more than the price of the animal; it had to be for sufficient payment for the owner to purchase another work horse. And if veterinary care could be offered at a nominal price, if not free of charge, for their sick animals, and subsidies provided for the period of the animal's hospitalization, this would incentivize poor men to bring their horses or mules in for care, because they would not need to worry about how they would survive while the animal was healing. Here, then, was a prime opportunity—perhaps the only one Dorothy would have—to educate the animals' owners in understanding how proper care could make a difference not just in the animals' welfare but also in that of themselves and their families. This, in turn, might induce the men to spread the gospel: that the best success lies in making sure all working animals are treated with care, respect, and compassion, just as their owners are, in order to halt the cycle of ignorance and suffering.

As mentioned, these considerations were revolutionary for the time and place, and not common in our own. In the twenty-first century, conservationists who include the human element in their animal welfare work are still few and far between. Those who do stand out all the more, integrating the needs of humans and animals who live in close proximity, encouraging a continuum of cooperation for the benefit of each other, of their families, communities, and nations, and ultimately a more harmonious world. They also work in an era when there is comparatively less need to justify such work on behalf of animals, work that in Dorothy's time was still seen to be the special province of the eccentric. Dorothy's idea of blaming poverty, not the humans who suffered from it and were, cruelly, blamed for its consequences, would become so deeply entrenched in the fiber of the organization she founded, and so effective in daily life, that it is still in successful use today, educating owners while improving the physical and emotional health of their equine partners in labor, making everything better for everyone.[16]

Within six months, Dorothy's photograph of Old Bill, the starved, overworked, and spiritless English war horse to whom she had given painless peace, would appear in the pages of newspapers lying open on the breakfast tables of thousands of people in Britain, people who paused over their tea and toast to contemplate visible proof of what many had only heard rumors of—that equines who had served in the Great War had indeed been left behind to a far worse fate than anything they had faced in a war that they had helped Britain win. And with him, Old Bill's fellow war horses, mules, and donkeys would not only stir hearts and consciences; they would open the pocketbooks of an entire nation to fund Dorothy's solution to their suffering. For the moment, though, a hard question remained. How was she to find all the other war horses, let alone purchase them and compensate their owners if and when she did, in the middle of a world gripped by the Great Depression?

The chairman of the Cairo SPCA managing board, whom Dorothy was to meet, work with, and part from in equally unusual circumstances, was a short, sturdy, opinionated Englishman named Dr. Alfred E. Branch—A.E.B. to his friends.

Born in Colchester, Essex, in 1862, Branch was educated at the Royal College of Veterinary Surgeons in London. Founded in 1844 by royal charter, which recognized "veterinary art as a profession" and the need for regulation of veterinary standards and ethics, the RCVS was staffed by professionals who had graduated from the Royal Veterinary College of London and the Veterinary College of Edinburgh. Passing the test of membership in the RCVS conferred recognition that a veterinarian was qualified to practice per the highest recognized standards. Branch passed his First Examination with "Great Credit" in July 1885.[17]

What brought Branch to Egypt is unclear. Perhaps the fact that as of 1881 Egypt was under British authority, and the attraction of a posting in a warm and sunny climate where the cost of living was low, made him, like many young Britons, eager to go abroad. However he got there, Egypt was to work a certain magic on young Branch. Somehow, and in short order, he acquired a massive knowledge of the Arab horse and its bloodlines, along with a better than working knowledge of Arabic, and through this knowledge, and the fact that the bluest of equine bloodlines belonged to the most royal of Egyptian princes, he would make useful friends in very high places indeed.

We know Branch was in Cairo by 1892, when he became involved in the Horse Commission, formed, writes Judith Forbis, out of "necessity to continue breeding Arabian horses for the overall good of the country."[18] With the founding of the Royal Agricultural Society in 1908, Branch was appointed administrator, where his main task, writes Forbis, was "to persevere and perpetuate the Arabian horses descending from Abbas Pasha I, Ali Pasha Sherif and others of Egypt's royal family," in addition to his other duties. The Agricultural Society was a locus of research into agricultural practices and animal diseases and treatments thereof. "Gruff but good-natured," Branch took to his many jobs with gusto, forming in the process close friendships with Prince Kemal El Dine Hussein (1874–1932), for whom Branch's son, Newton Kemal, was named, and Prince Mohammed Ali Tewfik (1875–1953), who would serve as regent for the youthful King Farouk and live to see the end of the royal dynasty. Both princes were descendants of the first Turkish khedive (viceroy), Mohammed Ali, who had transformed Egypt and especially Cairo into a society leaning more toward Europe than Asia, the West rather than the East, with benefits and drawbacks for the people and the animals of Egypt. Under Mohammed Ali, Egyptians were sent to Europe to be broadened and westernized. The khedive's relatively enlightened descendants, in turn, brought men like Branch to Egypt, not simply for their knowledge but because they knew they could get things done in what even to Egyptians seemed a slow-moving version of reality best summed up in the Arabic expression *maa'lesh*—"whatever."[19]

Branch did not live happily in a "whatever" world. His order for solving a particular problem needed to be instantly be put into place, or there was hell to pay. It was a side to him that Dorothy certainly came to see—"He liked to have his own way," she would write later, "and his own ways were often peculiar to himself"[20]—and it was a bullheadedness that was cleverly harnessed by the Egyptian authorities, starting with his first official appointment. Branch was assigned as director of the Cairo Zoo, where his home sat "in the middle of what had once been the vast pleasure gardens of the Sultans," recalled his son, Newton Kemal Branch.[21] In 1878 a census was taken of the animals living in the complex, which was more a royal menagerie than a scientific collection of animals brought together from exotic international locales. The Cairo Zoo held over 630 animals in total, from a giraffe and a hippopotamus to 300 "varied birds" and a large contingent of blue, white, and plumed peacocks, gathered in what Alan Mikhail describes as the "first bureaucratic listing of a collection of animals in Egypt owned solely for purposes of display, recreation, and exhibition rather than for any productive agricultural, laboring, or economic function."[22]

It had come to the government's attention that animals in the Cairo Zoo were either suffering from malnutrition or were disappearing from their cages altogether. In other words, somebody inside or outside the zoo was stinting on feed to appropriate the money elsewhere and was selling off or even eating some of the animals. With unerring aim the zoo's head keeper was first to be fixed in Branch's sights. In what would become a known characteristic, Director Branch told the head keeper that if the animals' physical health and body fat content did not improve spectacularly on an extraordinarily tight timeline, the keeper would be the first to pay the ultimate price, which would involve being thrown into the den with lions so in need of the nourishment his overfed body would provide. This threat rapidly achieved the desired results. In another example, when Branch discovered that the man who was supposed to take care of the chimpanzees was a hashish addict who habitually offered smokes to the apes and neglected their needs, Branch locked the keeper in a special cage (presumably without his drug of choice), marked with a placard designating the occupant "Homo hashhash. Rare specimen."[23] The humiliation of this punishment can be best appreciated when we realize that zoo caretakers were routinely allowed to use empty cages as rest areas during their shifts. These were cages that they, unlike the animals they looked after, could enter and exit at will. So it became clear that under Branch's regime, the Egyptian staff of the Cairo Zoo were as apt to be placed behind bars as the peacocks, giraffe, or monkeys if they did not toe the line. And as a result the zoo soon reached heights of professionalism it had never known before.[24]

Branch's wife was also a person who meant what she said. Ada Loomis Hill from New Haven, Connecticut, had charmed Branch, eighteen years her senior, atop a horse-drawn bus while he was on leave in England. As Mrs. Branch, Ada was delighted to live in the flower-covered bungalow in Cairo, surrounded by a wild variety of animals, including the peacocks whose discarded feathers were used by ordinary sparrows to make extraordinary nests, bundles of iridescent color high in the sunlit trees. Like her husband, Ada brooked no abuse of the animals among which she lived. When the Branches' Sudanese cook, having had too much to drink, tried to prepare one of the peacocks for the dinner table, Ada reacted with aplomb worthy of her husband. "Mother bounced an iron skillet on his bald head," recalled son Newton, "and, for the next 20 years, they shared a deep respect for each other."[25]

Branch's most truly important moment on the stage of Egyptian animal welfare took place two years before the Brookes' arrival. In 1928 African horse sickness broke out in Upper Egypt, the corridor of Nile Valley between Cairo and Aswan, over five hundred miles apart. Spread by insect bites, the pulmonary form of the virus can kill an infected animal within twenty-four hours. In our time annual vaccines control the disease, but in the 1920s the only way to contain an outbreak was to quarantine visibly sick animals, along with any others that may have come into contact with the insect vectors transmitting the illness. By the time Dr. Branch took charge of the situation, some twenty-three villages were already infected, and the danger of further spread was very great. Branch "threw out patrols across Egypt," writes Judith Forbis; in these controlled areas, he had some forty-five thousand horses, mules, and donkeys specially branded for identification and their temperatures recorded in precise detail, comparing from day to day to monitor for any signs of disease progression. By any standard it was an extraordinarily organized response to an epidemic, unfolding under conditions very difficult to control, and one previously unknown in Egypt. Branch made sure that all details of each animal's owners were also recorded, so as to be able to scientifically map out areas of infection and non-infection. All equid owners were warned, as only Branch knew how to do, that if an animal marked by his team as belonging to one restricted area was brought outside of that area or allowed to stray beyond that boundary, it could be euthanized instantly or removed to more stringent quarantine, depending on the circumstances. Nobody cared to test Branch's authority in the matter. Branch himself made it clear "to the headmen of each village that they would be caned in public if any horse or mule was caught straying out of bounds," his son Newton remembered. As a result Branch is credited with having saved the equine population of Upper Egypt from perishing in an epidemic and Egypt itself from financial ruin. This, of course, only increased his prestige and, for some, his fearsomeness.[26]

Though her schedule was largely taken up by her social duties, Dorothy had managed to spend what remained of her time at the SPCA, where more Old Bills had come limping through the gates. "Invariably they were arrested cases," Dorothy wrote—meaning that these animals, like Old Bill, had been forcibly removed from owners because they were seen being worked publicly despite incapacitation.[27]

Dorothy continually tried to talk the SPCA staff into euthanizing some of the most desperate of these animals, and when they didn't, she bought them herself and had them put down. When this method soon became too expensive, Dorothy asked friends to help financially. Some gave freely; others preferred not to get involved. "How inconvenient the stirrings of a conscience can be," Glenda Spooner remarked with the understandable bitterness of one who had watched Dorothy too often plead in vain. It was growing more clear each time she visited the SPCA paddocks that there was a dire need for an organized effort to help the abandoned equine veterans of the Great War. How to make this help available, given the costs involved, was part of the problem. The other part was far more difficult to work out—what was to be her role, if any, in this effort? Just what that role was would come to her in the least promising of settings.[28]

When Dorothy was not visiting the SPCA she liked to go horseback riding, accompanied by Geoffrey and her daughter Pamela (the future Mrs. Blenman-Bull, who went by the nickname Pinkie), in the desert wastes that bordered clipped and orderly Heliopolis. Surrounded as she was by every comfort, Dorothy had a thirst, which many in her circle might well have viewed as perverse, to see the opposite side of every situation—to step outside her comforts to where there were no comforts for anyone, beast or man. Like many people for whom compassion is more than just a passing fashion, Dorothy could not forget poverty or pain once she had witnessed them herself, and like such people, her memory of them never left her, especially in circumstances that for most people would conveniently screen them from view. In the walled gardens of their villas, Heliopolis residents were spared many sights they would rather not see, but had they gone out with Dorothy on her rides into the countryside, they would have had to face, as she did, the realities of the real Egypt surrounding them—the poor hutments, the street beggars or street vendors whose sparse offerings placed them only a notch above begging, the starving stray dogs and cats, and the horses, mules, and donkeys, battered by lives of unending toil.

On these morning rides, off hovering in the distance, Dorothy would have noticed the craggy outcrop of the Mokattam Hills, which Gustave Flaubert took the trouble to visit on Christmas Day 1849, only to write, "there was nothing to see."[29] To those who knew better, the Mokattam Hills constituted a microcosm on the edges of the universe of Cairo. Called "Broken Off Mountain" in Arabic, Mokattam today is the location of both a comfortable suburb of Cairo (Muqattam) and, at the base of the mountain, the slums of Cairo's Christian trash collectors, known as *zabaleen* ("garbage people"). Since just before the outbreak of World War II, young people from this community have driven donkey carts to collect trash from the streets of the city, which they bring back to Mokattam for sorting, a part of the job typically taken on by women.[30] The animals are often neglected in a specially miserable myriad of ways. They are worked for hours in intense heat and, back at Mokattam, in surroundings piled high with combusting garbage that can resemble a vision of hell. These animals are often singed and even burned by these flames while working in the sun, in an atmosphere fetid and caustic. For food, they get whatever scraps are left over after people and pigs are fed. Hungrily eating whatever they find among the rubbish in which they live, they can develop bowel obstructions and colic, which, if not treated immediately, leads to painful death.[31]

At the time when, in the first year of the 1930s, Dorothy was riding through the deserts around Mokattam, quarrymen there were putting horses and mules to much harsher uses and conditions at the summit as they dragged huge loads of limestone from hilltop quarries. All who knew about these animals shared the same opinion: the Mokattam Hills were where horses and mules were routinely worked to death.

In the era before obscuring smog became the accepted norm in Cairo, the broken mountain would have appeared picturesque in the morning light; indeed, from its heights, one could look back at the rumpled golden carpet that was Cairo to the three pyramids, their broad planes reflecting light and their angles casting sharp shadows on the opposite bank of the Nile. But Dorothy had heard too many stories about the abuses inflicted on the horses who worked in the hot, squalid conditions of the quarry pits, and the sight of the mountain on her morning rides would have provided no particular pleasure, any more than the Pyramids would to anyone who had seen the squalid and cruel conditions suffered by many of the animals that carried tourists to see them. Perhaps this was one of the reasons why Dorothy took her rides in the featureless deserts east of the city. The landscape provided a bare canvas on which to paint her daybreak emotions. And out of deserts have come many a visionary seized with a new and compelling view of reality to share with the world at large.

It was while she was riding in these wastes one such morning, pondering how to help the animals at the SPCA and the ones laboring in the pits of Mokattam, that her horse took her across a patch of random weedy field. And there, among the dust and dead vegetation, she saw the skeleton of a beast, "lying on a pile of rubble." She noted the large size of the bones. She knew they were not so big as to belong to a camel, but they were not the fine bones of a native Arab pony. Then she glimpsed the skull. "The teeth were very long and protruding," Dorothy remembered. "It lay on its side and had without a doubt belonged to an English horse." A decade or six months ago, this animal had wandered out here, laid itself down, and not risen again.[32]

Dorothy had the gift of a highly developed imagination linked to an empathic heart. This gift gave her a theoretical sense not just of an animal's suffering, but it seemed to transfer directly to her how it felt to have lamed or broken legs, untreated sores, hunger and thirst, what she believed was an English horse's longing for the green and temperate island that was its native home. At the sight of any former war horse in Egypt, she would work back through time to what the animal's life may have been—from fields or hunting or the easy routine of pulling a milk float; then to the mud and sand of European and Middle Eastern battlefields and later being auctioned away from everything familiar, with years of toil and pain to follow for those too strong to die quickly. For the bleached bones of the desert skeleton, she didn't need imagination to know that the body that had clothed it had not started its life where it had ended, in a rubbish-filled field outside the Egyptian capital. This horse had been one of the survivors of the Great War. Sold or abandoned, it had worked for who knew how many weeks, months or years, and then it had died here amid the stubble and rubble, its bones picked clean by scavengers, sun, and wind.

This long-dead horse gave Dorothy a revelation different to what she had experienced with Old Bill. She knew she could probably have gone on doing what she was able to do for the war horses brought in to the SPCA. She could comfort the animals as best she could in the time she had available, could keep finding the money to buy and euthanize the hopelessly disabled or sick or those who had given up. After all that she had already done, Dorothy could have easily sat back and said to herself, "At least I've kept a few of them from dying in the desert, on a rubbish heap, like this animal did," and she could have felt justified in believing that she had done as much as could be expected of a foreign woman in a country with many more pressing problems to solve than the fates of a few hundred old war horses. But Dorothy Brooke was not a person to sit back and be satisfied with the results of any endeavor. She had felt the pull of a superhuman responsibility, not unlike what had driven her two husbands and countless men and women to offer their lives in service to the Great War, not unlike what had brought Alfred Branch from what could have been an untroubled existence in England to a daily battle with recalcitrant cultural obstacles and entrenched traditions in Egypt. Or, considering where she had found the horse's bones, the pull was like the story of a famous local holy man of whom Dorothy perhaps had already heard—the legend of Simon the Tanner, mover of the Mokattam Hills.

In the tenth century the Caliph Abu Tamim Ma'ad al-Mu'izz Li-Dinillah, better known as al-Moezz, sponsored a religious debate between the Coptic Christian patriarch Abraham and a Jewish vizier to the Fatimid court named Yaqub ibn Killis. The latter invited the patriarch to prove the truth of one of the best known parables in the New Testament. In Matthew 17:20 Jesus is quoted as saying, "If ye have faith as a grain of mustard seed, ye shall say unto this mountain, Remove hence to yonder place; and it shall remove; and nothing shall be impossible unto you." Prove it, said Yaqub to Abraham. The caliph agreed with his vizier, proclaiming that unless the patriarch could move Mokattam, the entire Coptic community would be slain. In prayer, Abraham had a vision of the Virgin Mary, who told him that if he could find a one-eyed water carrier in the marketplace, this man would move the mountain. Abraham found such a man in Simon the Tanner. So strictly did he hold to Old Testament precepts that he had once dashed out one of his eyes for some sin rather than suffer the torments of hell. Taken to the mountain by Abraham, in the presence of the caliph and his guards, Simon the Tanner told the patriarch to cry for mercy three times, and the mountain would be moved. Abraham did this, and the mountain shifted, to the wonder of all. But when he looked for Simon, he was nowhere to be found. The moral of the story: his physical presence was not needed. His faith had been great enough to move the mountain and save his community.

That day in the desert, looking down at the skull of an English horse, Dorothy recognized the tiny mustard seed of her own belief—the seed that, though smallest of all, could grow into a tree large enough for birds to roost in. Riding home to Heliopolis later with Geoffrey and Pinkie, she resolved on two missions. First, she would write a letter that would alert the world outside Egypt to the horrors she had seen in the streets of the city and in the stables of the

SPCA. Second, she would arrange to meet Dr. Branch, chairman in charge of the SPCA, whose help she needed if her plan to save the lost war horses of Cairo was ever to succeed. She had no reason to believe that either plan would work out. But for the sake of Old Bill and of the bones of an English horse bleaching in the desert sun, she had to try.

3. Old War Horse Fund

The fate of animals is of greater importance to me than the fear of appearing ridiculous; it is indissolubly connected with the fate of men.

—ÉMILE ZOLA

Dorothy went to see Dr. Branch at his office at the Royal Agricultural Society (RAS), a triangular complex of whitewashed European-style office blocks and exhibition halls located on the lushly green southern tip of Gezira Island in the Nile. Founded in 1908, the RAS was set up to ensure breeding standards for Arabian horses, writes Judith Forbis, "and the Horse Commission was established in 1892 with Prince Omar Toussoun at the helm." Through these means, and with the guidance of Dr. Branch, "the best descendants of the horses originally imported by Abbas Pasha and Ali Pasha Cherif were gathered together by its dedicated leaders."[1]

Besides the breeding and care of royal Arab horses and Egyptian bulls that came under his supervision, Dr. Branch oversaw animals such as sheep and chickens. Indeed these animals, as Dorothy recalled, were not always properly located in their pens but were often literally on the loose in Branch's office. This was partly due to the fact that when Branch was at his desk, his door was open to all and sundry. "One walked without ceremony into his sanctum," wrote Spooner. It was a sanctum in which one might find Branch at his desk, surrounded not just by ordinary office furniture but often by such creatures as a friendly fat-tailed sheep, some turkeys pecking at the flies which buzzed the room or at one's clothing in passing, and a playful young dog whose gamboling offered sharp contrast to Branch's habitually serious expression.[2]

This was how Dorothy first laid eyes on him, surrounded by some of the animals under his care.

To complete the endearing eccentricity of this first impression, Branch sat amid his menagerie wearing an incongruously formal coat of pale silk, coolly unwrinkled in the torrid heat, on his head a red tarboosh, the tasseled conical felt hat worn by Muslims and non-Muslims alike. Most men wore their tarboosh with a dignified verticality; Branch's was habitually cocked slightly to one side. Coupled with his challenging stance and direct gaze, the tilted tarboosh seemed to state, "I'm not like anyone you've ever met before, or will ever meet again." Rumor had it that Branch was known to be a "character," befitting this appearance, as an American visitor discovered around the same time as Dorothy's visit. When entrepreneur and horse breeder Henry Babson visited Branch at his office in 1932, he and a friend were taken down a corridor, at the remote end of which sat Branch, immersed in a sheaf of documents. Only when the men stood in front of him did he suddenly bark at them, "What do you know about Arab horses?" then grinning at their startled discomfiture.[3]

Branch seems to have delivered much the same performance for Dorothy. After she had circled her way past the fat-tailed sheep and the friendly pup, Dorothy arrived at Branch's desk. All at once he looked up and bellowed, "Well, and what can I do for you?" chuckling at his joke as he offered her a seat.[4] Spooner hints that some of Dorothy's anxiety about requesting Branch's help lay in the fact that he was chairman of the SPCA managing committee; his own opinion undoubtedly informed the committee's decision to allow seized war horses to return to their owners if judged to be still "useful," a position with which Dorothy could not have disagreed more. It was possible he would tell her that her ideas were worthless, that there were no more war horses left, or that they were too difficult to find and would cause red tape for the SPCA that he would rather not bother with. There was also the fact that Branch, having lived in Egypt for so many years, so long he was more Egyptian than English, might laugh at her expat naïveté. Did she actually think she could make a difference in a culture she couldn't begin to understand, which he with all his years here had yet to bring under his own control?

But Branch surprised Dorothy. He told her that he already knew all about the war horses of Cairo. In fact, their suffering was "the most damned-awful scandal that could be found anywhere in the world," he pronounced angrily, tarboosh tassel swinging. That these horses were still in circulation was, Branch said, an outrage on humanity. He confirmed something else. Dorothy told him she had been assured that there were no more than a few hundred former war horses extant throughout Egypt, making it seem to her a relatively easy job to gather them up. Branch insisted that this was the correct number—but as Dorothy was to discover, he and received wisdom were off by thousands. But for now, she took comfort in this confirmation that the task of rescuing the animals might not be as insurmountable as she assumed.

The next challenge was to show Branch a letter she had brought with her.

Returning home from her ride in the desert, Dorothy had sat down at her desk in Heliopolis and poured out her heart to the English public in a letter appealing for financial help to rescue the war horses of Cairo. She had never written such a letter, or anything intended for public distribution. So she chose her words and her strategy carefully. For one thing, she was up against another crucial and popular appeal for funding. Dorothy's letter, which she planned to send to the *Morning Post* (later the *Daily Telegraph*), opens by referencing a war horse awareness campaign that was then spreading through Britain. Concerned citizens had expressed a common wish to fund a monument in memory of the horses who had served and died in the Great War, for which a large amount of money was needed. And there was a parallel movement: other British people were lobbying for bringing back to England war horses left behind in France and Belgium, where many had been seen laboring or, worse, being conducted to the abattoirs that had horrified Ada Cole. "Letters to the press were full of suggestions" about all sort of memorials, writes Sarah Searight; already a monument had been raised in Brussels to memorialize messenger pigeons. One letter writer suggested that Grand National winnings should be channeled toward funding an equine monument in England. There seemed to be little room in people's imaginations or hearts for the horses still living in the east.[5]

Dorothy assumed this apparent dearth was because the public were understandably uninformed about a scandal that the British government was not particularly keen to advertise. In her letter, she uses this topic of memorials as her jumping off point. Making it clear that she respects the idea of a war horse monument, she points out that there were still alive in Egypt hundreds of horses, mules, and donkeys not made of bronze but of tired and elderly flesh and bone, animals whose service in the war should have ensured them release from work, not to mention relief from pain. Carefully but firmly, Dorothy explains that such comfort could best come through the funding not of monuments in an England most of these horses would never live to see again, but of care for them in their last days in Egypt, the place British forces had chosen to leave them behind.

The letter, published on April 16, 1931, is worth quoting in full, as it lays out Dorothy's entire vision—the problem she faced as well as the solution the public could help her achieve:

There have been several references lately in the columns of The Morning Post as to the possibility of raising a memorial to horses killed in the War. May I make a suggestion?

Out here, in Egypt, there are still many hundreds of old Army Horses sold of necessity at the cessation of the War. They are all over twenty years of age by now, and to say that the majority of them have fallen on hard times is to express it very mildly.

Those sold at the end of the war have sunk to a very low rate of value indeed: they are past "good work" and the majority of them drag out wretched days of toil in the ownership of masters too poor to feed them—too inured to hardship themselves to appreciate, in the faintest degree, the sufferings of animals in their hands.

These old horses were, many of them, born and bred in the green fields of England—how many years since they have seen a field, heard a stream of water, or a kind word in English?

Many are blind—all are skeletons.

A fund is being raised to buy up these old horses. As most of them are the sole means of a precarious livelihood to their owners, adequate compensation must, of necessity, be given in each case. An animal out here, who would be considered far too old and decrepit to be worked in England, will have before him several years of ceaseless toil—and there are no Sundays or days of rest in this country. Many have been condemned and destroyed by the Society for the Prevention of Cruelty to Animals (not a branch of the RSPCA), but want of funds necessitates that all not totally unfit for work should be restored to their owners after treatment.

If those who truly love horses—who realise what it can mean to be very old, very hungry and thirsty, and very tired, in a country where hard, ceaseless work has to be done in great heat—will send contributions to help in giving a merciful end to our poor old war heroes, we shall be extremely grateful; and we venture to think that, in many ways, this may be as fitting (though unspectacular) a part of a War Memorial as any other that could be devised.

Dorothy passed her letter to Branch, who read it in silence. If there was much about him that was inscrutable and unpredictable, it was obvious to Dorothy that he recognized the need for publicizing the problem and that he appreciated the logic of Dorothy's plan for how to solve it. When he finished, Branch told her he approved of everything she had written. Indeed, Branch was so moved he promised Dorothy that he could find all the former war horses that existed anywhere in the region around the capital. "I know every blackguard in Cairo," he claimed. "I'll lay my hands on every English horse." There was just one catch. He could do his part only if she did hers: raise the money necessary to buy all the horses he found.[6]

Money was already at the top of a long and troubling list that Dorothy carried around in her head, and it had to be addressed before she could begin to grapple with any of the other issues. The important thing right now was that she had Branch's promise of help. She had verified his real concern for the horses, and he had given her letter a passing grade. She assured Branch that she would find the money he needed to fulfill his side of the bargain.

Folded, sealed, stamped, and addressed to the *Morning Post*, the letter, which included a photograph of Old Bill, was dropped by Dorothy into a post box near Branch's office.

The Brookes employed a butler, Ahmed, whose duties included retrieving and delivering the daily mail, and Ahmed was as keen to watch for a response to the *Morning Post* appeal as Dorothy was.

Glenda Spooner implies that in the first few weeks after Dorothy had mailed her letter, she and Ahmed were constantly on the qui vive for what they assumed would be at least a few letters and, perhaps, donations to the cause. Then, when nothing came, they turned their attention to the respective exigencies of their lives. Dorothy's "social chains," in particular, bound her to a round of entertaining, sporting events, and parties, in between which she spent her free time at the Cairo SPCA, trying to help the battered old war horses brought in by owners or police and trying to find money in order to buy the ones that needed help the most.

Waiting for a response to her first letter didn't mean Dorothy stopped writing other appeals, and she was doing just that when Ahmed entered the drawing room one morning with the mail. She acknowledged him, then did a double take. Ahmed was carrying not a tray with a few envelopes on it but a stack of them just barely held in place between his arms and chin. "Much post, more outside," Ahmed told her in delight. "Postman very pleased—think madam's birthday."[7]

Dorothy had never received so many letters at one time. She asked Ahmed to place what he had on the dining table and bring in the remainder, while she sat down armed with her letter opener. There was no telling what the envelopes might contain. Would there be notes finding fault with her suggestion that living, starving horses deserved at least the same attention and monetary support as memorial bronze ones? Would there be people who assumed she had a lot of money and wondered why she wasn't spending her own fortune on caring for the animals, whose care she so easily commended to the public's attention? But she need not have worried. Without exception, the tenor of the correspondence was complete support for the war horses' rescue; and almost without exception, each note contained a donation to be used for that purpose.

Ahmed, smiling ear to ear, happily heaved another stack of mail onto the table.

"The campaign caught the public imagination," writes Sarah Searight. In fact, it prompted letters to the *Morning Post* from supporters asking for more help on Dorothy's behalf. One of these, a Mrs. Hall, wrote what stands as a good example of most readers' reactions to Dorothy's original electrifying letter. "We must dash at the business," she insisted, "and not let one needless pitilessly hot week prolong [the animals'] suffering." And readers paid attention; more than that, they, too, paid in donations to the cause. Even King George V and Queen Mary would be moved to donate funds from this time forward.[8]

A gift truly without price arrived from Scottish Australian poet William Henry Ogilvie (1869–1963), whose deep love for horses was as much a part of his being as kookaburras singing in a gum tree:

Honour, indeed, we owed to those lost, neglected ones,
Sold to a heartless people over a broken trust,
Those who carried our husbands, brothers and sires and sons,
Those who toiled in our wagons, those who galloped our guns
Left to stagger and strive in the desert's burning dust.

Out of the scorching sand, out of the quarry pits,
Out of the meaner streets and the muddy flats of the Nile
Pitying hearts have gathered them home to where Mercy sits,
Shoulders galled by the collar, poor mouths torn by the bits–
Lapped them with loving kindness, bidden them rest awhile.[9]

When Geoffrey returned home that afternoon of the first mail drop, Dorothy shared the good news as well as the challenge. Together they added up the checks and money orders, which amounted to £600—a small fortune in 1931. And now initial surprise and joy turned to sobering reality. "It was then she realized what she had taken on," Spooner wrote. "No longer was it a small and rather amateur and personal affair." The money itself needed to be divided into individual budget items for specific uses, and the ebb and flow of each budget line kept track of. This meant engaging the services of an accountant to audit the funds on a regular basis. And each donor had to be thanked and issued a receipt. No amount was so small or anonymous that it was not acknowledged with public sincerity. A supporter who accepted donations made within England would state in the *Evening News*, "I have pleasure in gratefully acknowledging the receipt of a shilling P.O. from 'A Lover of Animals.' Were he not anonymous, I would gladly write to him." Another published an acknowledgment in the same paper for a ten-shilling donation.[10]

But Dorothy realized her biggest responsibility would be to account to her donors for how their gifts would be used. This meant developing a system for gathering statistics based on the charity's ability to make good on its promises and evidence of positive progress for the animals in its care, and presenting the information in a way that made methods transparent and achievements measurable. All of this faced the woman who wrote, "I had never done any office work, and I had no training whatsoever."[11]

Luckily, some of these most basic difficulties were cleared up immediately. When it came to managing the funds deposited in the National Bank of Egypt, Dorothy was invited to turn the responsibility over to officers from the Royal Army Pay Corps, who volunteered to look after the accounts for her. For an office, she simply set aside a corner of the villa's drawing room, while the dining table remained a broad, flat surface for opening of mail in between the Brookes' frequent dinner parties.

The one task that flummoxed Dorothy was deciding what her charity was to be called. For Dorothy, the term "war horse" was problematic. It seemed to conjure not the animals she was rescuing, veterans of the desert campaigns of the Great War, but rather knights and steeds in armor from the age of Agincourt. While the condition of many of the horses Dorothy helped and the knowledge of how to care for them on the part of their owners could aptly be described using medieval terminology, Dorothy preferred to stay clear of language that might distract or mislead present and future donors or the press. She considered "Old Army Horses" but discarded it, as not all army horses took part in battle (though all equines harnessed into the service of war can be seen as war horses, whatever job they filled). In the end, Dorothy was most comfortable with a variation that had undertones of the kind of organizations formed to assist elderly and infirm human veterans—Old War Horse Fund. The subtle equation of four-hoofed and two-footed veterans in need of support in their final years was heart-reaching without being sentimental, and ultimately the proof of the pudding was in the eating: after the name was selected and made public, more donations came in than ever.[12]

Dorothy's next big job was to assemble a committee along the lines of that which governed the Cairo SPCA.

It was to be first and foremost a buying committee. Its members needed to have an expert understanding of equines and of the conditions from which they were being rescued; the members also needed to enjoy connections within Cairo society that could help the cause, as cooperation was vital not just from the horses' owners but from all levels of legal enforcement, municipal and provincial government, and anywhere else that might prove useful. When Dorothy solicited Dr. Branch, not only was her request accepted with alacrity, but Branch offered the spacious RAS grounds for reviewing and accepting the war horses brought in for sale. This was a most promising beginning, as was the generous acceptance of Dorothy's nominations of some of the most prominent members of Cairo's British society: Maj. Gen. Sir Charlton Watson Spinks, Sir Alexander Keown Boyd (director general, European Department, Ministry of the Interior, Egyptian Government, 1923–37), Col. Paul Hornby (Twelfth Lancers), Col. Arthur Main (Royal Horse Artillery), Maj. Gen. Meade Edward Dennis, Maj. Roland Heveningham, and Maj. Joseph Bell (Royal Army Veterinary Corps).

In addition to these men, Branch urged Dorothy to include on the committee several men from the Cab Drivers' Union, members of which, as we have seen, boarded their animals at the Cairo

SPCA for a nominal fee and for the animals' benefit. "These men, [Branch] maintained, were prosperous but quite decent," wrote Glenda Spooner. They were on the side of the average poor driver and had intimate knowledge of market prices for working horses. There may have also been a certain realpolitik on Branch's part. During 1906–7 there had been increasing agitation among the gharry drivers of Cairo. Denigrated as among the lowest and most violent members of Cairene society, both by foreigners and by modern-minded Egyptians who considered horse-drawn transportation an embarrassing anachronism in a developing nation, finally the drivers of Cairo had had enough, and they organized and mounted a strike action. The virtual shutdown of this vital transportation service forced the government to promise never again to imprison drivers whose animals had suffered serious injury, and the action served to reduce punishment for infractions to fines rather than deprivation of a driver's license. While this softening of punishment undid much of what the RSPCA had achieved to protect drivers' animals from abuse, the restrictions these older regulations had created had put many gharry drivers out of business, resulting in increased misery for their horses anyway, defeating the purpose on all sides. Branch was in Egypt at the time of the strike; he understood the need for balance between the welfare of animals and the complex exigencies of people, so as to mitigate the suffering of both. By involving members of the Cab Drivers' Union, Branch would have preserved that balance while exposing union members and their fellow drivers to the humaneness and practicality of ensuring working equines received the care and attention they deserved.[13]

Dorothy had also come to a realistic conclusion on this issue. She and, perhaps, Branch were among the few on the committee who had really looked into the dark heart of abuse of the elderly war horses they intended to rescue. As such, they knew how easy it could be to let their emotions get the better of good sense. "It was essential," writes Spooner, "that in their anxiety over the horses, the committee did not overpay."[14] What they feared and indeed anticipated was that hope of financial gain might tempt some horse owners to cripple otherwise sound animals and present them for sale to play on the heart strings of the committee. Apart from the suffering inflicted on horses (thanks to such superstitious practices as "firing" or applying flame to painful joints or skin infections, and nostril slitting), purchasing these animals would drain funds earmarked for authentic war horses. The cab drivers were there to better help identify horses, at the same time proving to the native owners who brought their animals for sale that there were Egyptian voices as well as English ones at the buying table, and that the prices offered could be trusted. Though the tarboosh-wearing Egyptians never sat with the English at the table but off to one side, they were still as much a part of the negotiations as their English counterparts, and they prevented abuses while lending keen eyes and experience to the overall selection process.

Sir Charlton Spinks was chair of the Old War Horses Fund buying committee, and as Dorothy said, with characteristic frankness, he was "the man for me."[15] Not only was he inspector general of the Egyptian Army—the last sirdar of Egypt (1924–37)—and spoke fluent Arabic, but Sir Charlton had almost as thorough a knowledge of horses as Branch. Branch and Sir Charlton would seem a dream team on the buying committee; as time passed, Dorothy would find to her consternation and her despair that for Branch, no committee was big enough for himself and another powerful male presence to occupy at the same time.

Each Thursday the committee members would take their seats at a series of tables in the shade and be presented with horses for sale. "These animals are brought before two or more members of the Committee," Dorothy explained in a letter to the *Morning Post*, "who assess their value, which ranges from £6 to £12 approximately. The higher prices are paid for those in better condition, who consequently must be considered to have greater capabilities for labour before them for an indefinite period of time."[16]

Those purchased were walked to an open shed that stood within sight of Branch's office door. Those still waiting always formed an ever-lengthening queue. "The animals collected for sale gathered in dejected lines about 50 yards distant," wrote Glenda Spooner. Their owners sometimes accompanied the horses, but often they simply tied them up to posts along the way to the SPCA gates and left them in the sun, with no water. Some, ill and old, couldn't stand; they lay on the ground. Some died before they could be presented for selection.[17]

Dorothy would later describe the scene herself in a report to her donors. "Let us imagine we are standing in the blistering sun by our stable door on a buying day," she wrote. "The horses brought for sale are carefully examined on arrival, noting the old war brand on its quarters, its condition and lameness, or comparative soundness."[18] In addition to the picture of misery in front of them, as far as the eye could see, the buying committee had the added struggle of making rational offers for the animals, all the while hoping that by the time they reached the ones in the worst condition they would still be alive. A syce (pronounced "sice" as in "ice," from the Arabic word for "groom") carried water and berseem clover up and down the lines for those horses able to partake of them.[19]

Spooner points out that Dorothy was never absent from these Thursdays, though even she had her limits. Returning home one afternoon following a long morning during which everyone at the buying table had been gutted by heartrending examples of neglect and abuse, Dorothy simply fainted. This was, she later stated, with typical humor, a "rather silly performance," but the stress that had caused this collapse was very serious. "I will not attempt to describe to you the condition of the old English horses we purchased in that first and other innumerable buying days," Dorothy wrote in a letter. "I can only state without a shadow of exaggeration that so appalling is the work and so horrified all the English members of the committee, including tough Mr [Branch], that at times it is almost beyond our power of endurance to continue." Indeed, if Branch could barely handle some of the sights on buying day, there is no reason to assume that Dorothy was exaggerating; actually, she herself said often that there were no adequate means to describe the sufferings of the animals whose fates she presided over each week.[20]

Thursdays were a trial for everyone, including the horses, who until buying was moved to the SPCA often had to be walked long distances, in lame condition, to reach the Royal Agricultural Society grounds. But they were nothing compared to what happened the day after. Dorothy called this day "black Friday."

Following the purchase of war horses, Dorothy took upon herself the responsibility of inspecting each animal individually to determine which ones would need to be euthanized. A more businesslike person might possibly have taken one look at the entire collection bought on Thursday and sent them all to be destroyed, but Dorothy felt otherwise. To her, the first order of business was to treat these damaged but gallant old warriors with respect. This meant offering them a quiet, shaded place to rest. Many had been kept in the opposite conditions, crowded gharry stables with hard floors and poor ventilation. When Dorothy was later to visit some of the places from which her patients had been brought, in all of them she found horses left to lie "on wet mud or cement in their own dung which, in that climate, gave out even more acrid fumes of ammonia" than had they been stabled in normal conditions. She was determined that her patients would never have to endure this again.[21] From the beginning, to Dorothy the animals under her care were no different from human patients in a hospital or hospice. Their immediate suffering needed to be addressed; and while some of them might be brought back to some semblance of health through adequate diet, rest, and veterinary care, others were dying or in such compromised condition that death was to be preferred, sooner rather than later. They must be offered all the food and water they could take, which many of the patients received with obvious surprise. These were cases to be managed because they could not be cured.

Walking into a box, the floor of which was strewn with sweet, fresh straw, "they would lower their heads and sniff as though they could not believe their own eyes or noses," Dorothy wrote in her diary. "Memories, long forgotten, would then return when some stepped eagerly forward toward the mangers piled high with berseem, while others with creaking joints, lowered themselves slowly on to the bed and lay, necks and legs outstretched."[22]

Some never got up again.

Dorothy's daughter Pinkie captured one of her mother's patients in a watercolor dating from around 1931–32. As demonstrated throughout her work, Pinkie had a keen understanding of how to depict a horse. It was almost as if she painted from the inside out, starting with the animal's spirit and personality, then capturing it within a body of gleaming muscle. The horse Pinkie chose to memorialize at the hospital was very different from her portraits of the blooded Arabs of family friends. What we see first is the interior of a large, cavernous stable in which horses with jutting hipbones stand with faces to the wall, munching their hay. Just enough light spills through shadow to reveal the almost flattened figure of an emaciated chestnut horse, a white stripe down its nose. This is not a horse that has eased itself down comfortably into its hay; it has literally dropped, unable to stand. Its scrawny legs are splayed as if it had not been able to walk in the first place, or was too weak, once down, to rearrange its limbs. As it rests there in the bar of sunshine, its nose deep in a bucket of bran mash, the horse fixes a dark, wary eye on the beholder. It is an animal that has forgotten what it was like to take rest or food without interruption or to labor without pain, and it has not forgotten the whip that fell on it should it be unable to continue. Yet as its tired head arches up to eat what is in the bucket, even if it had been summoned with shouts or blows, there was no way this animal would have been able to get on its feet.

To the pages of her diary Dorothy confided what it meant to her to serve these traumatized animals not just as angel of mercy but as angel of death:

> It is a heartbreaking business and one which I dread beyond all words. To see one suffering or starving horse gives all horse lovers a pain in the heart. Imagine being faced, day after day, with rows of such animals, each more pitiful than the last. And in so many cases one can sense the remnant of a gallant spirit and a nervous anxiety as to what fate may yet befall them. So accustomed are they now to the endless demands of their owners, they nervously prick an ear or roll an anxious eye when I approach, which adds immeasurably to my own misery when I simply have to order the syce to lead this one or that out to a distant shed to be put down. If only a green English field would miraculously appear

outside that blistering, dusty yard, a field with shady trees and a brook running through it, what heaven it would be! If only I could say to the syce who is my fellow executioner, "Lead them into that field, let them lie down and roll to their heart's content, let them crop the sweet grass and drink the cool running waters." If I could have said that and left them there for even a week, I would not have minded so much. But to have to give the orders—one after the other and after only a few hours' precious rest in a shed and with the dread of tomorrow still in their eyes—caused me infinite pain. Only the knowledge that it just had to be done, that their suffering must cease . . . only this makes it possible for me to do it and go on doing it day after day.[23]

4. Black Friday

Good-bye, old man; I wish that you could answer
And tell me all your brown eyes try to say.

—LUCY LAWRENCE[1]

Facing suffering on a weekly basis gave Dorothy insight into equine psychology. She came to realize, even more so than she had ever done before, that horses were not so different from human beings who had lived through similar hardships—that, in fact, they were often far more sensitive to affection, gallant under strain, and able to summon trust after years of betrayal, than most human beings were capable of after surviving such trauma.

Anyone who has spent time around horses knows they have unique personalities and display a vivid range of emotions, with sudden loves and just as sudden antipathies. There are passionate attachments, not just always to other horses or to human beings but even to other animals with whom they have formed relationships, often under difficult or lonely conditions. There are those who could not be bribed to draw close with all the bran mash in the world, who lived in a wild-eyed solo drama of their own, often prompted by unforgettable mistreatment. There are the nobly poised and the warily skittish, the quietly affectionate and the sweetly shy. By studying the different interrelationships she saw, it became apparent to Dorothy that some of the war horses brought to the buying committee were bonded pairs. They had perhaps served together in the Great War, or they were from different regiments but were sold together when the British Army departed Egypt. Whatever had joined them, they had established a critical dependence on one another, propping one another up lest both fall. But she only discovered this after inadvertently separating two inseparable mates.

"One day a very sorry pair of old gharry horses were brought, one of which was a piebald," wrote Glenda Spooner. She referred to a type of horse with a black and white splotched pattern over its coat. On seeing the animal, even in his present condition, Dorothy wondered whether he had once been a regimental drum horse.[2] A drum horse, seen today in Trooping the Colour ceremonies, carries just behind its mane two silver drums, which are beaten by the horse's rider to maintain consistent march time for a cavalry regiment, while the rider's feet manipulate special reins connected to the stirrups. Piebalds are sturdy, quiet, grave, and handsome animals, and this patient was all of those, despite the fact that he was in such damaged condition Dorothy feared that with all his will to live she would still not be able to save him. Yet the horse with him was in even worse shape, if possible. In fact, it was difficult to imagine how he had survived the trip to reach the Royal Agricultural Society grounds to be offered for sale. Clearly he had persevered because his piebald friend had accompanied him on the long walk from wherever they had started.

Dorothy later believed it was the stress of "black Friday" that caused her to forget that the piebald and his mate had arrived together. From her first inspection of the piebald's companion, she knew it would be criminal to make him suffer one more instant, and she asked a syce to take him to join the others scheduled for immediate euthanasia. This was done with all the gentleness Dorothy could summon from the grooms under her supervision. These animals were gathered in a yard with an outbuilding where they could be out of the hot sun and away from the other horses. There they were given bran mash, a comforting, filling meal that also hydrated the water-starved, a treat no doubt familiar to those who could still remember what life had been like before 1919. Satisfied by this, each horse was then led away to its instant death.

No sooner had the incapacitated horse limped to the shed than Dorothy heard the piebald whinnying as if in pain. She hurried into the stables, where she found him "in a terrible state of mind," she recalled, "pawing desperately at his straw with his battered old legs and deformed feet. . . . Moreover he was shaking all over and, as he was blind in one eye, he had his head turned over his shoulder on the side he could see," stabled as he was in the Egyptian way, with his face toward the wall. Still unsure what to do, Dorothy had bran mash brought to distract him, but the piebald wanted something else and was so desperate for it that this treat, something that in his long life of Egyptian labor he can never have hoped to taste again, meant nothing to him. This is when Dorothy realized that he was looking for his old friend.[3]

Dorothy had a syce bring over from the "condemned" yard a horse the groom thought might be the piebald's mate. But it was not. He led several over, each in their turn. None were the mate the piebald was seeking; and it was terrible to watch as he continued to strain to see over his shoulder, stamping and whinnying in agitation. Desperate to fix her mistake, Dorothy asked the stableman to lead the piebald himself over to the condemned yard, to see if he could find his friend himself.[4]

"Anxiously, the old boy shambled across the yard," Dorothy wrote, "and along two rows of waiting horses . . . until, coming to a miserable old crock, he stopped and nickered softly."[5]

The piebald and his mate, noses bobbing against the other, had been reunited.

Both horses were taken back to the stable. They were given bran mash, which they ate happily, heads together, tails twitching. Then they were taken out again and euthanized simultaneously.

In his 2007 book *The Emotional Lives of Animals*, ethologist Dr. Marc Bekoff quotes the director of a primate research center who, when asked if animals were capable of experiencing and expressing emotion, replied that far from being so capable, animals were merely a "neutral palette on which we paint our needs, feelings, and view of the world." Having observed firsthand too many instances to the contrary to take this admittedly biased opinion seriously, Dr. Bekoff writes, "When we deny that animals have feelings, it demeans both them and us."[6] But Dorothy had seen this for herself. And she made a vow that never again would any bonded pair be separated. As they had lived and labored—and suffered—together, they would also rest, eat, drink, and sleep forever, together, too.[7]

In the meantime, funds to keep the Old War Horse Fund running were rapidly running out.

The Brookes went home on leave in May 1931, frustratingly soon after the committee had begun its work. This was also a time when with the shortage of funds came evidence that there were many more ex–war horses in Egypt than Dr. Branch had originally estimated. He was Dorothy's main source for war horses, but she began to have suspicions about his sources of information—he had claimed to know for certain that there were no more than two hundred old war horses in all of Egypt—when the numbers so clearly argued against him. Also, verifiable ex–war horses were being offered to the buying committee from sources outside Branch's own, bumping the numbers far over the figures he had originally given.

Thus far the committee had purchased over three hundred war horses; along with these were many army mules. As we have seen, Dorothy was concerned about the horses and mules being worked in the limestone quarries in the Mokattam Hills. But she would not blame the men, at least not in theory. "The everlasting necessity," she wrote of the quarries, "of almost superhuman effort on the part of man and beast render the men callous to all suffering. . . . So shocking is the condition of the horses that once they set foot inside these dreadful places, I am told on good authority, they are never seen outside again. The appallingly overloaded, great two-wheeled, badly-balanced carts used by the merchants, have to be dragged from the quarry head over deep sand and stones to where the road to Cairo runs. There these quite dreadful horses are unhitched and led back to fresh purgatory," made the more hellish through the heat in the quarry canyons and the little or no water available to either the men or the animals. The thought of elderly or thirsty or underfed animals being worked to death under these conditions haunted Dorothy intensely. But to get them out of the quarries to the buying committee meant not just pressing Branch, with his connections to "all the blackguards in Egypt," and recruiting the local police to her cause but also raising more money to pay for the animals, and now the fund was low on resources to help any. So the Brookes' return to England for a vacation was hardly restful.[8]

Dorothy's original fundraising appeal had done wonders to make the public aware of the plight of former war horses in Egypt. Now, only a month after her April 1931 letter to the *Morning Post*, Dorothy wrote another, which the *Post* duly published on May 19. She was mindful that not everyone could handle details, let alone photographs, of the sights she had to see on a daily basis—"I have always tried not to harrow the feelings of the public overmuch," Dorothy insisted, having lived in an England that saw soldiers returned from the Great War rendered faceless by bullets or shells. Or, rather, an England that did not want to see them, so that some donned beautiful, lifeless masks, submitted to the excruciating and not always successful medical marvels of pioneering plastic surgeon Dr. Harold Gillies, or just bravely faced the averted or shocked stares (except, it should be noted, among child spectators, not yet invested with all the prejudices of maturity). Dorothy knew that this tendency to avoid intolerable truths was still a factor with which she would have to deal. And in this thank-you letter/renewed appeal to that public, she achieved a masterpiece of considerate understatement and stark outline of truth that would be the envy of any fund development manager today.[9]

Sir—It is difficult to find words with which to thank you for printing my letter on April 16 and the innumerable kind people who so readily and generously responded to our appeal for funds. . . .

At the time of writing we have received £870–including a generous donation from Our Dumb Friends League—and I am happy to say, subscriptions are still coming in. . . .

I wish all those kind-hearted persons who have given us their invaluable help could see the animals we buy, and feel the thankfulness we ourselves experience at having it in our power to release them from their weary bondage and from so much suffering. Many are nearly thirty years of age: their sunken faces and shaking legs tell the story of their sorrows. Many have been beautiful horses in their day; even now their fine skins and carriage of their heads, as they shamble past, tell us plainly that no misfortune nor adversity can quite break their pride of race. It is a heart-rending sight.

Now that the administration of the Fund is on a firm footing, we cannot help entertaining a real fear that our present funds—thankful though we are to have them—will not carry us over half, nor a third, of the work before us. It is impossible to compute the exact number of old War Horses still alive in this country, but it can be estimated at many hundreds and, until we have the money, it will be impossible to call up more than a limited number of these poor animals in the country districts, where their sufferings are acute and where any form of inspection or supervision is out of the question.

At a rough estimate we shall need at least £3,000 to deal adequately with the work before us. Subscribers may rest assured that every penny given to this cause goes to the rescue of the horses, pays a fair price for each animal and for a few days' forage and attention before he meets a painless end.[10]

Dorothy and Geoffrey spent four months in England, without any real rest from their Egyptian responsibilities. The piles of mail she had had to deal with in Heliopolis seemed to follow Dorothy inexorably. In fact they not only accompanied her to her own home but were carted along to the homes of friends and family to whom she and Geoffrey paid visits. Dorothy easily confessed she was "unmoved by their pained expressions when I appropriated their dining room tables," which, like the table in her Heliopolis dining room, was the only surface capable of holding all the paperwork. (To help ease this burden, her sister Cicely Gibson-Craig generously stepped forward to handle all English correspondence for the Old War Horse Fund.) Perhaps their pained expressions changed when relatives and friends heard how much Dorothy's second letter had raised—another £5,000, a large fortune at the time. Dorothy deposited the money in Lloyd's Bank, Fleet, the manager of which had volunteered all his services for managing the fund.[11]

People touched by Dorothy's account of the lost war horses of Cairo did more than just write checks. From Britain to the Dominions, animal lovers raised funds through a variety of events. There were whist parties, with all winnings going to the fund, and gymkhanas where English horses could play a role in helping their less fortunate relatives in Egypt. Florence, Lady Alexander, widow of famed actor Sir George Alexander and herself a former stage personality, organized a ball at the Dorchester in Mayfair, a luxury hotel in London that had just opened for business in 1931, to benefit the Old War Horse Fund. The RSPCA made a grant to the fund of £500, just the beginning of what would be widespread cooperation on the part of that organization with the work of the fund committee.[12] A prominent member of the RSPCA, solicitor E. Meade-King, even went out to Egypt to see if he could buy any of the former war horses who were judged to be in healthy enough condition to survive the sea voyage. His was the first of several such efforts, which would culminate in the return of a few old war horses to England over the next several years, giving Dorothy's supporters a very real sense of the good their support was doing for the animals they had helped rescue.[13]

The RSPCA chapter in Leamington, a spa town in Warwickshire, was particularly supportive of Dorothy's work. Capt. J. A. Durham, a member of the chapter, and probably another member, Mrs. George Bryant of Ashorne Hill (her red brick manor house would become "the Bletchley Park of the steel industry" during World War II) were behind a long article in the *Royal Leamington Spa Courier*, published in November 1931. Besides its quotes from Dorothy's committee report for that year, the article speaks in the more universal animal welfare language of the RSPCA.[14] With the celebration of Armistice Day and Remembrance Day, wrote Captain Durham and Mrs. Bryant, "with all their sad and hallowed memories" of soldiers lost and battles won, was it not all the more appropriate to encourage commemoration of those other soldiers, "our 'Long-Faced Chums,' who gallantly and so uncomplainingly bore with us the heat and the burden of the day during the drab and dreary times of the War?" Such reminders would not be needed, they added, were it not for the fact that the horses, mules, and donkeys who had served alongside human soldiers were unable to speak for themselves—indeed, it was because of that voicelessness that they had been conscripted into war without being given a choice. Yet that silence should in no way downplay the contributions, and sacrifices, of animals brought into human conflict through no fault or choice of their own. Who, they asked, had not seen wounded horses standing patiently in a battlefield, the sky overhead exploding, ready to continue to serve though their injuries were mortal and their lives now measured in the moments it took to bring a pistol up to their heads? Who had not seen these animals struggling to pull guns through mud and filth, obedient in their selfless service to human warfare?[15]

The writers appealed to the newspaper's readership to remember what horses had endured in the war. "Remember they suffered, suffered in the same manner we did, from wounds, from sickness, from dread diseases," wrote Durham and Bryant. And after the war, who thought of what happened to these soldiers? Who remembered the thousands of them abandoned or sold in countries without animal cruelty laws or traditions of care like those in the Western nations from which these animals had come? "Surely the bounds of common decency and humanity were passed when for filthy lucre we parted with some 22,000 war horses to the natives of Egypt. Were honour, conscience, virtue, gratitude all exiled? Was there no relenting pity?"[16]

Another letter of this type was published in the *Bucks Herald*, written by Great War veteran Gen. Sir George de Symons Barrow. Barrow had commanded the Yeomanry Mounted Division in the Sinai and Palestine Campaign and had been present for General Allenby's entrance into Jerusalem in December 1917, a Pyrrhic victory described by one historian of the period as having been "achieved after three years of wasteful conflict by a short war of movement with relatively few casualties."[17] Relatively few human casualties, that is. Like Geoffrey Brooke in France, Barrow had had plenty of opportunities to witness the heroism and the tragedy of horses in the battles of the desert campaigns. What makes Barrow's letter so important is that it was the first known publicly shared indictment since the founding of the Old War Horse Fund of the cruel method by which British and Allied forces had so casually disposed of the equines who had helped them beat the Central powers and win the war. "On the termination of hostilities in November, 1918, followed by the withdrawal of our troops from Palestine and Syria, several thousand horses and mules were left in the country. A large number of these were the chargers and troop horses of the Mounted Force which played such a great part in Lord Allenby's decisive campaigns against the Turks."[18]

Following the war's end, General Barrow wrote, these animals being of no further use to the government, and there being no funds to organize transport back to where they had come from, the horses were sold to Egyptians. Though many of these horses had since died, many others, over a quarter century in age, were still living and were, in the general's words, "miserably wretched." To make this all the worse, as age overtook them and their strength, bred into them for other purposes than dragging overloaded garbage carts or gharries filled to capacity with tourists, their value decreased, and, too often, so did their owners' interest in looking after a draft horse or mule that might die in a month's time.

Barrow, an eyewitness, painted in no uncertain terms the physical and mental deterioration of the equines left in Egypt to be worked in the streets, fields, and quarries. "Some are blind, some suffer from advanced forms of ringbone, which makes each step an agony; and one recently purchased had been worked for some time with a broken leg and was blind in both eyes," he reported. Most had never had enough to eat, and those in the worst physical shape were worked during the night, when their owners were less apt to be arrested by the police. "Such is the sad fate of these faithful old servants who carried our soldiers gallantly on many a long and waterless march and in many a combat," Barrow wrote. For these broken animals, death was sweet release, if it could only be given to them. And, it was made clear to readers, the way to help ease this suffering was to contribute to the Old War Horse Fund.[19]

Dorothy was grateful for the many voices that echoed everything she was trying to share with the world about the fate of Britain's lost war horses. "So many people persist in giving me all the credit," Dorothy noted in her diary, "that I want to make it abundantly clear that it would be absolutely impossible for me to achieve any fraction of success but for the unselfish, sustained and invaluable help rendered by a great number of other people, who never receive adequate recognition. I have been given many more pats on the back than I deserve."[20] Yet had she not undertaken the work, even with an obvious groundswell of public interest in the fate of the abandoned war horses and army mules, it is very possible that they would have been completely forgotten. This was never more clear than in a publication touting the official party line, the *Illustrated London News*, a standby of weekly news reporting in England that seemed content to edit the contributions of war horses out of the stirring narrative of the Great War.

In May 1935 the *Illustrated* published a deluxe edition celebrating the Silver Jubilee of King George V and Queen Mary (at the death of his father, King Edward VII, on May 10, 1910, George, then Duke of York, had acceded to the throne). Pages of commissioned art and vintage photographs were devoted to memorializing and celebrating Britain's role in the war. Yet aside from a brief, parenthetical, amused reference to animal assistance—"(horse, mule, donkey, camel, and even sleigh-dog)," as if describing a circus— the colored plates to which all readers would have turned, showing "Phases of the British Army's Part in the Great War," included none of these animals. They were not included even in the vignette titled "1917 Palestine," where horses, mules, and camels had been at least as responsible for driving out the Turks as British soldiers were, a fact that men like Geoffrey Brooke and Sir George de Symons Barrow knew all too well.[21]

This omission would continue to remain a sort of blind spot for the British government, much as it had been in 1919 when Secretary of State for War Winston Churchill discovered that war horses who had served in the European theater of war had been left behind to starve, die of disease, or become steaks in Belgian and French abattoirs. In a memo to Quartermaster-General Lieut. Gen. Sir Travers Clarke, Churchill had used a tone echoing Dorothy's own desperation of years later. "If it is so serious, what have you been doing about it?" Churchill demanded. "The letter of the Commander-In-Chief discloses a complete failure on the part of the Ministry of Shipping to meet its obligations and scores of thousands of horses will be left in France under extremely disadvantageous conditions." It is unfortunate that this concern, welcome as it is to see in a high-ranking British official, for the horses left in Europe (many of which were still to be found there into the late 1920s and early 1930s, this concern notwithstanding), does not seem to have extended to those left in the Middle East.[22]

For the present the growing success of the Old War Horse Fund, thanks to which help for the horses and mules in the Cairo stone quarries now seemed within reach, spurred Dorothy to take a more personal role in seeking out animals to rescue on her return to Egypt that fall. If she thought she had seen some of the worst of what individual human beings, and the larger scourge of poverty, could inflict on helpless animals, venturing into Cairo slums would reveal additional depths of despair. And so, to her shock, would her future work with Dr. Branch.

2

Adventure

I loved the wide gold glitter of the plains
Spread out before us like a silent sea,
The lazy lapping of the loose-held reins,
The sense of motion and of mystery . . .

—WILLIAM HENRY OGILVIE (1869–1963)

5. An End and a Beginning

Horses were all about heroines, not heroes.

—SUSANNA FORREST[1]

Dorothy returned to Cairo to find that over the summer many more war horses and mules had been identified and were ready to be brought to the buying committee's attention. This promised an even busier fall than spring. She also found that Dr. Branch had come up with an idea to improve on the buying experience for people and animals.

"In future," wrote Glenda Spooner, "[Branch] decreed they should collect not at the Agricultural Society grounds, but outside the SPCA Hospital." In another change of routine, Branch required that animals brought for sale be presented in discrete groups rather than strung out in long queues. How they were grouped is unknown, but it is likely that animals in worse shape than others were kept together and examined before those in better condition, which would have helped prevent the heartbreaking cases of animals dying before they could make it to the buying table.[2]

However, there was another side to these changes, as became clear to Dorothy and the committee at a later date. While Branch was clearly a man who loved animals, he also loved his preeminence among the Egyptian princes and officials who employed and relied on him. Perhaps, too, Branch was motivated by a certain amount of professional jealousy. To most who support animal charities and conservation work, the people who carry out missions of compassion are very near to being saints—think only of Dr. Jane Goodall and the chimpanzees of Gombe. And this is true of many like

Dr. Goodall. Unfortunately, among even among those who dedicate their lives to saving the last of an endangered species, there are those who must also always keep an ear to the ground for more funding and how best to acquire it to support their mission and its expenses. They must stand out from the herd of other conservationists in the fight for this support, without which, in a world of cash burned on as many bonfires of vanity as altars of compassion, the good work of one season can be undone by the poverty of the next, depending on economic factors and on the more sophisticated or attractive marketing of competing charities, as well as on politics, wars that take place in boardrooms as well as on battlefields, and other human-caused triggers for suffering that animals too often are made to endure.

And while most conservationists rise above the internecine warfare spawned by funding cycles and ever-tightening restrictions on ever-shrinking dollars, some descend to actively backstabbing their "rivals." These competitors are not necessarily bad people, but are rather good people driven to do whatever it takes to ensure the future of their particular work, even when this means ranging well outside the territory assigned to benign goodness. Indeed, this often calls on otherwise well-meaning people to ape the jungle creed of survival of the fittest, or worse, the human creed of vindictiveness and revenge.

To what degree professional jealousy played a part in what destroyed the happy medium of the relationship Branch and Dorothy shared we may never know. But it is clear that the term "amour propre," which Branch liked to use—in humor, it was assumed, by those who did not know how seriously he meant it—had something to do with his about-face.

It began with rumors. According to what Dorothy was told, Branch had been informed by various powerful personages in Cairo that the sight of miserable horses lined up on the RAS grounds and en route to the SPCA hospital for treatment or destruction had proved insupportably distressing to "various Egyptian officials," as Spooner tersely puts it. Tourists who had seen the horses had apparently also made "complaints." They had come to Cairo, after all, to see pyramids and to shop for fake but exotic trophies for the mantelpiece back home, not to have their heartstrings tugged or vacation ruined by dying animals. Spooner suggests these were less likely to have been complaints about seeing the animals as they were embarrassing enquiries of officials as to how equines in Cairo had been allowed to reach this level of misery in the first place. "[Dorothy] was told that not only did this sight cause distress to sensitive persons (who, as she points out, never lifted a finger to help)," Spooner says, "but that it embarrassed the Egyptian Government to have such animals paraded weekly before the public."[3] Branch informed the buying committee that operations would have to be moved to the grounds of the SPCA and away from the precincts of the RAS.

At the time, Dorothy had considered the move a boon and accepted Branch's reasoning on its merits. In truth, she was already casting her energies past any fixed place of collection in Cairo. She had realized that there were horses and mules throughout Egypt who needed help; the germ of developing several clinics was already active in her thoughts; indeed, one clinic was already in operation. A group allied with the Old War Horse Fund had been formed in Alexandria, where a number of former war horses were purchased and rescued. Dorothy was also increasingly drawn to working animals native to Cairo, who had not fought in the Great War but who each fought their own daily war of survival. "Driving through the streets of the town," writes Spooner, "she encountered heartbreaking cases of overloading and starvation of broken down little Arabs." Almost from the start of her quest, Dorothy had had the idea of setting aside some of the fund monies for the rescue and rehabilitation (if possible) of these Egyptian work horses, mules, and donkeys.[4] One major contributive factor was that many owners of former war horses were increasingly bundling into purchases their native horses, mules, or donkeys, often similarly neglected. "To look at these wretched little Arabs and donkeys was bad enough," Dorothy remembered, "to send them away well-nigh impossible. Very little had to be given for the cast-offs. A few shillings satisfied the most rapacious owners who had to admit the animals were useless." If, however, the committee members refused to buy any but former war horses or army mules, owners not infrequently held all the animals hostage. "Savagely tugging at the frayed rope that held the poor little misery and, nearly capsizing it in its weakness they would drag it away calling down curses upon our heads." She was powerless to call the police; an owner could only be held culpable if the animal were witnessed being worked in observably infirm condition.[5]

Branch, at least in the beginning, seemed to sympathize with Dorothy's concern for these *baladi* or "peasant" equines. He, like the other committee members, saw what happened when they refused to purchase two or three dying Arabs to get at one old war horse. A few otherwise powerless men often found themselves in a position to pose a shrewd bargain that was difficult for the committee to reject. "The owners of the gharry stables of mixed English and Baladi horses assured the committee that if only it would buy their whole stableful they would give up horses altogether and purchase a taxi," wrote Spooner.[6] So the group began to agree to these arrangements, using money Dorothy, as treasurer, had set aside in a neutral "Animal Assistance Fund." And when that account ran low, Branch authorized expenditure from the SPCA's funds, setting in motion an enduring relationship between the Cairo SPCA and Dorothy's own future hospital.

Then the trouble started in earnest.

In all her written references to him, Dorothy would protect Branch from his own well-known reputation, as best she was able to, by using a pseudonym for him, a practice carried through in Glenda Spooner's 1960 book *For Love of Horses*. (This pseudonymic reference only ceased when Dorothy's granddaughter Sarah Searight named Branch thirty-three years later in her book *Oasis*.) In the pages of her diaries, Spooner writes, Dorothy "is scrupulously fair and uses the fictitious name [Mr. Strong], an assiduity one might excuse her for not exercising on his behalf, given what he had done, and would continue to do, to set obstacles in her way."[7] But there may be more to the story of Branch's "defection" from the Old War Horse Fund than what Spooner assumes was merely wounded self-pride and accompanying vindictiveness.

For instance, if this turnabout was a personal matter for Branch, why had he helped Dorothy establish her charity in the first place, never missing a Thursday buying session or stinting in the time he devoted to the project? Why did he cooperate when Dorothy asked him to send his men into the slums and the quarries to locate all known or suspected former war horses or army mules, sometimes at risk to their physical safety? Why did he give his assent to expansion of Dorothy's mission to include fund expenditures on native animals?

What we should ask is whether Branch really did have a personal antipathy to accepting these additional native animals, or whether he was put under pressure from some higher source of power, for whom the embarrassment of international attention to the problem of the war horses had proved too sensitive for the Egyptian government to bear. Indeed, it is fair to ask further what role Egyptian nationalist fervor played in this effort to scuttle a charity founded by a British woman and staffed by Britons, most of whom had served past and present in the "veiled protectorate." Had Branch agreed to be involved as a means of surveillance or control over what Dorothy was doing? Or could it be that Branch of Essex, like Lawrence of Caernarvonshire, had become more Arab than the Arabs he served, to such degree that he, too, saw his fellow British as colonialist interlopers, publicly embarrassing the native Egyptians with their interference in cultural issues that were none of their business? Did Dorothy sense this—that she was dealing with political expediency rather than personal vendetta—and cut Branch more slack than his obstreperousness deserved? Or did she simply refuse to descend to Branch's level lest the fight compromise her work for the animals? Given the complexities involved, it may well have been some or all of the above.

Her first battle with Dr. Branch started at the buying table. One day, taking everyone by surprise, Branch suddenly objected to the quantity of animals being purchased. He blamed the acceptance of native horses along with war horses for driving up numbers and costs. But since he had agreed to this process from the beginning, the change in attitude confounded the committee members, setting off a chain reaction of disagreements and counterarguments that interfered with their duties each time a native animal was presented along with one of foreign origin. Branch then made the atmosphere more heated by taking the side of owners during arguments about prices offered for their animals, which naturally did nothing to smooth what were very difficult transactions at the best of times. He also took a stand for the peasants, claiming they couldn't possibly get on with their work when their sick horses were bought for prices too low for them to purchase replacements—an absurd objection inasmuch as the committee mandated purchase prices that would easily allow an owner to buy another horse or mule, a system to which he had not objected before this.[8]

Branch might have known better than any of the others on the committee that to renege on the offer to purchase native horses was, to belabor a metaphor, closing the barn door after the horses had fled. Pains had already been taken by the committee members to ensure that none of the horses presented as war veterans were purchased without verification of history and, at the very least, to ensure strict authentication of their brands, which were difficult to falsify. Now those men who did not own war horses but had old, sick animals on their hands saw an opportunity, as Spooner describes it, "to bring their animals into the hospital on the off-chance of a deal. . . . Most were victims of years of absolute starvation and neglect owing to some injury received in the past, which prevented them from working. They had then been cast aside to keep themselves as best they could." It was as pointless to stop buying native animals now as to push the Nile back toward Lake Victoria. And as it was a natural by-product of the buying process, it was impossible now to restrict or prevent it.[9]

In the beginning, consensus among committee members was that Branch's turnabout should be ignored as best they could. Yet this reticence only heightened the tensions and finally led to a scene made all the worse by the context in which it took place.

On that particular buying day General Spinks was seated at the table alongside Dr. Branch and Dorothy. She had already noticed the light skirmishes taking place between these two self-possessed males, but internecine disagreements are normal for any board or committee, and after a while they began to seem part of the fabric of how the men worked together. But the day of the clash had already been a distraught one. Everyone was heartsore, having presided over the purchase of several battered war horses and the protracted process of purchasing a sad former army mule, who had been worked for months, even for years, with a broken leg. The owner disagreed with the price offered. When he saw that his arguments were getting him nowhere, he had suddenly lunged at Dorothy with a knife—the first time she had ever been threatened in this way. The owner was subdued and taken away by police, and just when everyone was catching their breath, Branch chose to take a curiously forgiving approach to the attacker, puzzling and angering members of the committee. The mule, in the meantime, having been purchased, was taken away and put out of its misery. There could be no great mystery as to what its life had been like. Once the committee saw the violence of the mule's owner, the idea of how long it had suffered at his hands left everyone even more deeply shaken.[10]

It was shortly after this incident that a man approached with "two of the most awful-looking native horses it had been the committee's fate to see." "They stood before us shaking in every limb," Dorothy wrote, "their heads nearly touching the ground. No distance they might have travelled could have accounted for what was obviously due to weeks of lack of any food at all."[11]

Branch chose this emotional moment to put his foot down. He declared that neither these nor any other horses were to be bought that day or any other day. As he was in charge of the Cairo SPCA, his order, effective immediately, was that no more native horses were to be allowed on the premises at all, and those purchased that day should be ejected with the rest. Dorothy asked him what he thought would happen now to the horses that had already been bought, which were resting in a nearby yard. "What happened to them," Branch told her brusquely, "he did not care or wish to know."[12]

"As a rule," Dorothy would state later, "the more incensed I become the less I am capable of saying."[13] General Spinks, too, seemed to be a person who said less the angrier he felt. But his rage was shown in another way. The general stood, then lifted the cane he habitually carried with him and slammed it down on the table top "with such concentrated fury" that even Branch flinched. Spinks then stalked off with his aide-de-camp. At that point everyone else left the table except the recalcitrant Branch and Dorothy. There was no way to overestimate the predicament that had just descended on the committee. Branch's dictum had effectively broken it up and ended its purpose, since if they could not convene at the SPCA to purchase animals, their work could not be carried out. Stunned, Dorothy also rose and walked back to the yard where the two miserable Arabs were temporarily penned. She couldn't let them go back into the street. She bought them from their owner using her own money, then sorted through the other animals and purchased the most desperate cases from among them. The pair of Arabs had reached her just in time. When she and General Spinks returned next morning, they found that one of the two had died during the night. As the other little one lay beside the corpse, he was euthanized then and there.

Having cooled off, General Spinks was of the opinion that for the short term, the Old War Horse Fund buying committee should accede to Branch's request and deal only with verified war horses, in the meantime looking for another location to achieve their broader mission. Finding a new location was a depressing prospect for Dorothy in a city she didn't know, having only just moved operations from the Royal Agricultural Society. But now that people knew about the Old War Horse Fund, the animals would only keep on coming. A solution had to be found, and fast.

Conscious of the damage it could do not only to her search for war horses but to funding, Dorothy could not afford to let Dr. Branch have the last word on her work. If he succeeded in turning people in Egypt against her, rumors might reach abroad and dissuade overseas donors from support also. As this support was essential, Dorothy couldn't afford to lose any of it. So going to meet with Branch at his office, she begged him to reconsider his decision. But her olive sprig was not well received. Branch quixotically complained that he was "sick of the whole business and that she had bought enough horses." Further to this, he threatened to obstruct any further buying, adding that he would find a way to stop her even if she managed to find another location for her charity on her own—in itself a significant threat to the future of the buying committee and its work.[14]

The heat was turned up a few days later when a letter arrived from the Cairo SPCA. It was about two former war horses Dorothy and General Spinks had found who, though they had served in the war and were no longer young, were strong enough to work for the fund as draught horses for the equine ambulance Dorothy was planning to purchase. Without this ambulance, such a vital feature of future Brooke work, it would have been impossible to transport downed patients to the hospital who were unable to walk or stand. Now, however, according to the SPCA, this pair of horses had tested positive for glanders, the bacterium from which was lethal enough to be considered for germ warfare in World War II. The letter made it pointless for the committee to argue that the animals they considered to be infected had been fully inspected by them and judged free of disease. It was obvious to Dorothy that there was no room for discussion. There was now an embargo on bringing any more war horses to the SPCA site. The Old War Horse Fund effectively had no home to do its work in.

After informing the committee of the decision, Dorothy hurried again to the SPCA, where she found the gates crowded with owners and their elderly and ill horses. None had been told that there was no longer a buying committee. "It was bad enough when one knew one could at least put an end to their suffering," Dorothy recalled. "But then I realised that I could do literally nothing—nothing but tell the men who had dragged them there and who even now were fighting for positions nearest the gates, to take them away again." She went to see Branch in his office and for the last time tried to reason with him. She explained the problems, why it was vital to continue the work, and told him about the group gathering at the gates even as she spoke. Branch had no intention of giving in. He told Dorothy they needed to all go back to where they came from. "The war horse work was finished," he thundered. He again warned her that she had best not try to set up her own organization anywhere in Cairo. "He said that she would be unable to do so as the

Ministry of Health would never permit the housing of a large number of horses anywhere in the city," wrote Spooner. Any attempt to gather up suffering equines would not be "a good thing" as, aside from not being allowed to do so on her own, she would find the law against her if she tried to euthanize animals on site. "They would all have to go to the public abattoir to be killed by the butchers in the ordinary way," Branch told her. It was a curt statement that called forth to Dorothy's mind all the horrors of butcheries in Egypt.[15]

This seems to have been the last time Dorothy met with Alfred Branch face to face. She walked out of his office, trembling with anger and anxiety for the fate of the many working animals that needed her help, not to mention those waiting in vain outside the SPCA grounds. Her first inclination, however, was not to sit down in despair, though that was what she most felt like doing. Instead, she drove straight to the Ministry of Health—in this case, seeing what Branch had threatened, this was tantamount to walking straight into the dragon's mouth. There Dorothy was received by a British official. He "listened with patience and sympathy," Spooner wrote, "to her request for permission to house the war horses in Cairo should she find a suitable place." At the end of the conversation Dorothy asked whether, in the event she secured a new site, she could receive permission to have animals euthanized there rather than sending them to the public butchers. The official assented to this, saying that if her new hospital met all the Ministry of Health's requirements and that the carcasses would be disposed of according to law, she would be permitted to put down sick animals on site. This was more than Dorothy had dared to hope for. Now she only had one more mountain to move—finding a new location, and soon.[16]

1. Portrait of Dorothy
Brooke by Olive Antrobus.
Searight Collection.

2. Riccarton House in Edinburgh, home of Dorothy's Gibson-Craig ancestors. From a 1904 postcard. Courtesy of Ben Jackman.

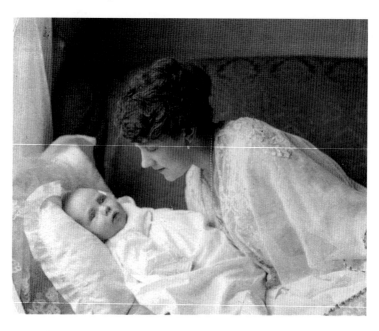

3. Dorothy Searight with infant son Rodney, pre-1914. Searight Collection.

4. Geoffrey Francis Heremon Brooke, Dorothy's second husband, with canine companion. Searight Collection.

5. Geoffrey Brooke and Combined Training. Searight Collection.

6. Dorothy Brooke on board a ship, likely going to or from Egypt. Searight Collection.

7. (*opposite top*) Felucca on the Nile River. Behind this exotic beauty lay human and animal misery. Myron Bement Smith Collection. Freer Gallery of Art and Arthur M. Sackler Gallery Archives. Smithsonian Institution, Washington D C.

8. (*opposite bottom*) A view to the cliffs at the Mokattam Hills. It was near here that Dorothy saw the lonely skeleton of an English horse and conceived her letter to the *Morning Post*. Myron Bement Smith Collection. Freer Gallery of Art and Arthur M. Sackler Gallery Archives. Smithsonian Institution, Washington D C.

9. Dr. Alfred Branch, wearing his habitual fez,
sitting at Dorothy's left at the buying table
in happier days. It is easy to see that amour
propre was of great importance to him.
Richard Searight Collection.

10. Two elderly patients at the Brooke Hospital, Cairo, showing the friendship so often bred in adversity. It is believed this is a photograph of the two horses Dorothy accidentally separated and later reunited. Searight Collection.

11. A pair of working horses that look to have been brought to the Brooke Hospital too late. It was images like this one that Dorothy assiduously kept from the public eye. Unfortunately these sights are still a daily reality for animal welfare charities. Searight Collection.

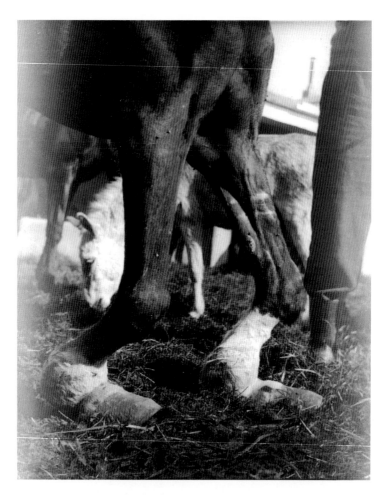

12. That a horse would have been allowed to suffer, let alone work, with this kind of injury is unthinkable to today's world. But this (and worse) is what Dorothy Brooke faced every week at her hospital, and it is faced by her vets' successors even today. Richard Searight Collection.

13. *Ransomed*, a watercolor of a rescued war horse feeding on the floor of the Brooke Hospital stable in Cairo by Pamela Searight, daughter of Dorothy Brooke. Searight Collection.

14. View to the boxes or stalls, Brooke Hospital, Cairo. The two horses peering out at the photographer would have been well enough to stand. Many remained on the soft straw where they first lay on being admitted. Searight Collection.

15. Dorothy Brooke, sitting outside the hospital with one of her patients in Cairo. Richard Searight Collection.

16. Dorothy Brooke's deep compassion for her equine patients is on full view in this photograph, dating to around 1934. Searight Collection.

17. A section of Old Cairo not much removed from its medieval origins, looking very like the vibrant slum area where Dorothy established her hospital in 1934. Author's collection.

18. Dorothy, center, at the buying table outside the SPCA hospital, with Egyptian members of the committee. Dr. Branch sits with chin in hand, considering the offer before him. The condition of the animal brought for their inspection has clearly left them all aghast. Searight Collection.

19. A view from the buying committee's perspective. Dr. Branch, in fez, and Dorothy can be seen at the table examining the horse being presented for sale. Richard Searight Collection.

20. (*opposite top*) Jordan, one of the handful of former war horses Dorothy's hospital was able to make fit enough to return to the country he had last seen almost twenty years earlier. Searight Collection.

21. (*opposite bottom*) This photograph, taken at the Cairo train station, shows Dorothy Brooke in later years. Her frailty is apparent here. George Gibson stands to her left. Searight Collection.

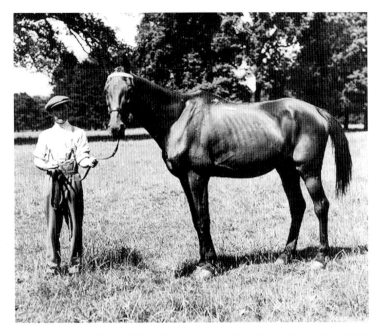

22. (*opposite top*) Dorothy Brooke, center, speaking with chief veterinarian Dr. Murad Raghib and other members of the hospital staff. Police captain Rushdi Effendi holds the umbrella. The charm she exerted on her staff is evident here. Richard Searight Collection.

23. (*opposite bottom*) Geoffrey and Dorothy Brooke in Salisbury, their final home together in England. Searight Collection.

24. (*above*) Taken in England, this photograph shows Dorothy pushing a pram containing her granddaughter, the future travel writer Sarah Searight Lush, and a canine traveling companion. Searight Collection.

25. Dorothy Brooke's grave, located in Cairo War Memorial Cemetery. Searight Collection.

26. A view to the Brooke Hospital today. Courtesy of Mohammed Abd-Elhay.

6. Street of the English Lady

Compassion gave her the authority to interfere.

—DR. PETRA MARIA SIDHOM

O ver the next three weeks Dorothy visited corners of Cairo that she had never imagined existed.

With her went Farrier Sergeant McCullock, "a large and brawny Scot." McCullock had managed the Army Veterinary Stables at Abbassia camp between Heliopolis and Cairo, base of the Imperial Camel Corps during the Great War, so he was well familiar with the world into which he and Dorothy were about to enter. Armed with McCullock's size and his fluent Arabic in the passenger seat, Dorothy drove the car, searching all over Cairo for new quarters for her war horse hospital.

Her must-have list was a long and possibly impossible one.

First of all she had to secure a stable of such size it would permit shelter for as many as fifty animals at a time, with space to lie down if needed. The location must have good ventilation, and it should have facilities on site where euthanizations could be carried out safely in accordance with official regulations and far enough away from the other patients to not distress them. It should also present none of the problems that had caused trouble with the sites at the RAS and the SPCA—there must be no lines of haggard equines to disturb those who preferred not to see such suffering, or to give the government more ammunition with which to close down the new hospital. And time was of the essence. Dorothy remembered the animals waiting outside the gate of the SPCA the day she had gone to Dr. Branch's office. News reached her that animals were still being brought into Cairo for sale but were being turned away by the SPCA, proof that Branch was holding to his bitter resolution. This both frustrated and invigorated her. "The realisation that instead of mitigating their suffering she was adding to it, goaded her on to further efforts to find accommodation," Spooner wrote.[1]

It was difficult enough for Dorothy to maneuver her car through people, animals, peddlers, horse-drawn gharries and carts. Streets turned to alleys, which themselves became passages better suited to foot traffic, where building facades seemed to lean toward one another overhead, blocking sunlight and congesting all activity below as the vehicle slid slowly forward.

Glenda Spooner describes one occasion when, having been guided too far down an increasingly narrowing street to what proved to be a property entirely unsuited to Dorothy's purposes, she and McCullock found themselves literally stuck there. Even if Dorothy could have driven the car farther, there was no exit to the alley; it was too narrow to turn the vehicle, and backing down the long way they had come was not an option. As Dorothy and McCullock sat, uncertain of what to do next, a crowd gathered, which "filled even the imperturbable McCullock with misgivings," wrote Glenda Spooner of what Dorothy had told her. Then McCullock had an idea. "Having sorted out twenty of the strongest-looking young men," recalled Spooner, "he told them to lift the car up and to heave it round till it faced the other way, at the same time telling Mrs Brooke to remain where she was at the steering wheel, as he was not at all sure of the temper of the crowd"—though how safe she would have been held aloft in a motorcar above a raging mob is certainly debatable. Thrilled to be asked by the foreign soldier to come to the rescue of the English lady, these young male Cairenes hefted the car over their heads like a coffin in a procession, turned it in the opposite direction, and set it down again, all with Dorothy still coolly upright. Dissuaded by McCullock from handing out tips to the young men, Dorothy recalled, all she could do "was to endeavour to express my gratitude with smiles and signs and by uttering the Arabic for 'thank you' which happens to be one of the biggest tongue-twisters in a language which to this day I have failed to master more than half a dozen words." (This was probably *mamnoona gedaan*, the formal expression of thanks.)[2]

In all, during their peregrinations about Cairo Dorothy and Sergeant McCullock visited some thirty stables, or what were described as such. None was suitable, and frustration was running high. So it was all the more heart-rending when in one of these lightless holes, which normally were empty by day as their occupants were working in the streets, Dorothy found a large black horse at the back of the stable, barely distinguishable in the darkness. The animal was evidently injured in some way, but it was difficult to tell what was wrong with it. McCullock felt over the horse's body and found out why it was half-standing, half-crouched against its manger: one of its hind legs was completely broken. When McCullock asked the owner about this injury, the man told him that the break was about two months old. So for eight weeks, unable to stand properly or move, this animal had been leaning against its food trough in agony, which nobody had done anything to alleviate.

The owner added that the horse was one of a pair he had bought shortly after the Great War—leading Dorothy and McCullock to conclude that the injured horse had served, like its mate, in the conflict. Both had been worked together, but with this one unable to walk, the other was out in the streets working and was the owner's only means of livelihood, which in any case appeared too insufficient for him to do without the injured animal, though it would never be able to labor for him again.

The man told Dorothy that the two horses were devoted to each other. Remembering the piebald and his mate, she worked out a deal with the owner to purchase both horses together. A horse with the this type of injury would have normally merited a few pounds from the buying committee, but Dorothy was not interested in dickering; she felt she had been directed to this stable for a reason, to ease the pain of one injured war horse and to free the other from its labors. She and McCullock waited till the other animal returned to the stable, noticing that when he did, the injured one, though unable to cross the stable floor to greet him, nickered to him softly from the darkness in a heartbreaking example of an animal's affection for friends and ability to endure pain. Dorothy paid the owner over and above the rate for both horses, and McCullock put down the black horse as soon as the money had changed hands. Arrangements were made to transport the sound horse to a safe place, but sadly, before this could be done, he fell into depression and refused to eat. The owner, who had no other means of contacting Dorothy, and of course could not reach her through the now off-limits SPCA, was conscientious enough to travel out to Heliopolis to tell her about the situation. Dorothy had McCullock return to the man's stable to put the horse down, its grief "further proof," Spooner noted, "that friendships formed under such adverse circumstances are stronger than those made under normal ones."[3]

Despite the fact that she had rescued two war horses she had not even known existed, Dorothy was still without a new home for the Old War Horse Fund, and there was no sign of any rescue for *her* on the distant horizon.

The Cairo Manure Company stood a few miles outside the Old City, and came well recommended for all the needs of the new hospital. Driving out to see it with Geoffrey and Capt. Meade Dennis, Dorothy arrived to find a site and location that could not have been a less adequate answer to her prayers. "The Manure Company was one of these nightmare establishments which disposes of carcasses of animals unfit for human consumption, chiefly horses," she wrote. Certain aspects did recommend the location for use as an equine hospital. It had stables erected to house the mules who transported the carcasses from the abattoir. There were obviously facilities for disposing of these carcasses. The trouble was the horrible stench, "an appalling atmosphere" that clung like a London pea soup fog.[4] The smell made everybody physically sick, even officers who remembered the corpse-strewn battlefields of the Great War. Horses are not believed to have as strong a sense of smell as of sight, but what appalled Dorothy was the notion of old, weary, and sick animals having to spend their last hours so close to a place of such concentrated misery, the stench from which would be miserable for the humans who had to work there.

Dorothy turned down the property, against the stringent objections of both Captain Dennis and her husband. For the entire drive home, they argued the pros and cons. To reject the location might mean Dorothy would not have another chance at any place at all. The future of the hospital was at stake, along with the donations so many had made to the cause, which she would be failing along with the animals that needed rescue. So Dorothy made herself a deal. She would try one last property, which, like all the others, had been warmly recommended but which she had avoided up to now, because it appeared to be too close to another public abattoir. If this one did not meet her standards, she would hold her nose and agree to the Cairo Manure Company site.

Next morning Sergeant McCullock accompanied Dorothy to look over the new contender. The property was located in Sharia Bairam al-Tunsi street in the busy district called Sayyida Zeinab.

A granddaughter of the Prophet Mohammed (peace be upon him) and patron saint of the city of Cairo, Zeinab (b. 626 CE) was a figure of defiance in the face of inequity. A woman of heroic character, she "may never have set foot in Egypt," writes John Reynard, "but Egyptians, though virtually all Sunni, celebrate her heroism during and after the battle of Karbala," the AD 680 clash between what would eventually divide sharply into Sunni and Shia sects of Islam. "People seek out Sayyida Zaynab, who was a champion of justice for the oppressed, to obtain relief for eye ailments and to gain access to the heavenly council of Friends who are believed to converge on the shrine."[5] According to tradition, a mosque, later to flower in refulgent Mameluke style, was built in Zeinab's name not long after she arrived in Egypt. Tradition claims that she was buried in or around the mosque, where her mausoleum shrine exists today. The neighborhood bearing her name had itself a colorful history even by Cairo standards. It was a place where you could find the mansions of upper-class families as well as the modest dwellings of working-class people; this amalgamation of classes and the sharing of mutual grievances helped lay the powder train to the 1919 revolution against British rule, which started in the square adjacent to the Sayyida Zeinab Mosque.[6]

As Dorothy wrote of her introduction to the neighborhood:

With a ruffian of a guide we drove to the uttermost end of one of the byways of old Cairo. The road was wide and led straight to the sand hills skirting the town on that side. At the end of this road, we were conducted to two very large garages and two unusually roomy livery stables. Beyond these buildings was a wide open space, rough and stony, but airy and about four hundred yards wide. A small, unoccupied house stood in the centre—the rest was just rough ground. The abattoir I had so dreaded was a quarter of a mile away, up a side street. The traffic to it went along another road, and not, as I had feared, past the stables.

Our guide led us to the furthermost stables and there we found the owner who had obviously been warned and was waiting for us. A big double door gave access to a very large stable indeed. This was of course filthy, but it was at least high, airy, and well lighted by several tall windows. It was evidently used to house gharry horses that, at the time of our visit, were out working in the streets. Big mangers lined the two sides of the walls. The floor was in the same filthy state, but by now I was accustomed to that.[7]

The property, located at 2 Bairam al-Tunsi Street, was located in the middle of a poor and crime-ridden part of the city in which, it was said, Europeans in military uniform (especially British) were not welcome. For the wife of a British officer, whose hospital would be staffed by British officers, this rumor must have given Dorothy pause. But there were good points to consider, one of especially happy significance: the abattoir that Dorothy hated was well down the street.[8]

It was obvious that much would need to be done to make the Bairam al-Tunsi premises livable for the animals and useful for staff, and the nightmare task still remained of meeting the standards of the Ministry of Health so that the hospital could be opened for business. But all taken into account, Dorothy had landed in a good place to start her work all over again and on a much surer footing. In fact, she could not have found a better spot had she tried. "Mrs. Brooke chose a very interesting site in Sayyida Zeinab," says German Egyptian veterinarian Dr. Petra Maria Sidhom, who was involved with the Brooke Hospital for thirty years. "She was where the working people are, where the working animals are. She would have had more support in richer areas of Cairo, or in the expats' district, but she wanted to be where the help was most needed." And because she was where the help was most needed, Dorothy could reach out beyond the slums where she provided that help and could in turn ask for help from those in the wealthier areas of Cairo. From the hospital in Sayyida Zeinab, Dorothy would tell the whole of the outside world about the animals in whose lives she tried to make a difference, and about the people for whom she made a difference, too. "Not too many upper class foreign ladies were taking their tea in Sayyida Zeinab," laughs Richard Searight. "And she was the wife of a general. When she spoke about what she saw and what needed to be done, even from a slum, people listened, and they helped."[9]

It was October 1934, three years since she had founded the Old War Horse Fund, and four years since she had seen her first war horses at Ramses Station. The unassuming site, hemmed in by tenement blocks on one side, their balconies hung with washing, and by a handsome European-style municipal courthouse block on the other, would be named the Old War Horse Memorial Hospital—now called the Brooke Hospital for Animals. In time, this modest equine cross between hospice, hospital, and respite care center would make famous a thoroughfare that would shed its original name honoring a nationalist Egyptian poet and take on a moniker memorializing the English lady who worked there.[10]

Before her arrival in Egypt in 1934, Glenda Spooner, who was to edit Dorothy's diaries and serve as one of her greatest supporters, had had a life stranger than fiction.

Born Glenda Graham in India in 1897, where the first sounds she heard were the shouts and clashes of a riot, she was to similarly find herself, or insert herself, in situations of high drama, first as an actress with the theatrical company of actor Graham Moffatt, later as supporter of women's suffrage just after the Great War, and then in a career in advertising on Fleet Street. Glenda would also become the author of several books for young people about ponies (with which she worked as a professional dealer) and horses. A devoted supporter of Ada Cole's International League for the Protection of Horses, Glenda also had a love for aviation, and it was through this passion that she came to know Captain Hugh "Tony" Spooner. Tony Spooner already had another heroine in his life: he was brother to the English aviatrix Winifred Spooner, who in 1929 was awarded the Harmon Trophy as outstanding aviator of the year. After cheating death on so many occasions in the air, Winifred died of pneumonia at age thirty-two in 1933. On the heels of this tragedy Tony met Glenda in Cairo in 1934 at an International Air Race; they married shortly afterward. Then, only ten months later, in March 1935, Tony died in a freak plane crash near the coastal town of El-Arish.[11]

Before Tony's death, he and Glenda had witnessed the return to England of an old war horse whom Dorothy had rescued. The Leamington branch of the RSPCA had sent Dorothy a very large gift of £1,000 to be used for whatever purpose she saw fit. Dorothy applied her windfall to finance the return of an elderly war horse she called Valiant, who had survived the war, years of hard labor, and finally the death of the gharry horse who had been his bonded mate. What made Valiant's return to England all the more moving was that he had been accepted to parade alongside other old war horses rescued from Europe at the prestigious Olympia International Horse Show in London. Spooner wrote, "[Valiant] walked round the arena looking simply wonderful, keenly interested in all he saw, his spirit unbroken, his temperament unspoilt by all the starvation and ill-usage he had endured."[12]

Intrigued by Dorothy's work, when Glenda and Tony went to Egypt afterward, they met Dorothy and toured the premises of the Old War Horse Memorial Hospital. Not only was it love at first sight between Glenda and the hospital's patients, but she developed a deep respect for Dorothy and her work. A key trait that seems to be shared among many who devote themselves to animal rescue is that of a personal history of having endured and overcome profound loss. Saving and caring for an animal in distress becomes a kind of compassionate therapy that works both ways, for the suffering animal and for the suffering human. The timing of losing Tony and finding the Old War Horse Memorial Hospital could not have been more significant for Glenda Spooner. She arrived on the scene just as 2 Bairam al-Tunsi Street was being made ready for patients, and even through the stars in her eyes we can see just what a huge job it was to bring the place up to both Dorothy's and the Ministry of Health's standards. "There was a tremendous amount of work to be done," Spooner wrote. "The walls, caked with filth, had to be scraped and cleaned before the whitewash could be applied. The mangers had to be restored and above all disinfected. Most were broken and half eaten by crib-biters and hungry animals. The stone floors had to be relaid and side drainage installed. It had to be borne in mind that everything [Dorothy] had achieved could be nullified if the Ministry of Health, who had to be invited in to inspect, took it into its head to reject the premises."[13] Maj. Roland Heveningham, the hospital's chief veterinarian, recalled what a challenge lay before Dorothy. "We took over some derelict buildings," he said, "with makeshift stabling, a combined office and pharmacy in a disused native house and one syce on duty to receive any animal brought in." This was a very small start for a charity with such a huge job before it, but it was a start. What emerged from this odd assortment of neglected buildings were premises unified by a coat of fresh whitewash and a thorough cleaning, the stables airy and bright and with roomy boxes for the patients, each piled high with soft straw. A pamphlet produced in the early 1960s describes the hospital's layout. Though in 1934 she had yet to add an operating theater or ambulance garage, the description given is much as it would have been in her time: "Three large wards containing 42 loose boxes (24 fly-proof), One isolation ward (3 fly-proof boxes), One dressing station and operation theatre, Two large kraals for convalescent animals, with boxes for mares with foals, Offices, dispensary, farrier's shop, ambulance garage and forage shed." The premises were virtually self-sustaining.[14]

Spooner describes Sayyida Zeinab as a dangerous slum, but to Dorothy, who had had a knife thrust at her in the relatively safe yard of the SPCA, it held no frights she hadn't experienced already. She was aware that proximity to the public abattoir a quarter of a mile down the street would expose the hospital to what Spooner termed the "quarrelsome and really dangerous men" who sold animals there, but she could console herself that there was a police station not far away, in fact quite near the abattoir's entrance, the chief of which was to become a good friend. Dorothy liked and respected Cairo's policemen. "The Egyptian police were a very fine body of men," Dorothy wrote, "smart, well-disciplined, and brave as indeed they had need to be." They likely did their best to live up to that description where Dorothy was concerned.[15]

In any event most of the owners who came to the hospital's gates were harmless men seeking help in one way or another, not to cause trouble. Dorothy met some whom she described as "genuinely poor but not heartless and cruel." She made many friends among them, helping some find jobs and helping to ease their difficult lives in other ways—another similarity to Florence Nightingale. The "black-guardly ruffians," as she called them, were to be found among the men who handled their animals roughly and caused fights on buying day, and it was because of them that Dorothy was glad for a police presence. The troublemakers tried sneaky tricks on each other in order to move ahead in the line, which led to arguments and fistfights. "I had no objection to the owners half killing each other," Dorothy wrote, "but I could never stand by and see the horses knocked about." When man-to-man fights turned into free-for-alls and the police jumped in to break it up, "the bewildered horses were pushed and punched in a way that infuriated me," Dorothy wrote. "Frequently the policemen's heavy bludgeons missed the men they were aimed at by inches only to fall upon the horses' boney quarters and backs," animals already in pain and barely able to stand.[16]

Perhaps the knife that had flashed in her face across the SPCA buying table, and certainly the suffering she had seen in stables and streets around Cairo, had hardened her nerves. Though it's difficult to imagine, given her upper-class origin and her natural abhorrence of scenes, not to mention the fact that many of the men may have had knives on their persons, Dorothy was no longer afraid to confront unruly owners and even involve herself in confrontations. She wrote:

My success in the brawls up the road was almost entirely due to the fact that word had gone round that I was mad. The mad "sitt" (lady) was the name I was known by, not only to every decrepit horse owner in Cairo but over a large part of Egypt itself. To the average Egyptian, a woman who spent all her time and great amounts of money seeking out old, crippled horses, giving them soft bedding, all the food and treats they could eat, the full care of a staff of stablemen, and then euthanize them a few days later, had to be crazy.

Spooner herself tells of seeing Dorothy vault from the buying table to protect the animals from squabbles among their owners and the police. "I had no need to do more than walk into the middle of the milling mass of men and horses and to command them to stop their nonsense," Dorothy explained. "They literally wilted before my wrath." Indeed, older men in Sayyida Zeinab still tell their children about the English lady who once grabbed away their whips.[17]

If a given troublemaker did not have the street smarts to wilt on command, Dorothy would grab his arm and glare into his eyes. This would usually do the trick. If the power of the white memsahib over groups of "natives" was waning, like the British empire itself, with each year, there was something about a foreign lady exhibiting bold eccentricities in the streets of Cairo that could still command astonished respect from even its staunchest criminal element.[18]

Dr. Petra Sidhom recalls that decades later, when her German mother and Egyptian father visited Cairo, certain expectations of behavior were still imposed on foreign women in the city and judgments were made about those who did not behave as they were supposed to do. "My mother was blond and blue-eyed," says Dr. Sidhom, "so she stood out anyway. But when she objected to horses being struck by their owners, which happened all the time, she told me she had more than once made a spectacle of herself in public." One day her parents were riding along in a gharry carriage, taking in the sights, when Dr. Sidhom's mother noticed the driver was beating both horses with a stick. She said something to the driver; he ignored her. Her Egyptian husband said, "Please, we're in the middle of the city." She was wearing an expensive white dress. "But she couldn't stand it," says Dr. Sidhom. "She climbed into the front where the driver was, took the stick from the man, broke it, threw it away, and told him to stop. People began to gather, wondering what this foreign lady was doing. So many years earlier, then, it was a really courageous thing that Mrs. Brooke did," she adds. "She would have had to be prepared to deal with a lot of disrespect, when people were half-amazed and half-laughing at her, and saying, 'It's only an animal, what are you doing?'"[19]

"Compassion gave her the authority to interfere," says Dr. Sidhom, speaking of both her mother and of Dorothy. "When you are so convinced of something, it gives you full authority. She didn't need backup of any man or police." Perhaps this authority, more than the ordinary Egyptian's fear of the mad or the subtle powers of the memsahib, is what protected Dorothy in the streets of Sayyida Zeinab.[20]

Presumed madness and compassion were excellent armor, but Dorothy did have a good policeman as backup if needed. The commander of the local police station was Abdul Moneim Rushdi Effendi (the latter a courtesy title), known to Dorothy simply as Rushdi, an Arabic name meaning "true faith." The name was apt. "He was our friend from the beginning," Dorothy recalled, "and not only supplied us with a police guard all day and all night for all the years we were there, but on buying days, he marched up eighteen to twenty of his best men to keep our crowds in order and to ensure our personal safety."[21] A handsome man with a neat moustache, tarboosh never off kilter, and nary a crease in his white uniform, Rushdi offered an amused expression that wasn't quite a smile but served as one on most occasions. He had a droll sense of humor: he enjoyed telling Dorothy that Sayyida Zeinab averaged about two murders on a given day, information she received with as straight a face as she could manage. This was meant to be reassuring, as without Rushdi's police force it was anyone's guess how many *more* murders there could be. Dorothy accepted the information in the spirit with which it was offered, marveling, too, that Rushdi managed to keep back the tidal wave of crime as well as he did. She saw him lose his composure only once, and it had more to do with his duty to her than to the mayhem in the streets. There was a murder case so uniquely violent that it required the commander to send out more men than he could well afford. Because this left the hospital unguarded, if only briefly, for a period of time, Rushdi saw this as an insupportable failure of responsibility on his part.

Murders aside, and even with Rushdi's assiduous presence at the hospital, there were a few instances where Dorothy could not sort out a situation herself. On just one occasion, though, she had to call on the official known to her as the Omda or chief inspector of police (al-Omda is Arabic for "mayor"). Dorothy was driving her car near the hospital, at her feet an attaché case crammed with cash donations amounting to several hundred pounds, when her way was blocked by a crowd. On investigating, she found that a water trough for horses had been damaged by a passing vehicle. The water was leaking out, and there were several thirsty work horses needing a drink. Milling around the horses were owners angry at the inconvenience. There were arguments among the men as to who was responsible for the accident and what was to be done about repairing the trough, while their horses stood with heads drooping in the heat. Dorothy sent word to the hospital for staff to come refill the trough, using the only water available, from a tap nearby. This, however, started another uproar, for when the owner of the tap saw what was happening, he interfered, shouting at Dorothy's staff and at her. Now afraid that there might be a bigger demonstration, and conscious of the fortune on the floor of the car, Dorothy took the attaché case with her into the Omda's office, which was located not far from where her car was stranded. She found him in the middle of judging a murder case. After she explained what was occurring outside, the Omda dropped what he was doing and walked into the street with her. On his own authority, he cleared the area and got into Dorothy's car to escort her to the hospital, never suspecting, as she later related, that a bag stuffed with a fortune in British pounds lay safely under his feet. Such was all in a day's work in the street of the English lady who spent all her money buying horses only to kill them.[22]

7. Going Home

Those that were past enjoyment of any sort were put down at once. But at least they pass on to the sound of an English voice, speaking kindly.

—DOROTHY BROOKE

Even before it could open for business, the Old War Horse Memorial Hospital had to be inspected and approved by the Ministry of Health. Knowing the most critical area was that part of the property set aside for euthanization and cleanly disposing of remains, Dorothy had put all her reliance on the advice of an expert in configuring drainage and establishing standards of disinfection. Her trust proved well placed. When ministry officials came to examine the hospital, "I held my breath during their minute inspection of the floors and drains," Dorothy wrote. "My relief cannot be described when all was pronounced satisfactory."[1]

This hurdle cleared, Dorothy could concentrate on who would run the hospital on a daily basis and, particularly, on who could be trusted to do so while she and Geoffrey were on leave. She hired Maj. Roland Heveningham as chief veterinarian; along with Col. C. R. Spencer, Heveningham would also carefully document each patient in photograph albums that are still archived at the Brooke Hospital for Animals in Cairo. Everyone with any experience with horses came forward to help, including Geoffrey's personal groom, Fred Baraby, who would pay visits on the patients and check on their general comfort. Soon the hospital even had its own guardian, Mohammed Aziz. A gravely handsome older man with a face as stonily inscrutable as Rushdi Effendi's was open and bright, Mohammed Aziz kept a strict eye on all security measures and stayed close to Dorothy.[2]

During her hours spent at the Cairo SPCA Dorothy had learned a great deal about veterinary medicine, and she had also picked up hints of how to run a similar organization. Though she had a hand in everything to do with the hospital, she realized that somebody had to be put in charge of the small army of syces who looked after the horses' everyday needs. Syces attended each buying day, leading the patients back to the paddock area; they fed and watered them in their stalls and took away those selected to be put to sleep. These men knew their jobs inside and out, but like any group they needed a supervisor to organize their activities each day. Dorothy discussed this with her committee members, who all concluded that the person in question should first of all be English. Egypt was no longer Britain's to boss around, but there remained as much an English as an Arab stereotype in which any situation requiring organization could only achieve it under English control. English horse experts proliferated throughout what had been the British Empire; they had held this preeminence for so long, whether in India or Egypt, that an understanding of hierarchy had developed between English and native horse people, and the English were usually the ones in charge. This part of the committee's recommendation would not have been difficult to fulfill, but Dorothy was unsure of the other laundry list requirements: that the supervisor not only speak Arabic fluently and have experience with accounting, but he must be able to oversee euthanizations.

George Gibson (circa 1908–72) was English and had horses in his blood. A short man with the bandy-legged, rough-and-ready stance of a jockey, George had actually ridden as one in Egypt, likely finding work through his brother, a well-known Cairo jockey himself. The death of their father brought George back to England to be of help to his mother, and by the time he returned to Egypt he couldn't find work anywhere and was living with his brother. Dorothy first heard of George through an English police officer and on the strength of that contacted him for an interview. At first, the job seemed like a dream come true. George knew a lot about horses. He knew how to manage Egyptian syces. He had learned to speak fluent Arabic. But euthanizing a horse was something he neither had done nor thought he could do. "I liked him all the better for this," Dorothy wrote of this first meeting—she couldn't have brought herself to put down an animal, either. In fact, this was what she was looking for, a man who shied from the job not through squeamishness but through compassion, who took no pleasure in doing what had to be done, but did so because it was far more cruel to leave an animal in such condition alive to suffer.

As early as 1895 the American Humane Education Society was including material in copies of Anna Sewell's seminal novel *Black Beauty*, describing in detail how to put down an animal humanely, as a way of normalizing the topic and to spread the word about humane methods of euthanization. Using an illustration of a horse's head, looking forward, with a dot placed between its ears, the pamphlet recommended shooting the horse first, bludgeoning it if shooting was not practical or a gun not available. It is unclear when Dorothy refers to the "humane killer" whether she means a gun or a captive bolt pistol (invented in 1903)—euthanasia by injection was not to come until later in the Brooke Hospital's history. But improved practices don't mean it isn't difficult even for a professional veterinarian to euthanize a patient. "Putting an animal to sleep has never been an easy thing," says veterinarian Dr. Mohammed Abd-Elhay, who works for the Brooke Hospital for Animals in Cairo. "The decision is much more difficult than the act. Once you find it in your heart that you are taking the right decision, the deed itself feels exactly like setting a trapped animal free from its cage." A recent patient, an elderly donkey named Chewie who had been rescued by Egypt Equine Aid, was very like the once strong, now battered old horses that George Gibson would have had to put down. "One can't imagine what kind of life a donkey like Chewie had lived," Dr. Mohammed says. "My last memories of him were from three days before he was gone. I was leaning on the fence at his yard gazing at him for I don't know how long. He was just sitting there on the sand with his head down and giving his thin body to the flies, like an old sailor on a wooden chair by the sea, unaware where he is."[3]

Nobody would argue that life in this condition was better than a quick and painless death, yet it was no easier to end the life of such a brave animal than it would be had he been young and healthy. That stalwart courage in the face of illness or old age ironically made one want to help the animal continue to cheat death, not succumb to it.

George Gibson badly needed the job, especially one that was relatively well-paying. When Glenda Spooner talked to him in 1956, he told her that this was his primary reason for accepting Dorothy's offer, despite his reservations about having to serve as "executioner" and the misery he would see every day, so different from the work he had done in the recent past. But George felt there was no recourse but to accept the job and do his best not only for the animals but for her. "There was something about her that 'got me,'" he told Spooner, "like it did everyone else from the highest official to the lowliest syce." Before he came to Egypt, George had grown up in England in a period when stratification of classes was still very strong, and people from a higher class did not mingle with those from a lower one, or stoop to do their work. Yet here was the epitome of an English lady, no longer young and not in the best of health, her whole life animated by a passion to ease the suffering of working equines, who had set up a hospital in a Cairo slum, and who bartered and sometimes battled with the lowest of the low as she tried to help their suffering horses, mules, and donkeys. She could well have told George in their interview that while the supervisor's job was to put the animals down, her job was the even less enviable one of choosing which animals had to die. She had a stomach to rival any man's, and the physical and emotional strength to do what had to be done, no matter how heartrending, without tears or weakness. If she could do what she did for the animals at the Old War Horse Memorial Hospital, then there was no reason George could not do his part. Very likely taking all this into consideration, he accepted her offer. It was an important choice he was never to regret.[4]

It was well past time for the hospital to have its official opening, not least because some two hundred old horse and mule war veterans were waiting to be purchased.

Ultimately, far more animals were taken in than there was accommodation for, but as these were the most critically compromised ones, space was made available on a regular basis. "All war horses and mules were put down within twenty-four hours and a few others not fit to work again," recalled Major Heveningham. "In a steady stream they came to their final rest."[5] Everyone had a role to play in the process of intake, examination, and care. Rushdi Effendi and General Spinks assisted Dorothy at the buying table, through the medium of a dealer who communicated with the owners presenting their animals under the eyes of a couple of Rushdi's police officers. Dorothy's task was to count the cash and pass it along when a deal had been sealed. George was responsible for taking the owner's thumb print (most could not sign their names) in a receipt book that was kept by Rushdi as evidence of the sale. There were the usual arguments over amounts offered, over whether the cash was correctly counted, or over the police presence, and there always was the possibility that some of the men would get into fights. Yet with these and any of the many other difficulties faced by any newly opened service organization came the small triumphs of saving another war horse, army mule, or donkey from a life of suffering and giving those who still had some life to spare the expert free veterinary care they needed as well as the education their owners needed just as much.

In all, on the hospital's first day they took in some seventy equine army veterans in the "Street of the English Lady." Dorothy described this in her diary:

> Often that afternoon I left the committee table and wandered into the stables for the pure joy it gave me to watch the old horses' faces. Long years ago they had given up all hope of having enough food and water, of a kind word, or any chance at all of evading the ceaseless round of

everlasting work accompanied by blows from their owners' sticks. They shambled behind the syces with drooping heads and sunken eyes.

Now, however, their lagging steps were directed with unaccustomed gentleness across the road and over the pavement to the double doors of the stables, thrown open to receive them. Here many paused and cocked an ear. Obviously distrustful of all interiors—as well they might be, judging by the sort of places in which for years they had been housed— they hesitated. But Gibson was there waiting. A pat on the neck and a little persuasion from him and the old horses walked in. As their ill-shod misshapen hooves felt the deep tibben bed beneath them, there would be another doubting unbelieving halt. Then gradually they would lower their heads and sniff as though they could not believe their own eyes or noses. Memories, long forgotten, would return when some stepped eagerly forward towards the mangers piled high with berseem, while others with creaking joints, lowered themselves slowly on to the bed and lay, necks and legs outstretched. There they remained, flat out, until hand fed by the syces. Once down, they stayed there, not attempting to get up for many hours.

I shall never forget the thankfulness in my heart as I watched them. The worst of our difficulties was behind us. Here we were at long last, running our own show with every detail under our own control. Every horse was carefully and understandingly cared for in the comfort and efficiency of our stable. . . . Each animal was given his own feed tin while all available syces and any volunteers joined in filling them. . . . They had not seen or smelt a mash since they left the army fifteen or more years ago, but they had not forgotten! The smell of the warm bran was enough. Immediately shrill excited whinnies echoed to the rafters. Ears were pricked and incredibly-aged faces, with nostrils quivering, turned on scrawny necks over bony harness-galled shoulders in an attempt to see what was going on.

The blind horses—and there were many—received special attention, as did the old ladies and gentlemen who decided to go to bed as soon as they arrived—and stay there. They were fed mashes where they lay, their head supported by syces. Those that were past enjoyment of any sort were put down at once. But at least they pass on to the sound of an English voice, speaking kindly.[6]

Around this same time, somebody took a photograph of Dorothy feeding one of her equine patients. Wearing a sleeveless summer dress and white open toe shoes, she sits alongside 2 Bairam al-Tunsi Street on an old wooden chair with rush seat. Her hair is short-cropped; there are pearls at her ears. She balances the pan on her lap while a horse with roached mane puts its nose tentatively among the contents, its eyes glancing up tiredly at its benefactor. Dorothy squints against the bright sun, or perhaps to hold back emotion, and her smile looks halfway to being a wince of pain. It is an intimate glimpse of a woman who had had an impossible dream become reality: that she could change the world for horses like the one she was feeding, horses that the world, for over a decade after the Great War, had chosen to forget. Sitting there in the shade, so calm and poised for being the "mad sitt" of the neighborhood, Dorothy radiates care and compassion, and she still seems enveloped in her dream, thinking about the English meadows to which she wished she could bring this horse and all the animals who were brought through the double doors of her stable. Yet another of her dreams was about to be realized—to send a former war horse back to England. It was a dream many a soldier had had years before Dorothy's work began. As Pte. Christopher Massie of the Seventy-Sixth Brigade, Royal Army Medical Corps (RAMC), would sum it up: "The warhorse is honest, reliable, strong. He is a soldier. . . . I want someone to take his case up and see that he falls 'cushy' after the war. It is only fair. . . . Don't ring a lot of bells and forget him. A field of clover, a bundle of hay, a Sussex meadow, a bushel of apples, a loaf of bread, a sack of carrots, sunshine and blue hills, clean stables, and trusses of straw, may they all be his, for he has earned them!"[7]

Dorothy had very real concerns about the safety as well as the practicalities of sending an elderly animal on such a long journey back home—the trip by rail to Port Said, by ship across the Mediterranean, offloading in Marseilles for another rail trip, then another ship across the English Channel. This trek was challenging even for a young and healthy horse; these horses may still have been prey to flashbacks from the frightening sea voyages that had brought them east nearly two decades before. Thus far Valiant had been the only war horse strong enough to return home, but soon there would be others able to retrace his steps. Three English horses who were brought to the hospital as "skeletons" had somehow found a will to survive, moving Dorothy to raise enough funds to send them back to Private Massie's "sunshine and blue hills."[8]

These lucky three were named Jorrocks (for a famous nineteenth-century racehorse), Jordan (perhaps because he had crossed that river during the Palestine campaign), and Ransome. Their return was made possible by the generosity of English donors and also, sadly, by Dorothy's inability to save another horse she had fallen in love with.

One of the Brooke Hospital's most devoted supporters was Annie Henrietta Yule, Lady Yule (1874–1950), a wealthy widow who was an avid breeder of Arabian horses. Lady Yule and her daughter, Gladys, who was also charmingly eccentric, spent lavishly on their travels together and shared a passion for big game hunting as well. But in spite of the latter interest, the Yule ladies were firmly on the side of happy lives for animals they loved, in this case horses. They lived at Hanstead Park, the family's estate in Hertfordshire, which was the location of Lady Yule's stud farm. Gladys Yule had been especially touched by the story of a polo pony Dorothy had rescued one particularly hot summer. Though the pony was purchased in poor health and did not seem likely to survive, she began to thrive under Dorothy's care, and the future began to brighten. Recognizing the pony as English-bred, Dorothy made a plan. "After the thousands whose destruction I had had to order, I had set my heart upon getting this little mare home," Dorothy wrote. But circumstances intervened, as they so often did in the unpredictable setting of Egypt. Because of the great heat of the summer and fearing the mare might not survive traveling on a ship's horse deck, Dorothy had sent her into the country to live with an Egyptian who would care for her. The plan was to retrieve the pony once the weather favored her to be shipped to England. But when that time came, the man would not give the mare up, and for reasons that Glenda Spooner, Dorothy's friend and compiler of her diaries, does not explain, the issue was not pursued (perhaps because the pony had died, news Dorothy would not want to reach Gladys Yule). The loss of the little mare haunted her, and she actively looked for other horses whose health would permit them to be returned.[9]

Dorothy's efforts, and those of the Our Dumb Friends League (now the Blue Cross), founded in London in 1897 to rescue abused working horses, as well as those of the RSPCA, began to pay off. From 1934 until the commencement of World War II, increased awareness of the forgotten equine warriors of the Middle East and in France and Belgium stimulated publicity and action to save and return them to England. Jorrocks, Jordan, and Ransome were the Old War Horse Memorial Hospital's contribution to this small herd that crossed the Channel for the last time.

Some horses had been as lucky on the battlefield as they were in being rescued years later. "The horse heroes of the War—who won ribbons and medals for gallant work on the battlefield just like soldiers—are spending the twilight of their lives in grassy meadows up and down the kingdom," reported Gloucester's *Citizen* in summer 1935. One of the luckiest of these survivors was Kitty, who entered the war on August 12, 1914, and was never wounded, though an officer was killed on her back, and she herself had had narrow escapes on more than a few occasions. Two days before Armistice "a shell struck the ground ten yards in front of her—but didn't burst," the *Citizen* explained. "Seconds later another shell fell almost at her feet . . . that one didn't explode either. Kitty was a horse with as many lives as a cat." Quicksilver was another fortunate horse awarded the Order of the Blue Cross, presented by the Our Dumb Friends League. Having survived the war, Quicksilver, a horse of "silvery white beauty" and sporting glittering medals, was ridden on several significant public occasions, including the funeral of the Unknown Soldier, the weddings of Princess Mary and of the Duke of York (future King George VI), the funeral of Queen Alexandra, widow of King Edward VII, and at every opening of Parliament.[10]

Wolseley Russell of the *Yorkshire Post* took the celebration a step further, reproducing in his column of June 18, 1934, a conversation between several elderly war horses who were presented at the International Horse Show at Olympia. These were Suzette (age twenty-nine), Taffy (twenty-eight), Grey Button (twenty-seven), and Ragtime (twenty-five). Russell depicted these elders as "deep in conversation," comparing scars and memories, when he interrupted them for an interview. "I saw the Somme, Arras, and Cambrai," says Grey Button. "I was wounded at Arras." "And Loos, and Neuve Chappelle, and St. Quentin," Suzette adds. "And d'you know, it's a very funny thing, but I was back at Mons on Armistice Day." "You and your daughter trotting round taking care of officers!" Grey Button sniffs. "Let me tell you what my idea of real war-work is. It's serving in the East as a veterinary pack pony, whatever."[11]

This is where one of the veterans Dorothy saved offers up his story: "'Listen, you chaps,' spoke up an aged horse in the corner. 'Jorrocks' was the name on his box. 'I don't mind hearing your reminiscences. But don't forget those ex-Service fellows who haven't been as lucky as you. Most of them are like me—our war records have been lost and our peace-time experiences haven't been such fun that we want to talk 'em over.'"

Jorrocks tells the other horses that he had been found in Cairo quite recently, working hard, and "I certainly never thought I'd see England again." He had been saved from hard labor and brought back to England thanks to the Old War Horse Fund Committee, "to represent the others, your old comrades and mine, who will never leave the East now." Jorrocks hopes, he says, that people who come to see him and the other former war horses will give a thought to those others.[12]

Ransome's biography was featured as contrast to the happier postwar lives of Quicksilver and Kitty. Described as being thirty-one years old in 1935, Ransome was one of the horses that Dorothy had purchased from the notorious quarrymen of Cairo. Not only was his rescue one of her greatest successes, but the fact that he was brought back to health and to England, after years of toil that few nonnative horses survived, was virtually unheard of.[13]

Three other English war horses, unnamed in the press, were reported as having been taken in by Maj. Gen. and Mrs. A. Solly-Flood and Lt. Col. and Mrs. E. J. L. Speed in Warwickshire and by the RSPCA branch in Birmingham. Lady Yule and daughter Gladys took two horses, a pair photographed on Armistice Day 1934 standing in a pleasant field, beside them a groom wearing medals from the Great War.[14] Jordan, too, would be taken in by the kind-hearted Old War Horse Fund supporter in Warwickshire, Mrs. George Bryant, who had coauthored a fund appeal with Captain Durham. Jordan was well in excess of twenty years old when he was found working in a salt mine, and only after protracted negotiations with his owner was he sold. Exhausted from pulling an overloaded cart uphill, Jordan had to be brought to the hospital by ambulance, and there was no reason to assume he would survive more than a few months. "Such was his marvellous constitution and his indomitable spirit," wrote Glenda Spooner, "that, after a winter's good feeding and three months out on that wonderful natural restorative, spring grass, he was soon as fat as butter and his legs remarkably restored." Photographed in England walking through a field, with Mrs. Bryant and her dogs strolling beside him, and greeting three curious neighbor horses poking their noses at him over a fence, Jordan still looks thin—his ribs can be seen under his gleaming coat—but his ears are pricked and his bearing alert. "I doubt if he ever forgot the past," Spooner wrote, "but was philosophical enough to put it behind him and to enjoy the present to the full." If only, she adds, all the others could have been so lucky.[15]

Jordan's and Ransome's good fortune in being rescued from mines and quarries, two of the most notoriously abusive environments for equines in the Cairo area, shows how much trust and how much prestige Dorothy's charity had gained since its founding only a few years earlier. She now did not need to fear approaching anyone in Egypt about the welfare of their working animals. She had a hospital that took in all equines in need, provided free veterinary care for them, and offered the incentive of subsidies for owners whose animals required hospitalization for extended periods of time. Dorothy and Dr. Branch had parted ways, and she could count herself lucky that he had not proved as menacing as he had threatened to be. Despite his opposition to her work, he had put no serious obstacles in her path and had even visited the hospital on the day of its opening, accompanied by members of the Cab Drivers' Union. Glenda

Spooner noted that they came by the location a few more times, and though they weren't seen again, their interest was assumed benign.

Dorothy should have known better.

Just when the Brookes' villa in Heliopolis was full of luncheon guests—invited to celebrate the Cavalry Brigade Horse Show—Dorothy's world, and the Old War Horse Memorial Hospital, almost fell to pieces.

She had been on her feet for hours already. "I had spent all morning on the show ground," Dorothy recalled, "and later several hundred residents in Cairo were to be the guests of 'The Brigade' when I had to be on duty with Geoffrey for many hours, ending the day by presenting prizes."[16]

Compared to everything else she had done that day, the luncheon was a time when she could relax, allow her staff to take care of the guests, talk quietly to one or two friends, and not be on stage at all. It was during this lull that an old friend approached her and asked if he might have a word. Lt. Gen. Sir John Burnett-Stuart was a formidable officer, awarded the Distinguished Service Order during the Boer War and lauded for his service in the Great War.[17] Burnett-Stuart, whom Dorothy knew as Jock, asked her if she had heard from Sir Percy Loraine, British High Commissioner for Egypt and the Sudan. She said she had not. Jock informed her that Sir Percy had given him the duty of informing her that he wished her to stop buying horses. According to Sir Percy, someone—it was not difficult to guess who—had complained to the High Commissioner's office about her work and requested official intervention to stop it. Sir Percy knew Jock to be a friend to Dorothy and Geoffrey and had asked him to break the news.

"The bombshell left me in such a bewildered state of agitation that I hardly knew what I was doing all the rest of the day," Dorothy wrote later. For the moment she had the presence of mind to tell Jock that the High Commissioner would need to communicate directly with General Spinks and the fund committee, not to her, as she could not make unilateral decisions, and they needed to discuss this incredible news at length. Jock, clearly unhappy to be the message bearer, asked her if "you want me to tell Loraine to go to hell." Dorothy may have been tempted, but instead she thanked Jock and tried to get through the rest of the luncheon, her head spinning.[18]

It was no surprise to discover that the petitioner to the High Commissioner was none other than Dr. Alfred E. Branch. He had written to Sir Percy "on behalf of the Ministry of Agriculture and the SPCA and the people of Egypt generally" to lodge complaint against Dorothy and the war horse–buying campaign. He accused the fund committee of seeking out and purchasing so many former army horses and mules that their owners, poor men, were suffering the consequences of having no animals to do their work—a charge that, given that owners were compensated sufficiently to purchase another animal, shows the speciousness of Branch's argument. He left no stone unthrown or unturned, including his opinion that just transporting these animals to Cairo from the four corners of Egypt was inflicting more cruelty on them than they were already endur-ing, compelling proof that Dorothy and her committee were tone deaf to the realities of the poor in Egypt as to the suffering of the animals they allegedly aimed to help. The irony of all this was that long before this letter's arrival, Dorothy and Sir Percy Loraine had had occasion to speak of her work, in social settings that didn't per-mit further explanation or exploration of Dorothy's work in Sayyida Zeinab. Having only a surface acquaintance with what Dorothy was doing, the High Commissioner could not be blamed for believing what Branch had to say in apparently damning detail.[19]

After a meeting of her committee Dorothy was chosen by the other members to write a letter to Sir Percy explaining what the Old War Horse Memorial Hospital was, how it had started, and how it worked—how the poor, far from being unconsidered, were compensated for the time their animals were hospitalized, how they were offered free veterinary care, and how they were paid above fair market prices for animals that could no longer work so the owner could purchase another animal with minimum interruption to his livelihood. She also pointed out that the hospital now took in all equines, not just those abandoned after the war. If Dr. Branch was correct, Dorothy wrote, and her work to rescue these aged horses and mules was undermining the Egyptian economy, how logical was it that the government should be depending at all on the labor of such elderly equines, most living their last few years or months, for heavy transport and haulage? How appropriate was it for the High Commissioner to play a role in ending work that had earned huge amounts of publicity, not only in Egypt and in Britain but farther afield, for helping those elderly equines? Was Sir Percy prepared to break the news to the War Office, which was an annual donor to the Old War Horse Fund, or to Their Majesties King George and Queen Mary, who had sent both funds and notes of support?[20]

There is much in this crisis that suggests interference from a few people at higher levels of the Egyptian government and to a certain gullibility on the part of Sir Percy Loraine. Appointed High Commissioner in 1929, after a career in diplomacy across Europe and the Middle East, Loraine had followed on the heels of Lord Lloyd, a conservative bastion of empire for whom any relinquishing of British imperial territory called forth groans about the last days of Rome. Loraine was more subtle and moderate. He was, however, perhaps too genial for his own good. Egypt's ruler, Fouad I, had raised himself from sultan to king in 1922, and with his waxed moustache and royal regalia gave a physical impression that lay somewhere between Kaiser Wilhelm II and a Gilbert and Sullivan stage despot. But King Fouad was not a king or a man to be pushed around, particularly by Britain, that thorn in Egypt's side. A year after crowning himself, Fouad gave himself sweeping discretionary powers. He considered his courtiers puppets and likely enjoyed being able to pull the strings of his High Commissioner, Sir Percy Loraine.[21]

King Fouad may have already pulled Dr. Branch's strings also over the matter of the abandoned war horses. We have seen that Branch did an about-face on Dorothy and the buying committee by suddenly registering his disapproval and just as suddenly pulling out as a key member of the charity; yet we have also seen that he was in no way a man lacking in compassion toward abused animals—he was, indeed, a man who loved animals. So there is something indefinably but indubitably redolent of political activity around what happened in 1933, when Branch distanced himself from the Old War Horse

Fund and went at length to denigrate its work to the highest levels of British diplomacy in Egypt. With this in mind, it is certainly possible there was pressure from Fouad or his courtiers, alarmed by the widespread publicity the hospital and its work were receiving. Many articles and letters in the British press addressing the abandonment of army equines in Egypt made a point of blaming the British government for not ensuring that they could all return home, but many others made statements such as, "There is no Arabic equivalent for the word 'cruel,'" submitted to the *Northern Daily Mail* in July 1933, "which, since our term conveys nothing to them, may account for the callous treatment old war horses in Egypt receive at the hands of their native owners."[22] In fact, there is a word for "cruel" in Arabic: *qaswa*, one that even appears in the Quran, just as the concept of cruelty was no less known among Egyptians than among the English, despite the ironically cruel Western belief that the Egyptian lower classes were insensitive to pain. For example, American clergyman Francis E. Clark, on a round-the-world journey in the 1890s, paused in Cairo to take in the sights and to make pronouncements such as this: "A traveler and resident for ten years in Egypt says that the sense of pain is very small among the lower classes, that their olfactory nerves are also extremely dull, that they cannot distinguish one person from another by his footsteps, and not easily by his voice, and that they never hear a slight or distant sound, or notice a whisper." These sensory handicaps were attributed by Reverend Clark to "centuries of oppression under hard task masters, and the subserviency to a false and degrading religion."[23]

Driven to despair by the cases of neglect she had to witness, and try to correct, if only with euthanasia, every day at the hospital, even Dorothy could confide to her diary on one occasion her impression of "this people's apparent insensibility to animal pain." Pain may not speak in riddles, but it rarely speaks rationally, and this was the voice of Dorothy's own pain, just as prejudices about Egyptian insensitivity were based as much on the trauma of culture clashes as on the dehumanization colonialism foisted onto the colonized.[24]

In the end what looked like a death blow to the Old War Horse Memorial Hospital was anything but. Sir Percy Loraine received

Dorothy's letter and report, read them, and then asked to meet with the Brookes the following day. After they had dined, Dorothy brought out for Sir Percy to see one of the picture albums she so seldom shared with anybody, mindful of most people's inability to look misery in the eye. Sir Percy leaned over the photographs assembled by Major Heveningham. He saw horses and mules with galled backs, deformed hooves and broken limbs, saw eyes blinded, eyes bright with pain or dulled to everything around them. He saw horses whose backbones stood up like ridges in the hot sun, with washboard ribs and jutting hipbones, septic sores gouging ragged hides. And he saw horses for whom there was more life to live, who were clearly flourishing under the course of treatment, the rest and care, being given them at 2 Bairam al-Tunsi Street. Closing the album cover, and obviously shaken by what he had seen, Sir Percy promised Dorothy he would lend his support. That he meant this was borne out by a letter that arrived shortly after the visit. The letter came from the office of the Egyptian prime minister, Isma'il Sidqi, and it left no question as to the government's approval and enthusiasm for what the hospital was doing. "My grandmother was politically very astute," recalls Richard Searight.[25]

It helped enormously to know that there was now understanding and acknowledgment of the hospital's work at the top of British bureaucracy in Egypt. Yet questions and misconceptions about what Dorothy was doing lingered, often among foreigners resident in the country. "Over and over again," Dorothy wrote, "I was seriously informed that, although many English residents of Cairo fully appreciated the excellence of my intentions and the self-sacrificing kindness of the members of the Buying Committee, it was common knowledge that at least sixty per cent of the horses purchased were faked Arabs, brought before us for sale as genuine old war horses by wily Egyptians, who were, of course, only too ready to take advantage of our gullibility!" This showed a complete misunderstanding of Dorothy's work and likely had a colonialist basis: to these people, "the natives" were constantly on the make, doing everything they could to swindle unsuspecting expats. After a while Dorothy stopped bothering to try to educate such people, who were in any case not part of the funding base for the hospital. For, best of all, she was reaching native Egyptians and, through the hospital's work, reaching the animals that needed help, while educating their owners in how to care for them. As for the visitors who came in increasing numbers to the hospital, she had a visual reminder of why what she was doing was so needed. Glenda Spooner writes that Dorothy had found a magazine illustration "of a cavalry charge in Palestine depicting the horses in all their youthful well-fed glory." She framed and hung this image in an area of the stables where those who saw it—including herself—could have the sad benefit of comparing it "with the pathetic remnant of the gallant army, standing in rows, starved, broken in spirit and in heart." It seemed the best way to make it clear to visitors that these heroes had also served, and because they had served, they deserved the best life possible at the end.[26]

One particular pony, and his unstoppable courage, seemed to sum up all the reasons why everything the hospital and Dorothy were doing in Cairo was worthwhile. She called him Dauntless. He was another of the old polo ponies discarded by some foreign owner, passed down the line of ownership and labor as his physical infirmities reduced his value, until he was being whipped through the streets, pulling a cart for a callous human himself degraded and devalued by poverty, sickness, and age. Of these discarded animals, Col. J. K. Stanford would write, "there is no sadder sight than somebody's old polo pony or half-starved racehorse, with little thoroughbred ears still cocked, putting all his or her gallant heart into the task of shifting a cartload of sand which might have daunted a Percheron."[27]

Dauntless was one of these gallant hearts, but his body had not been equal to the work to which it had been put. He was not simply bony; he had open sores on his withers, the area of a horse's shoulders at the base of its neck. The wounds resulted from a poorly fitted harness or a yoke attached to an unrelieved heavy load and were never cared for. Nobody had treated the sores, which were now seriously infected. But Dauntless still had spirit—it was what attracted Dorothy to him. When he was first brought into the hospital stable, he gaped in astonishment, as if he never thought he would see anything like this again. He was as happy to be in a box as a child with its toys, and he loved peeking over the half-door to see what was happening in the rest of the building, fascinated by the ongoing flow of life around him—a sign that whatever his present misery, Dauntless had at least when young been surrounded by happiness.

"He was the greediest horse for sugar that I have ever met," Dorothy remembered. The pony quickly learned to recognize Dorothy's voice and came to expect the kindnesses she lavished on him specially. "It must have been a pleasant change for the old boy to find his command instantly attended to," she wrote. As soon as he heard Dorothy coming, Dauntless would neigh and stamp. "He had me completely at his mercy," she recalled, "because his delight was so terribly pathetic. There was nothing one wouldn't try to do to give him happiness."[28]

She soon realized why he was so hungry for sugar—he had the charmed curse of a long memory. This old pony, his body in tatters, had once been the spoiled plaything of some polo player, born and bred in England and coddled in Egypt until, like the elderly dogs or cats still today dropped off for euthanasia at animal shelters on Christmas Eve as nuisances to family celebrations, the pony was sold, and sold again, worked out of all proportion to his age and condition, his physical ailments as neglected as his emotional ones. And now here he was, his life measured in a matter of days or even hours. Yet still he remembered something of the charmed atmosphere in which he had grown up. "This old pony had evidently, in happier times, been taught to hold up one fore-foot for a special treat," Dorothy wrote. "I can so well recall the expression of anxiety the first time he tried it on me. So many people must have ignored this gesture learnt when young, and which he originally must have regarded as infallible. . . . It nearly broke my heart to think how often he must have lifted that tired old foot to unheeding masters before he realised that it produced no results at all."[29]

Dorothy and George Gibson watched Dauntless's antics, charming and intensely poignant in a little pony with so many physical infirmities, with such an unhappy past. They observed his cunning escapes, as if he were still a saucy infant, from the stable to where the fresh piles of clover were kept, the billows of which he would swallow whole until led away; how he playfully strained to roll on his back in the sand of the paddock and had to be stopped from doing it, though the others were there doing it, too, because his sore-ridden withers were bandaged, and any healing that had occurred would be undone by the rolling.

Soon came the fly season, and Dauntless had to be placed in a meshed box, where his sores would be safe from maggots. He could only be let out into the paddock briefly and never unsupervised, and he couldn't see the other animals, which were as much a joy to him as Dorothy and her soft voice. Gradually Dauntless grew depressed, and with his physical condition not improving, Dorothy had to give an order that she had given thousands of times, but that in this one case desperately tore her heart in two. When the Quran adjures devout Muslims, "Do not take life, which Allah made sacred, other than in the course of justice," it refers to human life, but it could just as well have served to describe the decision Dorothy had to make for Dauntless. It was selfish to let him suffer because she loved him, justice to him to let him go.[30]

Dorothy wrote, "One could hardly bear to part with him. He was so brave, so full of zest for life." Some people thought all horses were the same, Dorothy added, "whereas in fact they are as intensely individual as humans."[31]

The only difference, when compared to most human beings in similar painful and deprived circumstances, was that the Dauntlesses of this world never complained.

8. World War

And this is how ...
What dies, dies
What passes, passes
What is lost, is lost ... under the layers of dust!
And you ask me ... And I shall not answer.

—DR. MOHAMMED ABD-ELHAY[1]

As Geoffrey and Dorothy Brooke arrived in Rawalpindi, Punjab (now in Pakistan), in 1935, when General Brooke was assigned as inspector general of cavalry in India, they arrived at a time when the jewel in Britain's crown was considerably less lustrous than it had been. "The English have not taken India," said Mohandas Gandhi, "we have given it to them."[2]

India was about to take itself back, but in 1935 Rawalpindi was still a British cantonment, or military garrison, located on the North-West Railway and the grand trunk road along the Leh River. When the Brookes stepped off their train at Rawalpindi Station, they would have seen a city of mostly low-storied structures, the sky occasionally pierced by minarets or church towers; there were crowded bazaars and broad streets lined with trees, and a statue of Queen Victoria, smiling benignly over all.

Glenda Spooner writes that it was not long after her arrival in India that Dorothy found working equines there just as much in need of care, their owners as much in need of education, as those at her hospital in Cairo. As if starting all over, she carved out time in her crowded officer's wife's social calendar to try to make a difference in these animals' lives, even commissioning large-scale plans for a hospital complex in Rawalpindi.³ Spooner tells us that these efforts were not to come to fruition, at least not at that time, perhaps because in Rawalpindi Dorothy was dealing with a completely different situation to what existed in Cairo. Spooner tells us that Dorothy did the best she could in Rawalpindi, but that always at the forefront of her thinking was the Cairo clinic, which she made a point of visiting every year, despite the arduousness of the journey.⁴

Fortunately in Dorothy's absence the hospital in Sayyida Zeinab proved to be in better than capable hands. Col. John Hodgkins, a retired RAVC surgeon who had served as veterinarian in the battlefields of France, had been put in charge of hospital administration alongside Col. Douglas Smith, RAVC, who in later years explained to Dorothy's granddaughter just how critical Colonel Hodgkins was to the hospital's very existence.⁵ During Hodgkins's ten years at the hospital, "he trained up his staff, trained a whole generation of Egyptian vets," recalled Colonel Smith, "reinforcing a code of good hygiene and animal management which has lasted to this day." Hodgkins was never a vet to give up on an animal, even when others saw no point in trying to save it; through this willpower as much as through skill, Hodgkins would help several patients pull through.⁶

A small, compact man, "by nature . . . shy and retiring," Hodgkins was good-natured and generous; he often gave kudos to the syces, typically a despised class of worker, and happily trained any family members who showed interest in working with equines or for the hospital.⁷ But he could be pushed to the wall, as would happen during World War II, when lack of staff threw most of the hospital's work on his shoulders. Dr. Murad Raghib, later chief veterinarian of the hospital, remembered Colonel Hodgkins running up and down the wards in a frenzy. "Get a move on!" he shouted at the grooms. "Hurry up! Hurry up!" Yet when dwindling funds and supplies meant cutting back on virtually all the hospital's expenses, Hodgkins would not hear of any economies being made at the expense of his patients, Dr. Murad recalled. And if he had to shout at anybody, it was for always the animals' sake. Completing this strong team was George Gibson, whom Dr. Murad would call "the principal doer," assisting Major Heveningham.[8]

"Links with Cairo University were encouraged by students from the University's veterinary department having a spell of training at the Hospital," writes Sarah Searight. One of these Cairo University students was to become a mainstay of the old war horse hospital, though the route he took to get there was circuitous at best. In 1938, three years after the Brookes departed for India, a young man named Murad Raghib arrived at the hospital. He was, says Dorothy's grandson Richard Searight, "to take on my grandmother's spirit, her mantle as it were."[9]

A Coptic Christian whose father was employed by the Government Veterinary Service, Raghib was one of a handful of students enrolled in the Veterinary College of Cairo University, founded in 1908 as a secular center of civil education. For Raghib 1937 was a hard year: his father's death and the weight of becoming overnight the sole source of support for his mother and siblings was especially draining as Raghib tackled his final exams. In a society so reliant on animals for transportation, it may seem there would always be a job waiting somewhere for a veterinarian, but the story is not so simple or easy. The profession was not only looked down on in the 1930s, but it had not gained much in public esteem over sixty years later.

Dr. Mohammed Abd-Elhay, Brooke Hospital veterinarian, who was born in 1984, describes navigating a similar rocky road on his way to a career of helping and healing animals many years later. "For all my life and since I was a kid I wanted to be a vet," says Dr. Abd-Elhay. "Being a vet wasn't a very popular profession in Egypt; you were more likely to get mocked and underpaid, so nobody really likes it except some fools like me!" Friends and family were discouraging, cracking jokes and predicting a life of difficulty for him. So he challenged them by beginning veterinary studies, "only to find it a really unpleasant place for students or animals," he explains. "But there was no way to pull back. It took me ten years to finish vet school; I was really lost sometimes and didn't know where my life would go. I discovered that not all vets work in National Geographic settings. I could see that I would eventually end up doing some unpleasant job for money, which wasn't an option for me. I'm a person who works to serve a higher purpose and get satisfaction by making a difference."[10]

At one point in his studies Dr. Abd-Elhay found a relatively quiet job taking care of cattle in the countryside—an ideal situation for a vet student who is also a published poet, but not for a man who turned out to be allergic to ruminants. "One day I was at the vet school and I asked a friend about a training place to make use of my free time," says Dr. Abd-Elhay. His friend referred him to the Brooke Hospital in Cairo. He was given a tour, "and that day I felt like I found my purpose in life. There I learned that I really could be a vet with a message and dedicate my time and effort to it." Dr. Abd-Elhay trained at the hospital for two weeks, then with the Donkey Sanctuary and with ESMA (Egyptian Society for Mercy to Animals), situated near the Pyramids. After more volunteering and working for a year for ESAF (Egyptian Society of Animal Friends), a vacancy opened at the Brooke Hospital in Cairo in 2013, and Dr. Abd-Elhay was hired.[11]

If a modern-day Egyptian vet's journey to a job he loved seems filled with obstacles, Raghib's journey some six decades earlier was even more so. Yet, as with Dr. Abd-Elhay, a friend of a friend smoothed part of the way. The Cairo University dean was a colleague of Major Heveningham and arranged for Raghib to be introduced to and taken on by the hospital on a volunteer basis. When it became clear that Raghib was unable to work for nothing, given his duties to his family, the hospital's treasurer, Major Burrill, found him employment on a pig farm owned by an English officer. After only eighteen months, however, Raghib was taken ill and was bedridden for several months. Then his mother died, and with his siblings to support, Raghib, who had not given up on his dream of working for Dorothy's hospital, continued to volunteer there by day while working a paid job at the Cairo SPCA by night. It was only in early 1944, the penultimate year of the war, that Raghib—known as Dr. Murad—would be paid for his work at 2 Bairam al-Tunsi Street, and not long after that he would meet Dorothy, who was finally free to return to Egypt in 1946. "Without this man," said Brig. Hassan Sami, a close friend, in 2003, "Brooke would have never survived." Though a "tyrant about veterinary methods," wrote Brooke employee Lynne Nesbit in later years, Dr. Murad was "saintly in his attitude to animals." And it did not hurt, she added, that "every female supporter who came within three feet of him fell in love with the man."[12]

The outbreak of World War II unfolded strangely in Egypt, where the influx of British personnel helped calm some people's fears of Axis invasion and yet inflamed the wounds of others who detested and distrusted the British. In the years 1940–45 the war refocused and reshaped what had been until then scattered pieces of anti-British feeling, Egyptian nationalism, religious factionalism, and social unrest. These competing responses tipped and twisted the flat Nile Valley landscape so that the disparate shards formed a pattern that, to those able to see it, spelled out the long-dreaded, long-awaited end of the old British order and a future that to some far-sighted Egyptians included neither the British nor the Egyptian royal family, but something revolutionary and new.

Other than a swift and alarming reduction in funds and supplies, the biggest hit Dorothy's hospital took with the outbreak of war was when its British staff left for military service almost as soon as hostilities were declared.

Major Heveningham was posted in 1940 to the Transjordanian Frontier Force, which had an extensive cavalry; Gibson entered the Royal Navy somewhat later, in 1943. What faced the Brooke Hospital during the war was a double threat: a sudden lack of trained personnel and inadequate supplies. While the former could be cobbled together from Egyptian sources, at least for the short term, the hospital owed its existence to donations, largely from abroad. Now it faced a crimp in that pipeline, as well as an increasingly public disaffection within the country as a whole for anything British. Without cash, supplies would dwindle, and without supplies—from food to medicines—the Brooke Hospital could not function. Yet somehow it did. Though Burrill, treasurer of the hospital committee, served as an officer at GHQ (General Headquarters of the British Army) in Cairo, he was always able to work part of what time he had at the Brooke. As the committee member who kept the accounts of donations received and funds expended, he had a combination of experience and talent that could not easily have been replaced or even temporarily covered by another employee. And, of course, Colonel Hodgkins was always on site, as he would be until felled by a heart attack in autumn 1945.[13]

Staff cutbacks meant leaning on volunteers, the backbone of any charitable organization. There were plenty of jobs to do for a volunteer, especially in the stables, easily performed by anybody who had any familiarity with horses. These volunteers offered something else just as vital during the war years as money and food: they maintained the hospital's credo of giving suffering animals a quiet rest, whatever the human conflicts raging outside the stable walls. Naval nurse Mary Carr-Ellis, a hospital volunteer, recalled for Sarah Searight her experience of the "wonderful atmosphere of peace and calm and care," noting especially, as Dorothy had done years earlier, how happy the patients appeared to be at the prospect of enough to eat and drink, a soft place to lie down.[14]

During World War II, "drugs were expensive and rare," writes Searight, all the more so when African Horse Disease, the sickness that Dr. Branch had prevented from destroying the equines of Upper Egypt in 1928, overtook Cairo's equines in 1943, possibly due to the movements of people and animals from the country to the city, depending on competing rumors of approaching Axis forces. The hospital was put under quarantine, unfortunately preventing intake of any new animals, yet out of the broader tragedy of the epidemic was born a key feature of Brooke's future services. Sarah Searight notes that animals were kept from the city markets. Instead, Brooke veterinarians were themselves sent to these markets outside the city center to provide mobile care, a salient feature of the hospital's work and also one that would later be crucial to the more wide-ranging clinics scattered across several Egyptian cities and then several developing nations.[15]

Most of the time, a shadow puppet show, like those then seen in the Cairo bazaars, flung flitting, imaginary figures of the war across the pale scrim of city and citizens, but never so darkly or realistically as in 1942. Field Marshal Erwin Rommel had made gains in Egypt that May and June, exciting Mussolini's yen for drama to such extent that he boarded a plane for Libya, another transport ship bringing his white horse, which he intended to ride into Cairo in triumph, not far behind.[16] Pro-German propaganda broadcasts had threatened an Axis air raid of Cairo that June, and while Prime Minister Mostapha El Nahas scolded "scare-mongers" in the Egyptian Parliament, Cairenes *were* scared. The British line that appeared impregnable was suspected of more than a few chinks in its armor. In the end, it was Alexandria that actually took direct bombings on June 29, and the resulting deaths and destruction were sufficient to flip Cairo, already on edge, completely on its head. GHQ burned so many files (to the despair of future historians) that July 1,1942, came to be dubbed "Ash Wednesday." A curfew was set over central Cairo, which did nothing to deter long lines of bank account holders eager to cash in and get out of town. Cecil Beaton, who was in Egypt as a commissioned war photographer, referred to the chaos, later determined to be an overreaction, as a "Flap," a calming yet sarcastic term that might better refer to a breakfast table disagreement.[17]

Not that this panic was without foundation. A bomb had fallen on the city two years earlier. At that time people had dumped everything they owned into carts and headed for the hills. Yet in testimony to how integral the Brooke Hospital had become to serving their needs, before they left, they stopped at 2 Bairam al-Tunsi, where the vets gave the horses or donkeys a checkup, water, and provisions to last until they returned, acts of kindness for which the hospital by now was well known. The Brooke Hospital's vets also did their part for the war effort. In the "Flap" year of 1942 Dr. Murad assumed the job of overseeing trench digging as well as fire drills at the hospital, "causing considerable interest and some consternation in the crowded neighborhood of Sayyida Zeinab." Colonel Hodgkins's task was to demonstrate the wearing of gas masks, again attracting a great deal of local attention. Whatever fears the hospital's neighbors may have had for their own safety, at least they knew that they and their horses would have a fighting chance should the war come to their district.[18]

Colonel Hodgkins kept Dorothy, then in England with Geoffrey, constantly apprised of all that was going on at the hospital, so that from her residence in Salisbury Close she could know what was happening in "English Lady Street."

Even, as Glenda Spooner writes, "while Rommel was at the gates of the city," Hodgkins was dutifully penning reports, "full of enthusiasm and of all the little details she so loved to hear." These details would have included what can only be described as a triumph under any conditions, but especially during time of war: citywide efforts to rough up and sand the streets of Cairo, so that donkeys, mules, and horses, beaten in order to force them to drag heavy loads up inclines, would have less chance of suffering the kinds of injuries that caused the hospital to euthanize so many animals far too much of the time.[19] Only a week before his death, Colonel Hodgkins had written to Dorothy with a number of ideas for how to "furbish up" the hospital once the war was over and life could return to an even keel again (he was not to live to see the coming storms of Egyptian nationalism and anti-British violence that the hospital would have to weather).[20] The day before Hodgkins died, remembered Dr. Murad, the colonel had called him on the telephone, setting out explicit instructions on the protocol required for receiving a dignitary from Sudan.[21]

Not only were thousands of humans conscripted into the second global conflict of the century, but animals were once again called to serve. The war machine had been thoroughly mechanized—it was largely due to this push, as we've seen, that horses and mules were disposed of in Egypt in 1919. But as Sarah Searight points out, "horses, mules and donkeys still had a prominent role to play in World War II, especially as pack animals." Jilly Cooper characterizes Britain's response to the renewed need for equines in war and the clumsiness with which they went about it as reminiscent of "a foolish housewife, who as soon as she buys a washing-up machine, promptly chucks away her washing-up bowl and Fairy Liquid," then is bereft when the machine breaks down.[22] Total mechanization had theoretically carried the British military into the twentieth century, but even modern machines could not manage the desert and jungle terrains that made up the Second World War's diverse theaters of action. Cooper tells of the nightmare voyage in 1939 of nine thousand requisitioned horses, shipped off to Palestine despite lack of adequate veterinary staff to look after them. These horses were sent by rail across France in open cars during one of the coldest winters in memory, as if it were 1914 all over again. Hundreds of them died, and those that survived were tossed on sea transport that nearly capsized in a storm, so that in the end eight thousand animals made it to dry land, only to be put to patrol service that was by any measure anticlimactic. They were luckier than horses serving in the Russian cavalry, who froze and starved in snowy fields or were urged in suicidal charges toward German guns that mowed them down by the thousands.[23]

Mules had no better a fate in World War II. Bright, intelligent characters whose responses to a given situation were never predictable, they seemed to know they had once upon a time been the mount of choice of the kings of Israel and high prelates of the Catholic Church, treasured for their versatility and adaptability to varying loads and circumstances. They served faithfully as they bore ammunition, weapons, supplies, and just about anything that could be put on their backs, often in quantities that in peacetime would have been considered far too much for them to carry and in terrain that was risky at best, even for a sure-footed and logical mule. Such were their individual personality traits, combined with the heroism of their effort in the war, that when men had to part with them it was somehow more devastating than leaving a horse behind. Cooper describes a case of unwilling abandonment at Dunkirk in May 1940. When rescue vessels arrived, there wasn't space for the mules, who had to be left to the Germans. She speculates, with good reason, that there were not a few mule drivers in tears as they sailed away to safety, their animals stranded on the beachhead.[24]

There were innumerable heroes among the mules of World War II, but the prize must go to Mitzi, who served in the Burma campaign, having had her vocal cords severed, like all the rest, so her braying wouldn't alert the enemy. Though Mitzi was ornery, she served her driver, Douglas Roberts, with sturdy, even heedless, bravery. Running from Japanese troops, Mitzi and Roberts ended up in a river that nobody was able to cross. As Roberts gripped her tail, Mitzi fought the current. She pulled him to the other side and up on the bank to safety, only to die from the effort. That was courage for which a human soldier would have received a posthumous medal. Mitzi's body was left behind as Roberts was evacuated to a hospital, her only reward the saving of his life.[25]

The situations in which these World War II animals served were admittedly quite changed from 1914–18, yet the same threat hung over them as over the equines Dorothy had spent thousands of pounds and thousands of hours saving—what would happen to them after the war ended? In the war's first year, Dorothy seized the opportunity and sent a letter to Anthony Eden, secretary of state for foreign affairs. Born in 1897, Eden (later British prime minister) had lost two brothers in the Great War, in which he had served himself, in France, becoming the youngest brigade-major in the British forces. He had seen what war horses and army mules were exposed to in battle. Interestingly, he later served as member of Parliament for Leamington Spa, locale of staunch RSPCA and Old War Horse Fund supporters in the early 1930s. So Eden probably knew Dorothy and Geoffrey, if not socially then by the work they were doing in Egypt, and when he received Dorothy's appeal—that none of the horses, mules, or donkeys serving in the war effort would be subjected to a repeat of 1918–19—Eden assured her that this would be the case.[26]

Dorothy, writes Glenda Spooner, "had not forgotten how similar vows . . . had been broken." When Eden was succeeded by Leslie Hore-Belisha, Dorothy sent him a letter of concern as well. In October 1940, she received a reply from the War Office, stating that "in the event of cavalry horses becoming surplus in the Middle East, the pledges regarding their disposal which have in the past been given in Parliament, will be observed."[27] This did not, of course, appear to cover the Yeomanry and draft animals, and Dorothy was smart to take nobody at their word. Just around the time she had arrived in India, in 1935, Dorothy had received an alarming cable from a friend, alerting her to a plan underway to dispose of British cavalry and artillery horses in Egypt, essentially replicating what had happened at the end of the Great War, and again in Egypt, of all places. Dorothy pulled together a collection of documentary and photographic evidence of what awaited these animals, should they be put to the same fate as their elders, and sent it to the authorities whose decision this was to make. "At the eleventh hour," says Spooner, "the order was rescinded." Not only this, but the proof of the suffering these horses might well have endured had such an impact on thinking in London that the subject, as referred to in the War Office letter from five years later, had been raised in the House of Commons, and assurances were given there that "in future no English army horse would be disposed of to the inhabitants of any foreign countries under any conditions whatsoever." This influence, reaching into the halls of power, of a compassionate woman over the bellicose affairs of men, reminded Glenda Spooner yet again of the work of Florence Nightingale.[28]

Like a general calling in reinforcements, Dorothy also enlisted the good offices of General Archibald Wavell. Wavell was not only commander in chief in the Middle East but also had been a supporter of Dorothy's work for some years. He, too, assured her in no uncertain terms that "no branded horses were to be sold, all were to be either humanely destroyed or brought home." Another reassuring voice was that of Major Heveningham, who, as mentioned, served with the Transjordanian Frontier Force. As he wrote to Dorothy in November 1940, "I have not, nor ever will, forget our experiences when doing that great work of mercy out in these parts and consequently when horses first arrived out here I made contact with every possible officer and official to ensure that horses 'cast' [culled] for any reason at all, were all humanely destroyed and *not sold*."[29]

When Dorothy was able to return to Egypt after the war's end, she found that Colonel Hodgkins's plans for "furbishing" the hospital were well justified. Though 2 Bairam al-Tunsi Street was still the same place she had left, "cream-coloured, creeper-clad, its broad asphalt pavement edged with neatly clipped evergreen trees and square-box hedges," wartime shortages meant there had been no new paint, and that numerous repairs had been postponed. She had bigger plans, though, than patching plaster or resurfacing floors—she intended to build a real operating theater to the latest standards to replace the crude shed that up to then had been used for surgeries. All of this was a lot to worry about when money was as short as it had been during the war, but when Dorothy stepped through the modest entrance of the Brooke Hospital in spring 1946, seven years after she had last seen it, it was as if she had returned to paradise. "I have rarely known anything that has given me happiness equal to visiting the hospital again," she wrote. "To find myself there at last with so many old friends is almost too good to be true."[30]

There to greet Dorothy, besides two small dogs, hobbling happily on three legs each, was Dr. Murad, new among the familiar faces of Gibson, Burrill, and Egyptian staff, though he was not to have a chance to really meet and talk with her until at a tea party she gave at the hospital shortly afterward. He evidently expected her to be some sort of Amazon powerhouse, barking orders, organizing everybody's day. Dorothy was a superb organizer, but Dr. Murad's impression was rather that her iron hand was well concealed in its velvet glove. Far from being the stereotypical foreign memsahib, Dorothy was subdued, thoughtful, funny. "She spoke to us so quietly," he recalled. "And she was always optimistic. That wasn't easy in 1946. But even then, she could make us laugh."[31]

Not long after her return to Egypt, Dorothy received a visitor who was to play a vital role in the future of the Brooke Hospital. Kathleen Taylor Smith was born in Canterbury, Kent, in 1900; she had married and had a son, and she was living the quiet life of wife and mother when the war disarranged settled patterns and plans. While her husband Robert was in the service, Kathleen worked at the local soldiers' canteen as committee treasurer. In 1945 Robert was posted to Cairo, where Kathleen joined him a year later. There, as she adjusted to the heat, sandstorms, unfamiliar sounds and smells, and the postwar anti-British sentiment painted on walls and glaring from the faces of Egyptians she met in the streets, Kathleen fell in love with Egypt. She worked as secretary to the music officer of the

British Council, a charity founded in England in 1934 to offer educational and cultural opportunities and exchange in foreign countries, but the music of the written word was as strong in her, if not stronger. A poet of often striking artistry, Kathleen also wrote witty, keenly observant letters later collected into a book, *Speaking of Palm Trees*. She saw clearly what was wrong with British-Egyptian relations; she did not blame Egyptians who demonstrated their anger against the British, though she never condoned violence on either side. "How I wish it were in my power," she wrote in June 1946, "to do some work which would bring Egypt and Britain together, or some work of real benefit to the poor of the country, brave and loveable as so many are, and who have so little."[32]

These words, indeed, could have been spoken by Dorothy Brooke, of both animals and people, when she arrived in Cairo sixteen years earlier. So it comes as no surprise that when the two came to meet, on April 8, through the kind offices of Brooke treasurer Burrill, their elective affinities led to mutual affection and trust.

They met at the hospital, where Kathleen was given a tour that sounds incredibly thorough. This may have been what Dorothy did for all visitors, but perhaps she sensed that this woman with a generous heart (Kathleen had brought along some of her friends, who later subscribed to donate to the hospital) was different from those who could only handle so much of the truth of what she and her staff had to face on a daily basis. As such, she spared Kathleen very little. Dorothy told her that what she had discovered in 1930 was not simply the tragedy of war horses who had been sold away from all that was familiar in language, care, or custom. They were sold without the bits and harness they had been accustomed to all their adult lives, receiving Arab bits that never fit comfortably. These led to painful sores and damaged teeth, with a consequent disinterest in food, even when the animals were hungry. Many animals, their mouths hurting, simply starved to death (a problem Brooke still works to remedy today). Dorothy told Kathleen that while the sale of English horses in Egypt had been a catastrophic failure of duty and decency on an individual scale, the volume of horses disposed of had resulted in a "market [that] was so flooded in this way with cheap horses that they were bought for next to nothing and worked to the death."[33]

Not least to be considered, Dorothy explained to her, was the plight of the owners. "Where the people are so poor," Kathleen wrote, "the animals are bound to suffer." Instead of lashing out at these men for their neglect and sometimes cruel treatment of their animals, the Brooke tried to teach them that an animal that is given care will deliver longer and more efficient service to its owner than if it is neglected—that, indeed, neglecting an animal on which a man's livelihood depended was exactly the same as neglecting his family.[34]

Kathleen Taylor Smith had visited the SPCA in Cairo, where the Brooke Hospital's work had first begun, and had seen the good work being done there along with a guest book displaying signatures of such august visitors as Lord Cromer, British consul-general in Egypt, as well as military heroes Lord Kitchener and Lord Allenby. Yet something about the Brooke Hospital stayed with her. Sensitive as she was to the fact that British occupation of Egypt was living its last days, she was nonetheless impressed that the Brooke—and Dorothy—had managed to bridge two worlds and two cultures so often in conflict, tapping a mutual love for animals and a mutual understanding that to care for them meant not disposing of ancient customs but leavening them with education to improve the lives of animals and their owners. As if to cap off this cross-cultural exchange founded on compassion in common, Kathleen noticed that the subscribers' list for 1946–47 was headed by none other than Prince Mohammed Ali Tewfik, Dr. Branch's old friend. This was a wise perception, because Dorothy's active search for ways to work with, rather than against, her Egyptian hosts was to prove useful to the survival of the hospital in the next decade.[35]

The woman who would write, as Kathleen did on leaving Egypt in 1947, "I only know you need to live in Egypt and love it to understand its special problems and how these have arisen," would become organizing secretary for the Brooke Hospital for Animals, visiting her beloved Egypt yearly until 1973. When she gave Kathleen a tour of the hospital that April day in 1946, rickety and war-worn though it was, Dorothy must have known that she had found another compassionate spirit to carry on the work beyond her own lifetime. As in so much of what Kathleen wrote, we can hear some of Dorothy in her last letter from Egypt: "Imagine what the world would be if love spreads all over it."[36]

Dorothy herself wrote of this love in one of her reports to the hospital's subscribers, describing the end of a busy day:

> The sun is setting when, after visiting between forty and fifty patients, we take our leave with a feeling that our efforts have not all been in vain. The teaching of the hospital is beginning to bear fruit but it is rather like tilling a vast waste, there are so many thousand owners to be converted. Those we do reach, increasingly appreciate the hospital and slowly but surely we are awaking a sympathy and a consciousness that animals have feelings like small children, and that it is the responsibility of every owner, so far as his small funds permit, to consider the welfare and comfort of his animals.[37]

This was a lovely dream at twilight. Would it withstand the heat of day?

9. Their Portion Is Gardens

They can't even deal with life. How can they deal with their animals?

—BRIG. HASSAN SAMI

I n late March 1946, on her first outing in the streets of Cairo, Kathleen Taylor Smith wrote, "A fine looking old man in a turban, his face like that of a Hebrew prophet, sits selling papers at the corner of this street. On the wall, over his head, is chalked: 'Down with England. Evacuation with Blood.'"[1]

"What a shock this gave me," she added. In fact, tears sprang as she remembered what the world had just been through, and been saved from, thanks to Britain and the Allies, and of how easily Egypt could have fallen to Nazi Germany but for those foreigners whom the graffiti artist wanted swept "in blood" from Egypt. Kathleen was also well aware, even at that stage of her stay in the country, of what would make Egyptians feel this way. Still, she admitted to the old man that the sign bothered her.[2]

"No, indeed, it is not good," he agreed. "I will wipe it off." But he didn't try very hard. When Kathleen was next in that street, she noted that though there was evidence of his effort to erase the slogan for her sake, his own belief in it was manifest in the half-hearted way in which he had gone about it.[3]

Try though even well-meaning and worldly Egyptians might, there was no way of completely erasing that sentiment. It went deep, down to cultural nerves that cannot be probed without pain, which no anesthetic can numb. Many Egyptians were angry with King Farouk, believing he had caved in to British pressure to unseat Prime Minister Nahas, an anger that was more than simple outrage against the British. War has always had a tendency to open hearts, minds, and mouths to subversive ideas in those of the population who disagreed with war in the first place and, in the second place, with war's dictatorial interference in civilian affairs. When the chessmen shifted places and the Soviet Union joined the Allied effort, this military alliance had social consequences for structures based on old-fashioned, hierarchical structure. If millions of voices were stilled by both world wars, those of the living began to question that hierarchy, and nowhere more so than in the countries where Britain still held colonial control. In Egypt the powder trail was being laid. "Every extremist, nationalist group, whether right- or left-wing, flourished in the general dissatisfaction," writes Artemis Cooper.[4] These groups merely stirred dissent already fermenting among dissatisfied peasants, who heard rumors of extravagance that few had seen but all could credit. It was at fever pitch among young students whose Egyptian nationalism grew in proportion to their educational opportunities, or their outrage at perceived or real restrictions, and also among the rank and file in the crowded streets of Cairo, where the "Evacuation in Blood" message would have been retraced in chalk or ink no matter how many times it was removed.

Five years after Dorothy had returned to Cairo and to her yearly trips to keep an eye on the hospital, the first trouble began around that locus of tug-of-war territoriality, the Suez Canal, and treaties in which Egypt had long believed it had received the short end of the stick. General unrest was focused on the British presence in Egypt, with cash incentives publicly offered for the assassination of British officers. Nor was the situation aided by British retaliation laden with colonialist codes of control over crazed natives. Egyptian propaganda held up its own side with alacrity, blaming the British for profaning holy places like mosques and cemeteries. Riots and threats were daily occurrences, and at last, on Friday and Saturday, January 25–26, 1952, hell opened. Well-rehearsed, well-dressed male mobs began assaulting foreign-operated and foreign-patronized nightclubs, hotels, shops, and banks. Shepheard's Hotel, a Cairo icon, went up in flames. British nationals were hunted down and hacked to death, as was the Canadian trade minister, Joseph

MacLeod Boyer of New Brunswick (a Great War hero in the battlefields of France). "Every cinema, bar, cabaret and wine-merchant in the city centre was destroyed," writes Artemis Cooper. Officers of public safety were seen slicing up fire hoses in use to put out the flames. Collusion with the rioters only whipped up both ruthlessness and panic. The madness streamed out toward the Pyramids and engulfed pleasure spots known to be frequented by foreigners and well-to-do Egyptians. As happens in many riots, aside from lives lost and property destroyed, some of it forever, thousands of ordinary Cairenes were put out of work, some for good, by anarchy deluding itself that it was the answer to working men's prayers. The king, too, was facing the end of the line. Exactly six months later Farouk was given orders to leave the country, which was now in the hands of the army, with Gen. Muhammad Naguib as leader of the Revolution Command Council. He was sworn in as first president of Egypt in June 1953. This was more of a fragile truce with the British than a solution to the problems that had led to Black Saturday, and it would only hold for a few years.[5]

As early as 1951, writes Sarah Searight, "most members of Cairo's British community, civilian and military alike, were talking of departure." Until he left Egypt in 1952, Dorothy's son Rodney Searight lived in Cairo, where he was general manager of Shell International Petroleum. For a month or more each year Dorothy would stay with him and his family. After he and many other British nationals left, she proved she had no intention of letting a revolution come between her and the patients at her hospital. "An obstacle is a mountain to the feeble," Dorothy said, "but a stepping stone to the strong."[6] There is a photograph of her leading President Naguib on a tour of the Brooke Hospital in April 1953. The president, in full uniform, salutes the crowds in the street while Dorothy strides beside him, glowing in the bright sun. Even the tough-looking security detail surrounding Naguib seem softened, more human.

There is another photograph of Naguib in the paddock with some of the donkeys, standing with hand outstretched and lips puckered in equine greeting as an alert little foal, legs apart in interest and apprehension, stretches out a nose alongside her mother. Naguib, who when under house arrest a year later would raise animals in his garden, was as much in his element in the paddock as on the revolutionary council—indeed, given what happened later, perhaps more so.[7] Naguib threw his support to the hospital, writes Sarah Searight, and until he died in 1988, the former Egyptian president made a gift to the charity every year. After his 1953 visit President Naguib sent Dorothy a note of appreciation. "The Hospital and its great deeds stand as the proof that in our world there are angels amongst its inhabitants. May God direct people here and in other countries to follow the same." Fouad Abaza Pasha, president of the Agricultural Society, told Dorothy he wished there could be a hospital like hers located in every district of Cairo—a significant indicator of the level of trust she had earned throughout Egyptian society.[8]

During this charmed interlude between one uprising and the next, Dorothy was able to realize plans she had dreamed of back in the 1930s. Since first arriving in Egypt, Dorothy had seen plenty of evidence that impoverished peasants in the fields outside Cairo and quarrymen working in the Mokattam Hills were not the only source of suffering for equines—tourists played a role as well, just as they do today. Out they went to the Pyramids by the thousands, and the only way to get there was via horses or camels, who were made to "stand on the wide cement and, therefore, baking hot pavement at the foot of the hill up to the Pyramids," wrote Glenda Spooner. "These animals wait here for tourists who all through the Cairo season stream out to see the Pyramids, the Sphinx and all the other tombs in that area. It is hot, exhausting work and until Dorothy Brooke thought of it, the animals were tethered and worked by the hour without a drop to drink."[9]

She had been thinking of how to address this problem for years, and every year she lived in Egypt, Dorothy appealed to the Ministry of Labor to erect a water trough for these animals. And every season, until the last few years of her life, the authorities had smiled and nodded and accomplished nothing. "At last she obtained permission for the hospital to install a trough so long as the ministry supplied the tap," Spooner wrote. Though the tap was eventually vandalized and stolen, the water was now piped there for the animals to drink, and the troughs Dorothy brought are still in place, just as needed this century as they were in the middle of the last one.[10]

Plenty of other problems remained for Dorothy to solve.

In 1947 Egypt stopped pegging its currency to the pound sterling. This meant the country was no longer a member of the Sterling Area, a consortium of nations that used the currency as their standard, and suddenly the Bank of England delivered the news that sterling transfers to Egypt were no longer possible. "This was certainly one of the most devastating obstacles she ever had to contend with," writes Spooner—indeed, it could have spelled the end for the hospital. But Dorothy had never had any compunction about aiming high. She went straight to Sir Ronald Campbell, British High Commissioner, who wrote a letter in support of the Brooke Hospital, and with this in hand Dorothy met with Bank of England officials in London. These gentlemen afterward related that Dorothy not only had a firm grasp of facts and figures, "but she made such pungent and often witty remarks," the officials could not help but give in to her request. Moreover, Dorothy was allowed to move an amount from the London account much larger than she had originally requested. Whether the president of the Revolutionary Command Council of Egypt or pin-striped nabobs who ruled the Bank of England, her combined assault of determination, information, and charm felled and, in the best sense of the word, seduced them all.[11]

After 1952, Dorothy's health began to fail.

Afflicted with emphysema—a legacy of long years of smoking, which itself was her calming response to years of unremitting stress—Dorothy was sometimes swamped with such weariness she had difficulty functioning. She was also getting on toward seventy. This was not exactly aged even by the standards of that era, but the decades of constant travel, of living and working in difficult climates, of dealing with daily and hourly problems, had caught up with her. Yet the "mad sitt" of Sayyida Zeinab pressed on. Her passion for the well-being of the suffering animals who needed quality veterinary care never abated; it seemed to most who knew her to flame even higher than in earlier decades, as if she knew her time was short.

Dorothy's last report to her subscribers is a case in point. Indeed it is as filled with the fire of compassion as any of her earlier writings about the Cairo hospital: "We cannot close one box. We cannot reduce our staff. Every inch of the hospital and every person we employ is essential to our work. We cannot contemplate turning a single animal away for want of room, for want of food, for want of sufficient skilled attention. For the sake of any animal you have ever loved I implore you to help carry on this great and needful work for suffering animals whose lives are ones of unremitting toil."[12]

In December of 1954, when Dorothy was at home in Salisbury, she asked Kathleen Taylor Smith to come for a visit. She was beginning to formulate succession plans for her charity. It was obvious now to Dorothy that she needed to form a committee in England to handle the administrative tasks that she herself had normally undertaken and that she, despite her poor health, was still managing on a regular basis. That could not go on forever.

After meeting with Kathleen, says Spooner, Dorothy "finally knew that Kathleen was the one person to whom she could hand over the care of the hospital in years to come." Dorothy understood from the start that she didn't need to do any serious convincing where Kathleen was concerned. It had been Kathleen's dream to be of service to animals and to Egypt, ever since her arrival in the country in 1946 and her first tour of 2 Bairam al-Tunsi. She had already proved her worth as an organizer, serving as chairperson of the Humane Treatment of Animals Committee of the National Council of Great Britain, for which Dorothy stood as representative in Salisbury.[13] In addition to the daily management of its affairs, the new Brooke committee would be able to shoulder the fundraising function that had been Dorothy's special province for so many years. Kathleen would eventually take Brooke's message farther afield on lecture tours she organized and presented throughout the United States. This was part of the effort to broaden Brooke's scope to North America, which would eventually lay the groundwork for Brooke USA, installed in Lexington, Kentucky, in 2015.[14]

In spring 1955, as Dorothy again prepared for her annual trip to Egypt, she asked Kathleen to accompany her. "How glad I am that

I went to Cairo when she asked me to," Kathleen wrote later. There was an urgency about the journey, as if there would not be enough time to do everything Dorothy had planned. As soon as they reached the hospital, Dorothy made sure Kathleen was given another tour of the premises and shown the improvements, or where improvements still needed to be introduced. It was made clear that all of these things would be her responsibility in the future. Dorothy also arranged for Kathleen to be driven down to the public markets to see the work Brooke vets were doing there, "giving first aid and instructing owners, urging them when their animals needed 'in-patient' treatment," Kathleen recalled. George Gibson, who had greeted Kathleen at the hospital after the war, was still there, heading out every day in the hospital's ambulance to rescue animals who could not be walked in for treatment.[15]

While Kathleen absorbed as much of the hospital's operational structure and its lengthening list of needs as she could, Dorothy began to fade and finally keep to her bed for lengths of time—an unheard of situation in prior years. Yet she remained obsessed with the administrivia that her committees in Cairo and London were supposed to be handling, unable to relinquish the reins. She had fears of another political upheaval. The 1952 revolution had certainly given fair warning. Sensing that more difficulties were to come in the not so distant future, Dorothy proceeded to work on ways in which she could increase the size of the hospital's emergency fund, so there would be cash on hand to live off of in the event of another crisis. Nor was she satisfied with her achievement of installing water troughs at the Pyramids: she insisted that more be placed around the city, which eventually was accomplished through ceaseless Brooke lobbying. Dorothy also reached out to Gen. Sir Richard Hull, commander of British troops in Egypt and the last chief of the Imperial General Staff, seeking his reassurance of the safety and care of any horses remaining in the Canal Zone should there be a revolution. Despite what she had been promised by the highest levels of British government, Dorothy clearly did not entirely trust that horses would not yet again suffer the consequences of warfare. She would not rest until Sir Richard vowed to see to the horses' safety.

And, finally, Dorothy's thoughts turned increasingly toward her own mortality. She told Geoffrey that if she should die soon, she did not want him to attend the service—it would only upset him, and she would not be there to comfort him as she would wish to do. It was a commentary as much on her love for him as on her innate need to organize events and people so that everybody was happy.[16]

When it came time for Kathleen Taylor Smith to return to England, Dorothy was too weak to go back with her. Taken care of in Cairo by daughter Pinkie and by Geoffrey, Dorothy was often in her bed, where she took pleasure in the only animals she still had the power to help. "She amused herself by keeping what she called 'maison ouverte' [open house] for the birds," writes Glenda Spooner. These birds regularly collected on Dorothy's windowsill— sparrows, doves, bulbuls with calls like the rattling of glass beads, and rainbow-colored bee-eaters, too—to dine on the bread crumbs that were left for them there.[17]

The bee-eater was an appropriately indomitable bird to be paying calls on the indomitable Dorothy Brooke. Before it devours its prey, which, as the name implies, is most often bees, the bee-eater thwacks the insect against a hard surface to defuse its stinger and remove its venom. And it has a gentler side: when raising its young, not only do both parents take part in the process but other members of the colony as well. It is a bird that has learned that cooperation, and always taking care to remove the stinger, are the habits of a good life—characteristics that Dorothy might have recognized as similar to her own.

And, of course, there was one last, lovely, poignant brush with a horse. The mare was a broken-down, abused, and elderly former polo pony that Dorothy called Rosie.

As Spooner wrote, the mare was the property of a farmer who, perhaps not understanding when George Gibson asked him to wait until he drove the ambulance out to fetch her, sent the miserable animal on a walk of fifteen miles into the city, his son rapping her with a stick the entire way. That day Dorothy happened to be at the hospital for a visit and was resting in a chair when she saw Rosie stumble up the street. She sent for water, then took Rosie's bridle and led her to the stable herself, two elderly and ill ladies leaning each on one another as they went. Dorothy was heard speaking softly to the suffering mare, whom she caressed and coaxed. Returning to the hospital the following day, Dorothy brought with her a treat at the sight of which "Rosie lit up like a torch." It was what Dauntless had loved, too—sugar. And as Dauntless had done, Rosie lifted a battered hoof, having been taught somewhere in her dim privileged past to say "please." Nobody could witness the two together without tears.[18]

Shortly after meeting Rosie, Dorothy was confined to bed for good. Yet every day she asked, "How is my darling Rosie?" Dr. Murad told Sarah Searight in later years that "[Dorothy] used to specially nourish destruction cases. 'Don't destroy them till I've left Egypt,' she would say."[19] She had never gotten over Old Bill, or Dauntless, or the thousands of other lives she had brought to a peaceful end. She could not cease worrying over Rosie. One of her last requests was that Rosie be allowed to live a month in the comfort she was forced to walk so far to find. And indeed, in the irony that was never far from anything Dorothy did during her life, Rosie was to actually outlive her, if only by a few weeks.[20]

In her last days Dorothy had grown more focused on hospital work, determined to get as much done as she could while her strength held out. Though she was ill, she still had a sense of humor. The secretary of the Cairo hospital committee was a Mr. Saxby. Needing to speak to him urgently on business, Dorothy sent Saxby an old visiting card on the back of which she had written, "I'm in bed but I must see you." Saxby hurried to her bedside and received his instructions, and then he found himself called back just as he was leaving the house. Dorothy wanted him to return the card on which she had written her note. "You might be run over by a tram or something," she said, "and it would be most compromising for our ambassadress." It turned out she had used the visiting card of Lady Stevenson, wife of the newly installed British ambassador Sir Ralph Stevenson, on which to ask a gentleman to come see her in bed.[21]

The evening of Saxby's visit, George Gibson also paid Dorothy a visit. He found her as gaily engaging as ever. But later in the night, her temperature fell dangerously low, a worrying symptom that Dorothy took with characteristic good cheer. "I've defeated the doctors again," she assured Geoffrey. "I said I would." Not long afterward she died, nine days past her seventy-first birthday, on June 10, 1955.[22]

In a letter sent to Kathleen Taylor Smith shortly before her death, Dorothy had written of horses like Rosie and the heaven she hoped awaited them, her words echoing the imagery of gardens and water that constituted the Islamic paradise: "But give glad tidings to those who believe and work righteousness," states the Quran, "that their portion is gardens, beneath which rivers flow."[23] "How I wish I could bring them back with me into a lovely green field, with trees and a stream," Dorothy mused. "Wouldn't it be wonderful. I always hope they find one when they wake up after we have said goodbye to them. I pray they do."[24]

Dorothy's burial, with a representative of President Nasser present along with the governor of Cairo and British ambassador Sir Ralph Stevenson, took place in the Cairo War Memorial Cemetery.

Located in the Coptic district not far from 2 Bairam al-Tunsi Street, its European-style marble markers overlooked by the flowing fronds of date palms, the property had originally been designated the New British Protestant Cemetery but had been opened in 1920 to take the remains of Great War dead. Thus Dorothy's ashes are companioned, one might say even guarded, by many of the soldiers whose horses, mules, and donkeys she had helped at her hospital.

Far more in need of protection, however, was her lifework, which not long after she died would be threatened again with political upheaval.

"Animals have neither nationality nor politics," wrote Glenda Spooner, echoing Dorothy's own belief, "and to allow these controversial elements to enter into work of this description is not only lamentable but petty."[25]

This is a fact we all know, or believe we know. The abuse of animals has occurred not only through direct use of them in human war. Even when far from the front lines, they suffer collateral damage, often in settings to which our need to collect, classify, and display consigned them. In August 2014, the *Daily Mail* reported on these other victims of the Israeli-Palestinian conflict. "The lions sit dazed in the shade of their damaged pen," writes Sam Webb, "while nearby the decayed carcasses of two vervet monkeys lie contorted on the grass of a Gaza zoo." Horrific photos revealed mummified animals dead for weeks, even months, frozen in a rictus of despair. "The impact on animals in war is huge," says Louise Hastie, former shelter manager for an animal welfare charity in Kabul. "Many just do not get that it isn't isolated just to companion animals such as cats and dogs but livestock and working animals, and war has a massive overall impact on all living creatures which in turn causes further problems for people as well."[26]

If this scene sounds familiar, something similar happened at the Baghdad Zoo over a decade ago. Eight days after the conclusion of the 2003 Iraq War, South African conservationist and "elephant whisperer" Lawrence Anthony entered the ruins of the complex, where he found the grounds littered with carcasses and wandered by half-starved, traumatized animals. He saved as many lives as he could, including what was left of Saddam Hussein's herd of prized Arab horses. Lest these conditions be presumed endemic to the Middle East, an example occurred right under the European Union's nose. Writing in April 2014 of the sufferings of captive animals in war-torn Ukraine, Jillian Kay Melchior of the *National Review* put the situation in words that could apply to all animals caught in the crossfire of war: "Exotic animals are among the unlikelier victims of a nation in crisis." The unlikelihood that these animals should even be in harm's way, not just caged and helpless but thousands of miles away from their natural habitats, is just part of the broader tragedy.[27]

For some animals, human conflict could spell the end of the line. As of this writing, rare northern bald ibises, whose breeding colony lies near the ancient city of Palmyra, northeast of Damascus, are now as endangered as the temples and palaces themselves by the pernicious presence of the self-styled Islamic State of Iraq and Syria, which first occupied the site in May 2015. "Culture and nature, they go hand in hand," Asaad Serhal of the Society for the

Protection of Nature in Lebanon told the BBC, "and war stops, but nobody can bring back a species from extinction."[28]

When she saved so many of the abandoned war horses of Cairo, Dorothy Brooke had done what she could to right some of the wrongs of 1919. But her grand experiment in compassion for working animals, though planted deep in Egyptian soil was, like that soil, just as apt to experience inundation, in this case from the political upheavals that washed over Egypt as regularly as Nile floods. Because of this political instability, the animals the Brooke Hospital worked to help continued to face further threats from troubles purely of human origin. These troubles would remain until well into the twenty-first century, and the jury is out as to whether they will ever really abate, or whether animals will ever really be safe from them.

At Dorothy Brooke's death in 1955 the staff of the Brooke Hospital could look back on their organization's history with satisfaction and pride. By the middle 1930s the hospital's original mission—to rescue all known living war horses and army mules left behind after the Great War—had been achieved. The hospital had grown beyond its original mandate because Dorothy saw how many native equines were just as much in need of aid, their owners just as much in need of education.

Nothing before that had been easy. Dorothy had fought and triumphed over substantial resistance put up by Dr. Branch and the myriad of problems carrying out her mission in a place where compassion toward animals was not the norm, and perceived foreign interference was not welcome. Her challenges had only grown with time. She had kept the hospital open during World War II and throughout the anti-British climate following Black Saturday and the revolution of 1952. The Brooke Hospital proved by every part of its work and the dedication with which the staff carried it out that it was not an alien concept implanted by a member of an alien culture, like mission schools in China or India, or a fly-by-night concern to exploit a vulnerable nation, but had been deeply integrated into, and accepted by, Egyptian society, from peasants and peddlers to the officers in uniforms at the top of the social pyramid—in fact, without the support of this topmost tier, even when social and political changes made it difficult for them to do so, Dorothy's dream might never have been sustainable. This appreciation had thus far proved a powerful defense for the hospital during the storms that had swept over a changing Egypt. However, not long after Dorothy's death the strength of the Brooke's reputation would be tested heavily, when the hospital could be said to be especially vulnerable without her special, respected presence to protect it.

Though he had sent a representative to Dorothy's funeral in 1955 and supported the hospital's work, President Nasser had it in for the British, and the feeling was mutual. He would be emblazoned on the cover of the March 29, 1963, issue of *Time* magazine, along with a sensible Arab proverb, "Keep your tents separate and bring your hearts together." Yet it is likely he was thinking of his fellow powers in the Middle East rather than of the Europeans whose interests in the region had admittedly largely benefited themselves. Nasser had made promises to the Egyptian people that he had to keep. One of these was to nationalize all foreign-owned property, and without doubt the most controversial act carried out was that of seizing the Suez Canal in July 1956.

As much a lifeline to global trade and political influence in the 1950s as it had been during the two world wars, the Suez Canal nearly became the crisis point for another. Israel, Britain, France, and the United States were drawn into the fray for a welter of competing strategic and economic reasons. Their threats prompted Egypt to freeze all foreign funds, which in turn led to the retaliatory freezing of all Egyptian assets abroad, spelling disaster for organizations like the Brooke Hospital. French and British troops, joined by Israeli soldiers, invaded and occupied the Canal Zone, and Egypt eventually withdrew under enormous international pressure. However, its nationalization policies held firm where foreign interests on Egyptian soil were concerned. Egypt also demanded that foreign nationals like George Gibson, cornerstone of the Brooke Hospital, must leave. All were expelled after being compelled to sign a document requisitioning any Egyptian property to which they held title.

It was a harsh blow to lose Gibson, in whose departure was abruptly discarded a quarter century of accumulated and hard-won Brooke experience and wisdom. Shortly after, the hospital itself was sequestrated. Yet the Brooke's luck held out: its sequestrator was none other than Major Ahmad Murad, a sturdy, broad-chested member of the Cairo Brooke committee. Major Ahmad was also secretary of the Gezira Sporting Club, which meant he was an Egyptian with friends in very high places. "Major Ahmad was a vital link with the Egyptian authorities," confirms Sarah Searight.[29] Others preferred to see a less tangible protector. "It is my opinion," a supporter wrote to Kathleen Taylor Smith, "that nobody dared to touch the hospital, and I dare say that Mrs Brooke saved the hospital even after her death."[30]

Though the property was sequestrated like any other foreign holding in Egypt, there was definitely something different about the way the hospital and its governing body were reconstituted. According to Ann Searight, a granddaughter of Dorothy Brooke, after sequestration the hospital "became an independent Egyptian Society with its own Board and Membership, though exclusively funded by Brooke UK (to all intents and purposes)."[31] So while the London office continued to direct funding streams toward the hospital, its fully Egyptian governance fulfilled the sequestration rules and kept the doors open for business, and when it was desequestrated in 1959, the hospital was the first such charity to be thus released from the regulations established after the Suez crisis. If it has never closed even for a day since it was opened in 1934, it is because the hospital had earned Egyptian trust and friendship from the beginning, despite the occasional stumbling block put in front of any foreign NGO in Egypt and dependent like any other on the variable political weather conditions to which Egypt has always been susceptible.

This new system was put to the test a decade later when the hospital was threatened not just financially but physically by the outbreak of the Six-Day War between Egypt and Israel in 1967.

The conflict led to food shortages in Cairo, which, of course, had a damaging effect on tourism, which in turn led to many cases of equine malnutrition. The hospital staff remained in Cairo and treated all sufferers, despite the very real possibility of invasion by Israel. (Years later long-term fallout from the Six-Day War was to interfere when veterinarians from the Brooke Hospital asked for government permission to take an ambulance to help animals impacted by Israeli-Palestinian warfare and were turned down on the grounds that their work could be seen to be aiding the state of Israel—another example of human politics prolonging animal suffering.) When Israeli jets dropped bombs on Cairo airport, only a little over thirteen miles away from the hospital, even the newer portions of the complex rattled under the blasts, frightening staff and animals. Yet their work continued without abeyance, as it had always done, as it always would, no matter the circumstances.[32]

Sarah Searight points out that throughout the administration of President Nasser (who died in 1970), the hospital struggled to stay afloat. This was in part due to the lingering aftereffects of the disappearance in 1956–57 of people and structures the hospital had depended on for so long—administrative resources like the British Army's veterinary arm, seasoned employees like George Gibson, higher-ups in the British command who could be resorted to as needed. It was also a by-product of Egypt's postrevolution political situation. "Adventurous foreign policies [of the Nasser government] did little for the Egyptian economy in the 1950s and 1960s," wrote Sarah Searight. Egypt remained a nation all the more reliant on draft animals to do their pulling and hauling.[33] Along with adventures in foreign policy were economic and social problems emerging under President Nasser, under whom a bureaucracy had been created to which even the bloated employment rolls of the defunct kingdom under King Farouk could scarcely compare, compounded by the fact that few employees showed up at their offices except to collect their pay. The paradise that was to open up to all who attained a college education had failed to materialize; students who couldn't afford or access electric light at home would sit with books, paper, and pencils, studying under streetlamps late into the night.[34]

The overall situation tended to widen rather than fill social fissures, at the same time giving the impression to the outside world that Egypt was swinging very much its way. This apparent change lent Cairo a multicultural, cosmopolitan sophistication that attracted more foreign tourists than before. A burgeoning tourism influx made money for men with horses while it placed heavy demands on these equines to carry or pull visitors out to the Pyramids, into the desert oases, or through the winding alleyways of the exotic Old City. As always, this demand meant that there were many overworked or injured animals who needed the Brooke Hospital's care. This is why, in part, it was determined that there was a need for the hospital's services not just in Cairo but in other tourist centers located well outside its boundaries.

The first expansion of the Brooke Hospital was to Alexandria. There, longtime supporters of the Cairo clinic, Gen. Ahmad Shawqi and his niece, had overseen for some years a twin but independent establishment. This clinic was reconstituted as a branch of the Cairo hospital in 1965. Though far smaller than its parent, the Brooke Alexandria was expanded in 1992 and in that same year treated more than two thousand patients. The next expansion was to Luxor, similarly motivated by the demands of the tourist trade. Amid the temples and palaces of the ancient city, animals suffered. Sarah Searight explained the terrible phenomenon, whether started by tourists or offered by their hosts, of rushing at great speed in carriages from one temple to another. Tourists were encouraged by drivers and guides eager to make a tip for guaranteeing this time-saving convenience. When Dr. Murad visited Luxor on behalf of the Cairo hospital in the late sixties, he was horrified by what he found. Out of the sixteen carriages waiting at the station for the arrival of the tourist train, Dr. Murad counted "at least fourteen destruction cases," meaning over 80 percent of the carriage horses in just that row would have been better off dead than alive—an echo of Dorothy's first sight of ex–war horses at Ramses Station in 1930.[35]

Dr. Murad, who was typically well ahead of everyone else in strategizing terms, cleverly made a case for having a Brooke clinic in Luxor, which touched the city fathers not just in the municipal pocket book but in terms of self-respect. He pointed out that foreigners coming to Luxor from the United States or Great Britain, who knew healthy horses from sick and neglected ones, would see these unfortunate animals waiting for them at the station and refuse to ride in carriages drawn by them. Moreover, these people who had paid no small amount of money to travel to Luxor had friends who would ask them about their travels, and they would tell their friends of the misery they had seen in Luxor, where draft animals were so poorly cared for. It might even get into the foreign newspapers, and from there, nobody could tell where the scandal would end, though canny gentlemen like those who governed Luxor must realize that it would do no good for business or reputation to allow this abuse to continue. Dr. Murad's warning did the trick.[36]

Aswan and Edfu, south of Luxor, were the next sites where Brooke expansion was deemed critical. The building of the Aswan High Dam—one of President Nasser's great projects, begun in 1960 and completed ten years later—had endangered the temple of Ramses II at Abu Simbel along with dozens of other ancient sites. UNESCO formed a project to move the temple to the Lake Nasser shore to prevent it from being swallowed up in the rising waters in a feat as vast in its own way as Nasser's dam. The newly re-sited temple and other archaeologically significant locations in Nubia drew tourists, and as they needed transport to these sites, working equines were required in greater numbers than before. By the 1980s these animals' sufferings clearly mandated a branch of the Brooke Hospital, a project that in this instance had the blessing and support of the provincial governor. As with Luxor there was a mobile clinic for cases in the marketplace or outlying districts.

It was the same for nearby Edfu, site of a spectacular Ptolemaic temple dedicated to the god Horus, deity of the sun, and many ruins that made the town a popular travel destination. For the opening of the Edfu clinic in 1992, Brig. Hassan Sami came down from Cairo. A gentle, compassionate man, Brigadier Sami was an army officer, as his rank implies, who had been a friend of Dr. Murad's for many years. In the early 1980s, Dr. Murad was readying himself for retirement from 2 Bairam al-Tunsi Street, and Brigadier Sami was hired as deputy director, though by roundabout means. "Brigadier Sami took over from Dr. Murad very gradually," says Dr. Petra Sidhom.

"He was in the army, he was studying philosophy and psychology to be an army instructor. He never wanted to replace Dr. Murad, but Dr. Murad was clever about it. He asked Brigadier Sami to fill in for a week, then two weeks. Finally, Sam slipped in and took over from Dr. Murad," becoming general director.[37]

Though not a veterinarian, Brigadier Sami was an organizer who, like Dorothy, intimately knew the problems of Cairene equines and their owners and also had a great love for animals. Of the men who worked their animals to the point of exhaustion, he said, echoing Dorothy's own view, "They can't even deal with life. How can they deal with their animals?" It was important, he explained, to understand the psychology of the owners and the animals and to appeal to the former on the basis of that understanding. "Our target is to listen to the suffering of animals, and to teach and educate owners how to treat their animals to maximise their own economic benefit," he said. "Good health is equal to good money," which was reasoning of interest to any owner surviving from day to day on what his animal made for him.[38]

Sarah Searight relates an anecdote about the opening of the Edfu clinic. After Brigadier Sami had opened the clinic, an impoverished elderly lady approached him. Was it true, she asked, that this was a hospital reserved strictly for animals? Sami assured the woman that the clinic was intended for treatment of animal patients only. She asked him who owned the clinic. Upon being told that Brooke was a charity, providing free care, the old lady could scarcely believe his words. Brig. Sami assured her that it was true, and that no, it was not run by mad people but by veterinary professionals who cared about the welfare of working equines and the education of their owners. That being so, the woman pointed out that though the poor who were aided by the charity could never repay the debt, God would richly reward the charity on their behalf.[39]

Dorothy's original concept—what Brigadier Sami termed listening to the suffering of animals—which had resulted in her reputation as the "mad sitt" of 2 Bairam al-Tunsi Street, still prompted some conservative-minded Egyptians like this elderly lady to question the sanity of a venture that gave the same care to working animals as that which working humans would receive in a hospital (that is, if they could afford it at all). Yet it's clear from the woman's parting words that through her bewilderment, she grasped the necessity of what the clinic was there to do for the suffering animals of Edfu. And she went away enlightened, perhaps to tell the other women in her street about what she had seen, what the officer had said, and to open other people's hearts, as hers had been opened.

By the time the Edfu clinic opened, Dorothy's grandson Richard Searight had become organizing secretary of Brooke, succeeding his aunt Pinkie. Pinkie's act was a tough one to follow. "She had my grandmother's same system of getting things sorted," remembers her nephew Richard Searight. "If she wanted something done, she'd ring you up at the same time each day, simply to chat about various subjects, and then bring the conversation round at the end to that thing she wanted done. It was gentle, but persistent. And nobody could resist." Just, he adds, like Dorothy.[40]

Richard Searight's own gentle and persistent vision and guidance helped put Brooke on a better financial footing, and so did his willingness to share just what services the Brooke Hospital for Animals performed each day for the working equines of Cairo and their owners—even when it meant sharing sights that many who saw them had never seen and who could not perceive the world the same way again.

In 1989 the BBC program *40 Minutes* broadcast "Cairo Vets," a documentary giving an overview of the Brooke Hospital's work in the Egyptian capital. BBC producer Mo Bowyer had visited the Brooke clinic located in Luxor and had come away both shaken and inspired by the work to be done and the work that was done, each and every day, to help animals in that city. Through Bowyer's auspices, *40 Minutes* became the vector for the Brooke Hospital and the charity as a whole to share what it did with the television viewing public and show to what uses donor dollars were put—not unlike what Dorothy's famous appeal letter in the *Morning Post* had achieved in 1931. "The greatest thing that could have happened," says Richard Searight, "was when the documentary was sold to the BBC. That broadcast and the subsequent ones made all the difference." "Overnight—actually, over two weeks—our supporter list grew from a mere 4,000 to more than 17,000," says Lynne Nesbit. It was not unlike that morning in Heliopolis in 1931, when butler Ahmed carried in stacks of mail to be opened on Dorothy's long dining table. "Six overflowing sacks filled our two little offices" in London, Nesbit recalled.[41]

Just obtaining permission to film in Cairo was a trial worthy of some of Dorothy's early struggles to set up her hospital. When the Egyptian government demurred, Richard Searight knew from experience what to do. "Mo and I went to the Ministry of Information, together with Brigadier Sami," he says. "And while Mo and I, formally dressed, chatted happily with the officials about nothing to do with the film, Brigadier Sami built the logistics off to one side. We received permission and nobody stopped the process of making the film." This was, again, Dorothy's technique in action. "Many overseas charities have problems dealing with the culture in which they are situated," Searight says. "As my grandmother knew, when in Egypt, you do things the Egyptian way."[42]

The profound effect "Cairo Vets" had on television audiences is difficult to overstate, even from this remove, when we are accustomed to almost daily gore on any news channel or social media platform we watch. No punches are pulled. Right into the film, a little donkey, once white, covered in scars and dirt, is brought in to the Cairo clinic, trembling and prone. It proves to be dying of tetanus after it had been left, according to its sheepish owner, flat on the ground in that condition for two days. Its life could have been saved had it been brought in sooner. The sad vets lecture the man, whose primary concern is, of course, for how he is to make his living if his donkey dies. There is no question that the donkey must be euthanized. Yet it isn't the owner who interferes but all the other equine patients of the hospital. They begin to crowd with obvious concern around the mortally ill animal and have to be shooed away so the dying donkey can be put down. Apart from anything else, this harrowing scene makes clear that the Brooke Hospital was a place of not only human but also animal compassion.

Other footage is just as terrible to see, showing a failing donkey, harnessed in tandem, still trying to help pull a load too heavy for two, kept partly upright only by its joined harness and the strength of its mate, its eyes glazing over even as it stumbles along. It is "dying in harness," as narrator Michael Dean quietly describes.

And there is the horse treated in a street by Brooke vet Dr. Salah Wahib Fahmy. In 2010 Dr. Salah was presented with an award for Most Inspirational Vet by Brooke president Her Royal Highness the Duchess of Cornwall for his thirty years of compassionate care for the working animals of Cairo. It is easy, twenty-six years earlier, to see this compassion and also the despair that often lives right beside it. In the "Cairo Vets" scene, Dr. Salah, visiting UK-based veterinarian Dr. Graham Munroe, and Richard Searight talk to the horse's owner, squinting against the intense heat of a Cairo noon. They ask him how the horse had got itself injured. He cut his leg on a rock, the man says. How long ago was that? Dr. Salah asks. Over two weeks, the man replies. Dr. Munroe shakes his head in disbelief; Searight looks quietly on, having seen and heard this all too often. Dr. Salah bandages the horse's leg, after cleaning and disinfecting the septic wound, and gives the owner more bandage rolls to use. Dr. Munroe asks the man to change the dressing often, and he agrees. The men move on, Dr. Salah with his purple disinfectant spray, and they are dealing with another couple of animals when they hear a commotion. Around the corner a horse is being whipped as it tries to pull a heavy cart, the wheels of which have been chained—a backstreet test of a horse's strength that has been banned in Egypt because of the real physical harm that could be done to an animal abused in this manner. Shouting and laughing men surround the desperate animal, and there, beside the horse, is the man Dr. Salah has just given the bandages to. In fact, it is the same horse. The camera follows Dr. Salah as he rushes into the crowd and stops the "contest," crying out at the owner, "You animal! Why should I care if your horse lives or dies if you do *not*?" The vet tries to reason with the owner, who stands abashed. The bandage has come off; Dr. Salah holds out a patient hand until the man hands over the unused roll; then he redresses the wound, a look of despair and a few tears on his face.

One stares at this scene and wonders. This vet has been here before, many times before. Unlike the viewer, who can turn off the television at any time, he has to see it all again tomorrow. He has to do his job, or try to, despite the stupidity and the cupidity of the human beings who do not see their animals as sentient creatures capable of feeling pain, or even as partners in the harsh game of survival, but only as inanimate machines. Because he does care whether this animal lives or dies, even if the owner doesn't. So he continues his work. He will do this again tomorrow, if he has to, and again the next day. Because, as he would say years later after that award in London, "My love and care for the animals made me not just focus on their treatment but furthermore on ways to prevent animal disease," on keeping them from being put in situations where there was no hope for anything better. Dr. Salah makes it clear that this is a world filled with pain and ignorance. But it is also a world of hope, because compassion can be taught just as cruelty can. It is a world where, thanks to the educational work of Brooke clinics, people are beginning to put their animals first, not just because they are a family's meal ticket but because they are a part of a human family. The garbage-picker children of Cairo are one example. Seeing their fathers whip overloaded donkeys, they are apt to do the same themselves, but they think differently when they, as Christians, are reminded by a Muslim vet that Jesus rode a donkey. Hearing his words as a revelation, they look at their animals with a new light in their faces. And they drop the whip.

Perhaps the most inspiring moment at the end of this often painful documentary is when the camera follows the oldest serving vet at the Cairo clinic, picking his way through the night-darkened grounds of the hospital, a swaying lantern in his hand. Long faces and bright eyes greet him from boxes along the way, as if they are all in on the secret mission. But it is not so secret. The old man's lantern light spills over hay on which a new foal has been born. "It will have a better chance of life," says the narrator, "thanks to a woman called Dorothy Brooke." The last frame is filled with the benignant, slightly puzzled gaze of the foal's mother, safe in the privilege of her maternal duty of caring for her offspring in this strangely peaceful place located in the heart of so much noise and misery.[43]

Still a practicing veterinarian, Dr. Graham Munroe has strongly colored memories of his experiences in Cairo in 1989. One thing he points out is that he was nowhere as controlled in his reactions to what he saw as he appears to be on film. "It is very easy to go to these places and be utterly frustrated by the mindset," he says today, "as it is completely different to a western concept of animal welfare. And it is very easy to get angry and condescending," he adds, noting that the scene of him with the man who put his injured horse through the back street endurance test did not include a few frames when he lost his cool. This underscores what Dr. Munroe believes is the jewel in Brooke's crown—its preventative work in the field. Admiring as he is of the hospitals and of the utter dedication of the vets and staffs in them, Dr. Munroe says, "You can help lots of animals through preventative education. I spent a lot of time with Richard Searight in Cairo. He's a lovely, gentle man; his vision is very much that of his grandmother—he carried that forward. He said to me, 'This is all about teaching people how to look after their animals. It's about how important it is for them to understand how economically crucial the animal is to them.'" He also points out Searight's apparent unflappableness in the face of harsh scenes of abuse or neglect of working animals in the streets and the patients in the Cairo hospital, scenes that made a seasoned vet from the United Kingdom wince. "He takes it all on the chin," says Dr. Munroe, "and, believing in what he is doing, gets up and tries his best. Again, very like his grandmother."[44]

Richard Searight remembers the event very clearly. "I recall how Mo Bowyer wanted to translate everything Dr. Salah shouted at the horse's owner," he says, "but they were such terrible swear words, many of them unrepeatable, that the subtitles had to be watered down considerably!" He adds, "The most important part of what is happening in that scene is that it takes an Egyptian to deal with Egyptians, just as it takes an Indian to deal with Indians and so on. It is the same principle in how one deals with people from a veterinary and preventative care perspective. One of the problems with the SPCA in Egypt was its legalistic approach to animal welfare. It was all about making people obey the rules. But that doesn't teach them how to do better. This is what made my grandmother's concept so successful, and makes Brooke so robust today. It is about the people *and* the animals."[45]

It is still about the people and the animals, and people and animals far beyond Egypt's borders.

After Geoffrey Brooke's death in 1966, Richard's father, Philip Searight, a former stockbroker, helped grow the organization in Egypt and then expand outside it as needs elsewhere were identified and recommended by others. One of the latter was Princess Alia bint Al Hussein, daughter of King Hussein of Jordan and an acknowledged expert in Arab horses, who was concerned about animals being worked at the famous site of Petra. Brooke was now able to look beyond Egypt's borders to areas where a combination of poverty and lack of education led to a cycle of misery for both animals and humans: Jordan, Pakistan, India, Kenya, Afghanistan, Ethiopia, Guatemala, Nepal, Senegal, and Nicaragua, the last in 2013.

These nations endure problems springing in some cases from overpopulation and consequent lack of opportunity and adequate resources to serve everyone equally; in other cases from sectarian violence inflaming towns, neighborhoods, and families with divisive civil wars based on religious schisms few completely understand, none of which are worth the anguish and bloodshed they cause; and in all cases from poverty that mandates the use of horses, mules, and donkeys in work that to people in First World nations can seem a throwback to medieval times and mindsets. Often without rest or food or water for long periods of time, these animals haul double hods of bricks from hot kilns under broiling sun for many miles each day, or pull carts overloaded with garbage or farm produce or carriages or carts for the tourist and trekking trades; they are worked in fields or as pack animals in the mountains and in mines and quarries. Where Brooke has gained the trust of these communities and educated its laborers, still offering free veterinary care and educational support for owners of working equines, it has begun to break this cycle using Dorothy's holistic philosophy. Yet while this philosophy has endured through world war and the local and national revolts, sorties, and coups that have made up the unending game of power in the Middle East over the past several decades, animals living in the region are as exposed to the dangers of armed conflict sixty years after Dorothy saved the horses that war left behind.

In 1990 Iraqi leader Saddam Hussein invaded the oil-rich emirate of Kuwait, touching off the Gulf War. "The Gulf war added a new dimension to the risks for animals as well as humans," writes John Loretz, "the use of oil as a weapon." Dumped into the Persian Gulf, crude oil devastated wildlife habitats, killing thousands of birds, while oil leaking from Kuwaiti wells and going up in smoke from oil fires poisoned the atmosphere, sickening and destroying uncounted wildlife. Perhaps worse, if possible, is what happened to the animals caged at the Kuwait Zoo. Over four hundred of them "were killed by Iraqi soldiers"—some tortured or used as target practice—while others "died of starvation and injuries, or were removed from the zoo to unknown locations."[46]

The Kuwaiti emirate was a tourist destination that, like so many, relied on horses and camels to transport visitors, and as in all upheavals, the owners and their animals became trapped in a situation where they could not work, and because they could not work, they could not get enough to eat. "In their straitened circumstances," wrote Sarah Searight, "owners were threatened with having to destroy their animals." This is where Brooke stepped in. Matched by funding from the kingdom of Jordan, the charity fed all the horses for free, saving their lives and the livelihood of their owners. Though Britain and Jordan were not on the best of terms, given that Jordan had thrown its support to Iraq, a parallel reality existed where the animals were concerned, mutual compassion for which ensured that relations "between government and charity remained warm and friendly." Thus the animals themselves proved able to negotiate diplomacy where human beings had failed.[47]

The Gulf War crisis was a trial run for disturbing events Brooke would face two decades later. The Arab Spring began in December 2010 with the suicide by fire of a Tunisian street vendor named Mohamed Bouazizi.

Life for this young man had never been easy. He was known to be kind, even generous with what he had for those in worse straits than he was. But everyone has a tipping point. Desperately poor and unable to bribe police to allow him to continue selling on the streets of his small town, Bouazizi was confronted by an official, who shut down his business. When Bouazizi complained to the local governor, he was spurned. Fetching gasoline, Bouazizi doused himself, lighting a fire that ended his own life but touched off a series of blazes, literal and political, starting in Tunisia and spreading across the Arab world.

It took a year for those flames to reach Cairo, and when they did, just after the fall of the Tunisian government, they met plenty of dry tinder, waiting to explode. These grievances had been lurching past the halls of Egyptian power like Boris Karloff's undead mummy, most of them dating back to the 1952 revolution and, depressingly, still as relevant decades later. Poverty, lack of employment, and lack of affordable food and shelter had been endemic to society throughout Egypt even before the ousting of King Farouk. Added to these universal ills were more particularly recent ones complained of during the rule of President Nasser and his successors, Anwar Sadat and Hosni Mubarak: accusations of unimpeded police brutality and fraudulent election processes, and perpetual "state of emergency" laws dating from the 1967 war with Israel, only briefly lifted before being restored after the assassination of Anwar Sadat in 1981 and the beginning of the rule of President Mubarak. Corruption at the highest levels, a sinking sense among the Egyptian people that they had no democratically elected government but yet another royal dynasty, and continued deterioration of services to the least powerful in favor of smoothing the way for the most powerful set tectonic plates grinding against each other long before January 25, 2011.

That day, however, was when the earthquake finally came. For two and a half weeks, Cairo was rocked by public demonstrations and increasingly violent official response. "Downtown Cairo is a war zone tonight," reported Jack Shenker; "as reports come in of massive occupations by protesters in towns across Egypt, the centre of the capital is awash with running street battles."[48]

A little over a week later the "camel incident" took place. On February 2, alleged supporters of President Mubarak dashed into Tahrir Square, epicenter for the uprising, on horses and camels. According to Al Jazeera, "In Dokki, in western Cairo, thousands of Mubarak supporters gathered in Lebanon Square, chanting, 'He won't go.'" The largest segment of this group positioned itself near the Egyptian Museum, where government guards had been placed to protect the collections, and "the camel and horse riders from Dokki galloped through the crowd," while their fellow pro-government supporters threw rocks at the protesters in Tahrir Square.[49]

Several of the mounted pro-government men charged into the protesters, beating them with sticks; a camel was seen to trip and fall. Gunfire burst out from the pro-government protesters, wounding animals as well as people, and firebombs caused burns for both. As video footage of this charge made its way to television and the Internet, there was outrage in Cairo as well as around the world. Mona Khalil, a board member of ESMA (Egyptian Society for Mercy to Animals), found herself shoved around along with animals. She would also see not just stray dogs and cats lying dead in the streets of the city but house pets left behind—more victims of human disorder—and she voiced concerns about the condition of animals in the Cairo Zoo, which, like the tourist sites, was a ghost town in the aftermath of the unrest in the city, impacting the budget and consequently the animals' care.[50] In her 2012 book *Cairo*, Ahdad Soueif writes of calling her sister, frantic from having seen the violence in Tahrir Square. All was well, Soueif's sister laughingly shouted over the din. "They attacked us with horses and camels, but we've captured them," and people were riding the no doubt terrified animals around, their festive tassels swaying.[51] Karen Reed, Head of Animal Welfare and Research at Brooke in London, did not find the incident amusing, commenting in barely restrained frustration, "Horses were ridden into the middle of the protest with little thought for the welfare of the animals. They were pelted with rocks and sticks. This should never have happened, using these animals in such a way is distressing for the animals as well as being both frightening, and dangerous, for the people around them."[52]

Veterinarian Dr. Mohammed Abd-Elhay of the Brooke Hospital was then volunteering with another animal rescue organization when the revolution came to Cairo. "It meant a lot to us," he says, "the young educated men who could see Egypt leading a better future. But these owners who came all the way from the Pyramids to Tahrir Square, driving their animals through the protesters, wanted to kill that revolution." They were, he adds, echoing the remarks of Mona Khalil, believed to be duped with the promise of compensation for their participation in helping put down the demonstrations. He recalls hearing that a few Brooke vets even went down to Tahrir Square to join the sit-ins after their daily shifts. When the "camel incident" occurred, some of the owners were recognized by these Brooke staff members. Later on, a few of these men came to talk with the vets, admitting that they had been encouraged in their actions by Egyptian government operatives.[53]

Most Brooke staff were confined to the clinic during the first days of the revolution, and the field clinics they would normally have conducted at the Pyramids and in the brick kilns were postponed for the time being (to be resumed in early February, a few days before President Mubarak resigned from office). But concern for the horses and camels used during the Tahrir Square charge prompted immediate action on the animals' behalf. On February 13, Brooke joined the Egyptian Society of Animal Friends (ESAF) and the Donkey Sanctuary (based in the United Kingdom) to feed animals left starving because the sudden drop in tourism had driven the cost of feed too high for most owners to afford, even if they had not already been deprived of their livelihood by that same dearth of tourist dollars. "We found that other animal charities that are working in the area of the Pyramids or became interested in feeding distribution had the same goal," says Dr. Ammr Mahmoud, communication and information officer for the Brooke Hospital. "So we developed a memorandum of understanding to organize the roles and responsibilities of each organization, avoid overlapping and maximize the impact of animal welfare." Such organization was vitally important for every animal as well as every human who lived off their labor. In November 2011 the *Daily Mail* of London estimated that the protests had deprived the Egyptian economy of over $3 million for each day of unrest—not a price even a wealthy nation could afford to pay, much less one on an insecure footing.[54] "For people working in hotels and bazaars it is bad," says Dr. Abd-Elhay, "but for people who own tourist horses for a living, it is a crisis because they not only have to feed themselves, they also have to feed their animals, who are now no longer bringing any money to put food on the owner's table."[55]

Harrowing photographs were published in the *Daily Mail*, showing gaunt, barely living horses as well as dead ones lying on the ground like garbage, their corpses torn by scavengers. Though a Cairo animal activist, Dina Zulfikar, would later clarify that many of the photos released to the press showed not animals starved by lack of tourism but those who had died of disease well before the revolution and been dumped in a carcass yard in the area near the Giza pyramids,[56] Dr. Abd-Elhay says he saw the neglect everywhere he looked. "Animals started to die of hunger and thirst at the pyramids," he says, "and you could see them in the street as you walked about." That said, he points out his impression that the tourist trade crisis of early 2011 was far more complex that it appeared. "I think it was more about panicking than loss of jobs," Dr. Abd-Elhay explains. Many of the owners solved their problem, in part, by selling their extra horses, keeping only those they could afford to feed. "The problem at the pyramids goes beyond the issue of feeding," he adds. "It is about changing the attitudes and a history of poor practices by the horse owners there."[57]

"The Brooke Hospital for Animals' approach was to provide 1 kilogram a day or 7 kilograms a week of concentrated feed," recalls Dr. Ammr Mahmoud, "to supplement each animal's diet. This represented 25–35 percent of a full ration, and was provided with weekly token to be exchanged with feed from the local feed seller's shop." By the time the feeding project was wrapped up in April 2011, almost eighty thousand tons of food had been provided to over eight thousand animals (with ESAF focusing on camels, not included by Brooke or the other charities), with double that number of veterinary care treatments for animals not just in Cairo but in Edfu, Aswan, and Luxor.[58]

"The whole story started in Egypt in 2005," says Dr. Ammr Mahmoud, "and began at the initiative of Mr. Sherif Foda, Brooke Hospital for Animals Egypt Chairman. The initiative was the inclusion of an article on animal welfare." Dr. Petra Maria Sidhom, who had retired from most of her animal welfare work in Egypt in 2008–9, assisted Brooke and several other charities brought together by constitutional mandate to draft this animal protection law. "The constitution required an umbrella of organizations for animal protection to come together and work on such a law," Dr. Sidhom explains.[59]

"The first conference I initiated was not about human corruption—it was about the degree of suffering and the ignorance of rules and regulations implemented in the Koran—rules that demanded that the slaughtermen must minimize the suffering of the animals during the slaughtering process, and regulations how to implement this, which were ignored on a daily basis; the second, to initiate the protecting legislation. But it was not really a homogeneous front," adds Dr. Sidhom. "In the end, it was mainly The Brooke and myself working on it."[60]

To develop the language, Dr. Sidhom, who took her doctorate in animal welfare at the Kriminologisches Forschungsinstitut (Criminological Research Institute) in Hannover, Germany, asked a variety of international charities to contribute their animal protection laws, from which the Cairo charities could pull what details were most useful for their purposes. But Dr. Sidhom began to have her doubts at the fourth draft, because the wording was becoming more and more diluted. Not all charities, in Dr. Sidhom's recollection, were particularly attentive to this. "I remembered from the World Organisation for Animal Health that wording is really crucial," Dr. Sidhom explains. "A single word can mean a world of difference. But the other Egyptian charities were so happy just to have an animal welfare law on the table they made huge compromises—regarding researching on live animals, product testing, appropriate penalties for violation of animal protection law. So I said, 'If this is the law you wish to fight for, fine with me, just try to have the best draft possible,' and she bowed out.[61]

The language ended up as a paragraph in the new Egyptian constitution, Article 45, but considerably watered down. "The whole article is much more environmental," Dr. Sidhom points out. "It is all about protecting resources. Prevention of cruelty to animals is at the very bottom."[62] Moreover, Article 46 also deals with environmental issues, making the prior article seem a sort of afterthought, or a last-ditch effort to insert some sort of animal protection language in the final sentence of what is really a law enshrining protection of natural resources of interest to the government of Egypt and to large-scale exporters of livestock. It awaited the reconstitution of Parliament, which had been suspended since June 2012, with promises from the current president, Abdel Fattah al-Sisi, that parliamentary elections would occur by the end of 2015. They did occur, but with notably low voter turnout. As for Article 45, in it the state commits to prevention of cruelty to animals.[63]

Dr. Sidhom points out one bright spark of light. "You don't see as many horses and donkeys as you used to," she says. "Cheap Japanese minivans come into the country now, and they can pay for them in instalments. Luckily, a lot of the garbage donkeys, horses and mules are fewer in number because of this."[64]

Yet social media, which has an unsleeping eye open to every square inch of planet Earth, is rife with the visible consequences of age or illness for the working animals of Cairo—a situation that in many respects has not changed a great deal since the early years of the Brooke Hospital for Animals.

People who follow the Egypt Horse Project, Egypt Equine Aid, ESMA, Brooke, and other animal welfare charities, on different days and sometimes on the same day, post to the Internet photographs of horses, mules, or donkeys in conditions not much different from the snapshots preserved in Dorothy Brooke's albums, images to be viewed only by those who have the stomach for truth. Many of these unfortunate animals are pictured after their owner has brought them in for treatment—sometimes late, sometimes too late, but at least they bring them in. Many others are seen standing or lying along roads, barely alive.

It's a testament to the work begun by the Cairo SPCA and Dr. Alfred Branch, and Dorothy's Brooke Hospital for Animals, and the many worthy animal welfare organizations scattered in and around Cairo, that it is recognized at all levels of society that there is no excuse for illness or injury to go untreated where there is free veterinary care available, where education reveals that the animal that is one's livelihood may also be the life of the family and the love of a child, and where it is understood more and more that compassion in the home sends out endless concentric circles of benefit to people and animals one may never meet.

Yet the specters pasted into Dorothy's early 1930s picture album continue to reemerge out of the dust and exhaust of modern Cairo's traffic-jammed streets. And they are not always brought in by a recalcitrant or remorseful owner. Many are simply abandoned, wanted by no one.

On the day this sentence was written, a photo is posted to a Facebook animal welfare page. It shows a thin, despairing donkey. No longer young, worn-out beyond human uses, he stands in a heap of hot sand alongside broken concrete and garbage at a busy intersection in a Cairo suburb. He is tethered by a thin rope too strong for the weakened animal to ever break, even if he had had the necessary will to live to do so, or a place to go for refuge, if he did manage to get free.

As many see this donkey, typed voices scream out of the Internet, in English and Arabic, in French and German: *Please save him!*

But nobody can.

Nobody can, because this little gray donkey isn't the only old, starving, thirsty, and despairing working animal left tethered to garbage, treated like garbage, in Cairo, or Hyderabad, or Mexico City, or somewhere in the hills of Montana. Of the many benefits the Internet brings, a specially dubious one is its bird's eye view of just how much animal suffering there is all over the globe, let alone in Egypt.

In Cairo our donkey is a mere speck in a human landscape so huge it would take hours to reach all the animals needing help, hours no one has to spare in the chaos of an overcrowded, stressed metropolis where even human life is lighter than the feather that counterweights mortal hearts on the scales of the Egyptian underworld. Against this, what is the substance of a little gray donkey that nobody wants, that nobody sees? And he is not Cairo's donkey alone. He lives in every society in every part of the globe where cruelty is tolerated and innocence exploited, where human suffering too often finds a scapegoat in abusing a defenseless animal. He has never fought a war, the little donkey—not the kind fought by Dorothy Brooke's battle steeds. But he is a casualty of the conflict between the limits to which one life can be stretched to meet unrealistic demands, ending at death without the decent benefit of the brief rest accorded even the poorest human being before the soul lets go. The donkey, and others of his kind, drop in the traces, stumble, and are beaten even when it should be clear the punishment will do more to kill than revive. His human tormentor has too often felt that same lash, similarly seen as valueless in the eyes of those safe on the rungs above him. So the little donkey is, in fact, a warrior of a kind Dorothy would have recognized, and one for whom she would have moved the Mokattam Hills in order to get him the green meadow he deserved—cool streams instead of hot sand, compassion instead of carelessness.

"The question is not, Can they reason?" wrote Jeremy Bentham, "nor, Can they talk? but, *Can they suffer?*"

The donkey suffers, and his suffering and that of working animals like him are all the proof necessary that the work of the Brooke Hospital for Animals, and of Brooke clinics it spawned around the globe, is needed, more than ever before—because little has changed since Dorothy Brooke arrived in Cairo in 1930 to find the ghosts of war shambling and suffering in its streets, alleyways, garbage dumps, and rock quarries, in a world where the wars of human beings are still exposing the innocents—the animals and the children—to violence they do not cause, do not understand, and do not deserve.

If the donkey *could* speak, he and all the forgotten animals like him might be forgiven for confessing, in the words of an ancient Egyptian poem younger than the history of human strife and animal pain, that "Hearts are greedy./ No man's heart can be relied on."[65]

In answer, Dorothy Brooke seems to respond from that green meadow of paradise she wished for all the horses, mules, and donkeys who came under her care: "From this community of suffering

I have never tried to withdraw myself. It seemed to me a matter of course that we should take up our share of the burden of pain that lies upon the world."[66]

Her guiding spirit, through the ongoing work of Brooke, the Brooke Hospital for Animals in Cairo, and all the clinics to which it gave birth bears, shares, and helps cool that pain still.

Epilogue

Brooke

Pray a prayer for the men at the war,
As the bells ring out at noon,
Pray for the reign of Love and Law,
For the World-peace dawning soon,
Pray for the mothers, and children, and wives,
For all who suffer and do,
Pray for the men who give their lives—
Why not the horses too?

—H.F.W. [1]

Brooke is an international charity that protects and improves the lives of horses, donkeys, and mules, which gives people in the developing world the opportunity to work their way out of poverty. For 600 million people in some of the poorest and most marginalized places in the world, 100 million of these animals are the backbone of communities and their best means of making a living. Without healthy working horses, donkeys, and mules, people wouldn't be able to put food on their tables, send their children to school, or build better futures for themselves and their families.

Brooke works hard to deliver significant and lasting change, even in some of the world's most challenging areas. We use our expertise to train and support owners of horses, donkeys, and mules, local vets, farriers, harness makers, and animal traders to improve standards of care. Operating in eleven different countries, and funding projects in many others, Brooke reaches more working horses, donkeys, and mules every year than any other organization. For more information please visit www.thebrooke.org. To support ongoing work to alleviate the suffering of working animals worldwide through Brooke USA, please visit www.BrookeUSA.org.

Brooke's Timeline

The Early Years: Forging a Tradition

1930   Dorothy Brooke arrives in Cairo, Egypt, with her husband, Geoffrey Brooke, a major general in the British Army.

1931   Dorothy Brooke writes a letter to the *Morning Post* to urge the British public to help relieve the suffering of thousands of ex–war horses she encounters in Cairo.

1934   The Brooke Hospital for Animals is established in Egypt.

1938   The first shade shelter and water troughs are established in Cairo. The first motorized ambulance starts to operate.

Decades of Change: Continuing Care

1961   Alexandria clinic opens, Egypt.

1966   Luxor clinic opens, Egypt.

1984   The first best horse competition begins in Luxor.

1988   Jordan clinic opens (Wadi Musa-Petra).

1988   Aswan clinic opens, Egypt.

1991   Brooke expands into Pakistan.

1992   Mobile teams begin operating in India.

1992   Edfu clinic opens, Egypt.

1994   Brooke Netherlands begins to raise money.

2000   Marsa Matrouh clinic opens, Egypt.

Today: Reaching Out

2001   Partnership programs begin in Kenya.

2002   Groundbreaking research program begins with Bristol University Veterinary School.

2003   Partnership program begins in Afghanistan.

2004   Brooke launches partnership program in Guatemala.

2005   Brooke carries out relief work with Mercy Corps, after
        the earthquake strikes in Pakistan.
2005   Partnership program begins in the Occupied Palestinian
        Territories (Palestinian villages in Israel and the West Bank).
2006   Brooke expands into Ethiopia.
2006   National Donkey Welfare Day is established in Kenya.
2007   Partnership with Action for Women and Rural
        Development is established in Kanpor, India.
2008   Partnership program begins in Nepal.
2008   American Friends of the Brooke is established.
2010   Brooke expands into Senegal.
2013   A pilot project begins in Nicaragua.
2015   Brooke USA commemorates its advancement with a visit
        to its location in Lexington, Kentucky, by Her Royal
        Highness the Duchess of Cornwall.

By 2016 Brooke hopes to have made life better for two million
working horses, donkeys, and mules and the millions of people who
depend on them for their livelihoods.

ACKNOWLEDGMENTS

Equines run by the herd through my family history. My mother was an expert horsewoman, as comfortable in English saddle as Western; as a girl in central California, she loved directing cattle with the aid of her eager dog Tiny. Something about a given horse's reticence, its basic impatience with being tied or stabled, its passionate resistance toward curtailment or control, and its heartfelt demonstration of affection toward those it loves resonated with my mother, who was very similar.

I learned to sit a horse as a child on the farm of a friend who had grown up with horses. Lisa rode an old mare bareback, gripping her mane; I held on to Lisa, and we three paced the low, hilly woods around the farm, clopping through peaceful stillness and dappled sunlight, kept safe by the mare's sure, untroubled steps over rocks or logs or gooseberry bushes, quiet but for her occasional snort or nicker.

At home we had a pony, Dickens, who preferred being in our house to the yard. The floors of the 1860s structure creaked but held firm, as did our open invitation whenever Dickens needed human company in human habitation. And my grandmother, though a devout Christian lady, confided to me she wanted to believe in reincarnation, because if it were true, she said, she hoped to come back as a wild horse, running forever over green fields.

Given this background, perhaps it was inevitable that I would come to write about Dorothy Brooke, whose love for horses and whose compassion for animals in need echoed my family's views on the subject. It was not, however, a given that even with a grounding in compassion for animals I would be able to capture Dorothy Brooke's life and her outlandishly beautiful idea, the Brooke Hospital for Animals, making her dream live again—showing why it has continued to inspire others—in these pages. If I have achieved anything close to this goal, it is because I have had the help of many friends and family who stood by me through many difficulties, faithful in all things, as I researched and wrote the book. Among them are these especial ones, given here in alphabetical order, as in no way could I assign each a level of consequence, when but for generous sharing of encouragement, inspiration, and wisdom by each (and by many I have not listed here, but who know who they are), this book would never have been written: Dr. Mohammed Abd-Elhay; Dr. Ammr Mahmoud; Dr. Marc Bekoff; Rachel Bhageerutty; Dr. Pamela Kyle Crossley; Elly Donovan; Judith Forbis; Susanna Forrest; Dr. Temple Grandin; Louise Hastie; Les Hayter; David Hogge; Petra Ingram; Rudi Klauser; Martin Laurie; William Luce; Joanna Lumley; Sarah Searight Lush; James Mayhew; Ronda Louise Menzies; Sean William Menzies; Dr. Alan Mikhail; Roly Owers; Monty Roberts; Cindy Rullman; Ann Searight; Richard Searight; Dr. Petra Maria Sidhom; Fiona Stevenson; and Maj. Gen. Sir Evelyn Webb-Carter.

Last but never least, Freddie, my rescue pup, has sat at my feet through the research, writing, and editing of several books, including this one, always showing me why animal welfare and the efforts of so many compassionate people to support it are so important, for animals and for humans—undivided, unconditional love.

NOTES

Prologue

1. Rodenbeck, *Cairo*, xvi.

2. Brooke, *Horse Lovers*, 1.

3. Marriage license for Geoffrey Frances Heremon Brooke and Vera Mechin née von Salza, Ancestry.com. *England & Wales, Non-Conformist and Non-Parochial Registers, 1567–1970*, piece 0284. Vera's marriage to Baron Mechin, a traveler and adventurer she had met when Mechin passed through Russia, ended in 1897. Vera's father, Gen. Anton von Salza, is listed in Otto Magnus von Stackelberg, *Genealogisches Handbuch der estländischen Ritterschaft*, vol. 1 (Görlitz, 1931), 245 (Saltza [Salza]).

4. Masefield, *Poems and Plays*, 446–47.

5. S. Searight, *Oasis*, 8. Brooke and Combined Training were illustrated in midjump by artist Lionel Edwards, reproduced in Lunt, *Scarlet Lancers*, 119. In 1920, according to the *Times* (London) of June 25 (p. 14), Geoffrey and Combined Training won the Connaught Challenge Trophy at Olympia.

6. Graham, *History of the Sixteenth*, 176; Murland, *Retreat and Rearguard-Somme 1918*, 205; Paget, *History of British Cavalry*, 209–10. Note: Warrior, the mount of Jack Seely, commander of the Canadian Cavalry, would not only survive the war but live till 1941. Warrior's obituary reads, in part, "The horse served continuously on the Western Front till Christmas Day 1918. Twice he was buried by the bursting of big shells on soft ground, but he was never seriously wounded." See Brough Scott, "The Mighty Warrior, Who Led One of History's Last-Ever Cavalry Charges," *Telegraph* (London), January 12, 2015.

7. Brooke, *Horse Lovers*, 38–39.

8. Brooke, *Horse-Sense*, xv.

9. Per Dorothy Brooke's gravestone in Cairo.

10. "Gibson-Craig Burial Ground," The Scottish War Graves Project, http://scottishwargraves.phpbbweb.com/scottishwargraves-post-6118.html (accessed September 5, 2016).

11. "James Gerald Lamb Searight," Cricket Archive, http://cricketarchive.com/Archive/Players/350/350340/350340.html (accessed September 5, 2016); "Name: James Gerald Lamb Searight," National Archives, http://discovery.nationalarchives.gov.uk/details/r/C13281310.

12. Mocavo, Findmypast, http://www.mocavo.ca/Repton-School-Register-Supplement-to-1910-Edition/957906/200 (accessed September 5, 2016).

13. Maj. Philip Searight obituary, *Daily Telegraph*, January 17, 2001.

14. Nicolson, *Great Silence*, 6.

15. Florence Nightingale quoted in Peters, *Unquiet Soul*, 401; Spooner, *For Love of Horses*, 6.

16. Christie, *Death on the Nile*, 333; Blunt's "veiled protectorate" quoted in Kirk-Greene, *Britain's Imperial Administrators*, 66.

17. Jarvis, *Back-Garden of Allah*, 124.

18. "Brave Norfolk Woman Who Gave Poor Horses a Voice," *Eastern Daily Press* (Norwich UK), July 29, 2011, http://www.edp24.co.uk/features/brave_norfolk_woman _who_gave_poor_horses_a_voice_1_978670 (accessed September 5, 2016); Cole's organization, World Horse Welfare, operates on three continents: "Our History," World Horse Welfare, http://www.worldhorsewelfare.org/Our-History (accessed September 5, 2016).

19. Khaled Diab, "The Middle Eastern Century That Wasn't," Al Jazeera, September 3, 2015, http://www.aljazeera.com/indepth/opinion/2015/09/middle-eastern-century-wasn -150902083410504.html (accessed September 5, 2016); Barker, *Neglected War*, 24–25.

20. Calcutta gharry description by Bletchly, "Cabs and Cabmen," 187; S. Searight, *Oasis*, 11, quoting Honor Baines in 1991.

21. S. Searight, *Oasis*, 11.

22. Alan Mikhail, email message to author, May 30, 2015.

23. Lao She, *Rickshaw Boy*, 229. Richard Searight is quick to point out that many owners of working equines are thoughtful and compassionate. Citing one example, he tells of a mare owned by a baker who adored and cared for her. The mare broke a leg in a tragic street accident, and the owner brought her to Dr. Murad at the Cairo animal clinic. It was clear she had to be euthanized, and the hospital's normal practice was to provide enough payment for the owner to buy a new animal and something to live on beside. But when Dr. Murad offered the man £100, he would not take it. "He told Dr. Murad he would no more accept money for the mare than if his own daughter had died," Searight recalls. Richard Searight, email message to author, September 4, 2016.

24. Forrest, *If Wishes Were Horses*, 116.

1. Cupid

Part epigraph: Translation assistance provided by Dr. Mohammed Abd-Elhay of Cairo.

1. Kennedy, *Life of Elgar*, 140. What should always be remembered is that equine soldiers were sent abroad from the United States to serve in the Great War several years before any human ones left American soil. "During World War I, Newport News [VA] was the biggest supplier of war horses for the British Army," wrote Mark St. John Erickson (*Newport News Daily Press*, November 29, 2014).

2. Badsey, *Doctrine and Reform*, 305.

3. Baynes, *Animal Heroes*, 35.

4. Baynes, *Animal Heroes*, 35.

5. van Emden, *Tommy's Ark*, 22–23; Laurie, *Cupid's War*, 34–35.

6. "Memoirs & Diaries—A Sapper in Palestine," firstworldwar.com, August 22, 2009, http://www.firstworldwar.com/diaries/sapperinpalestine.htm (accessed September 5, 2016).

7. Baynes, *Animal Heroes*, 68. Before the capture of Beersheba on October 31, 1917, when thunderstorms dumped enough rain to fill shallow pools for animals and men to

drink from, "several light horse regiments [of the Desert Mounted Corps] went without water for 60 hours, the New Zealand Mounted Rifles for 72 hours and a wagon team of the Cable Section for 84 hours," writes Ross Mallett in his M A thesis, "Interplay," 153–54.

8. Laurie, *Cupid's War*, 58.

9. Hadaway, *Pyramids and Fleshpots*, 138.

10. Hadaway, *Pyramids and Fleshpots*, 150.

11. Laurie, *Cupid's War*, 61.

12. "Memoirs & Diaries."

13. Hadaway, *Pyramids and Fleshpots*, quoting Corp. Victor Godrich of the Queen's Own Worcestershire Hussars (Yeomanry), 152.

14. "Memoirs & Diaries."

15. Laurie, *Cupid's War*, 91.

16. Hadaway, *Pyramids and Fleshpots*, 158.

17. See S. Searight, *Oasis*, 9, quoting Lt. Col. J. W. Winteringham of the Lincolnshire Yeomanry, who remarked on the animals he saw who were "often cruelly over-loaded."

18. "Memoirs & Diaries." Nor was it as if only the locals overworked their donkeys. "In the Near East," wrote Harold Ernest Baynes, "eight thousand little donkeys, carrying baskets of stone on their backs, helped General Allenby to build his roads along the front from Jaffa to Jerusalem"—the difference here being greater numbers of donkeys to do a scope of work that fewer ones had to do for local villagers. Baynes, *Animal Heroes*, 130.

19. Laurie, *Cupid's War*, 102.

20. Laurie, *Cupid's War*, 108–9.

21. Laurie, *Cupid's War*, 121.

22. S. Searight, *Oasis*, 10.

23. Laurie, *Cupid's War*, 121.

24. Woodward, *Hell in the Holy Land*, 171.

25. This was not the first instance in which demobilized men had to leave their horses behind. Earlier in 1918 General Allenby acceded to requests to send men who had already served through the Egyptian and Palestine campaigns (and some of whom had served in France before that) back to the western front. This meant having to leave their horses behind. "Yeomanry regiments had an especially difficult time abandoning their horses," writes Woodward, *Hell in the Holy Land*, 71.

26. Laurie, *Cupid's War*, 128.

27. Laurie, *Cupid's War*, 131.

28. S. Searight, *Oasis*, 10.

29. For the Hogue poem, see Dr. Jean Bou, "They Shot the Horses—Didn't They?," *Wartime* 44 (2008): 54–57, Australian War Memorial, https://www.awm.gov.au/wartime /44/page54_bou/ (accessed September 5, 2016).

30. Bou, "They Shot the Horses," 54–57. According to Dr. Bou, there is little evidence that men actually took their mounts into the desert and shot them, which is, he writes, "one of the most often-heard stories related with the often mythologised light horse."

31. Laurie, *Cupid's War*, 131.

32. In one famous case a mule named Mademoiselle Verdun by American troops was brought back to the United States in spite of stiff restrictions. Born in a battlefield in April

1918, Mademoiselle Verdun was not even a month old when "she hiked thirty miles in two days, and was in the thick of every subsequent major offensive pulled off by the Second Division. . . . Then the question arose as to how she was going to be brought to the United States, because of an ironclad rule which had been issued against bringing animals back. The boys of Battery E decided that they had not fought in France for nothing, with the result that Mademoiselle Verdun, mysteriously missing for some days, blossomed forth at Quarantine on this side of the Atlantic, too late to be sent back to France. A relentless veterinary officer thrust Mademoiselle Verdun into quarantine but she was later freed and became monarch of the regiment at Camp Travis [Texas]." Baynes, quoting from the *Boston Herald* of November 22, 1920, in *Animal Heroes*, 124.

2. Old Bill

1. Ann Searight, email message to author, March 10, 2015; Spooner, *For Love of Horses*, 6.

2. Spooner, *For Love of Horses*, 6.

3. Chalcraft, *Striking Cabbies of Cairo*, 165.

4. Chalcraft, *Striking Cabbies of Cairo*, 165–66.

5. Mikhail, *Animal in Ottoman Egypt*, 179.

6. Spooner, *For Love of Horses*, 8.

7. S. Searight, *Oasis*, 12.

8. Tooley, *Life of Florence Nightingale*, 27–31; Chaney, "Egypt in England and America."

9. Spooner, *For Love of Horses*, 8.

10. Spooner, *For Love of Horses*, 9.

11. Spooner, *For Love of Horses*, 10.

12. Spooner, *For Love of Horses*, 10.

13. Brooke, *Horse Lovers*, 11.

14. Spooner, *For Love of Horses*, 11.

15. Mikhail, *Animal in Ottoman Egypt*, 15.

16. Specifically, Dorothy's ideas have been echoed in the work of such women as Sally Jewell Coxe, founder of the Bonobo Conservation Initiative in the Congo, and Lek Chailert, founder of Elephant Nature Park in Chiangmai Province, Thailand. See Lek Chailert: Save Elephant Foundation, http://www.saveelephant.org/; Sally Jewell Coxe: Bonobo Conservation Initiative, http://www.bonobo.org/. Richard Searight adds, "This level of management helps lift people up out of slavery. I remember Bangladeshi workers, bonded labor men, whose horses were dead within months, yet were still paying off purchases for them five animals back. A system that helps people as well as their animals live healthier, more productive lives goes far toward improving their families' welfare, because you go straight to the bottom of the pile, as it were. And when families are helped to thrive, along with their working animals, society benefits. Everybody wins." Richard Searight, email message to author, September 4, 2016.

17. List of veterinary school graduates, *Veterinary Journal and Annals of Comparative Pathology* 20–21 (August 1885): 103. Forbis, *Authentic Arabian Bloodstock*, 101. Though Judith Forbis describes Branch as a Scot, based on impressions from horse fancier Henry Babson, who met Branch in 1932, he was an Englishman whose crustiness of character was without recourse to any known Scottish heritage.

18. Forbis, "Brief History," 23.

19. Forbis, *Authentic Arabian Bloodstock*, 101.

20. Spooner, *For Love of Horses*, 36.

21. Forbis, *Authentic Arabian Bloodstock*, 106.

22. Mikhail, *Animal in Ottoman Egypt*, 164–66.

23. Forbis, *Authentic Arabian Bloodstock*, 103, 107.

24. Mikhail, *Animal in Ottoman Egypt*, 165.

25. Forbis, *Authentic Arabian Bloodstock*, 106.

26. Forbis, *Authentic Arabian Bloodstock*, 107.

27. Spooner, *For Love of Horses*, 12.

28. Spooner, *For Love of Horses*, 14.

29. Flaubert, *Flaubert in Egypt*, 66.

30. Wallach, *Understanding the Cultural Landscape*, 348.

31. Fahmy, "Health and Husbandry," 238–40.

32. Spooner, *For Love of Horses*, 15.

3. Old War Horse Fund

1. Forbis, "Brief History."

2. Spooner, *For Love of Horses*, 17.

3. Forbis, *Authentic Arabian Bloodstock*, 101.

4. Spooner, *For Love of Horses*, 18.

5. S. Searight, *Oasis*, 14.

6. Spooner, *For Love of Horses*, 19.

7. Spooner, *For Love of Horses*, 20.

8. S. Searight, *Oasis*, 16; Queen Mary likely made the donations out of her private purse, as there is no record of these gifts in the official books, according to a letter to the author from Pamela Clark, senior archivist at Windsor Castle, January 6, 2015.

9. Quoted in S. Searight, *Oasis*, 16.

10. *Evening News* (London), September 19, 1932, 2, and November 8, 1932, 3.

11. Spooner, *For Love of Horses*, 20.

12. Spooner, *For Love of Horses*, 20.

13. Jasper Goldberg, "Egyptian Cab Drivers Protest Colonial Animal Laws, 1906–1907," Global Non-Violent Action Database, December 12, 2009, https://nvdatabase .swarthmore.edu/content/egyptian-cab-drivers-protest-colonial-animal-laws-1906-1907 (accessed September 5, 2016).

14. Spooner, *For Love of Horses*, 23.

15. Spooner, *For Love of Horses*, 22.

16. S. Searight, *Oasis*, 15.

17. Spooner, *For Love of Horses*, 68.

18. S. Searight, *Oasis*, 19.

19. Spooner, *For Love of Horses*, 68.

20. Spooner, *For Love of Horses*, 25, 40.

21. Spooner, *For Love of Horses*, 37.

22. Spooner, *For Love of Horses*, 71.

23. Spooner, *For Love of Horses*, 28.

4. Black Friday

1. *Book of Poems for the Blue Cross Fund*, 74.

2. Spooner, *For Love of Horses*, 28.

3. Spooner, *For Love of Horses*, 29.

4. Spooner, *For Love of Horses*, 29.

5. Spooner, *For Love of Horses*, 29.

6. Bekoff, *Emotional Lives of Animals*, 25, 28.

7. Spooner, *For Love of Horses*, 29.

8. Spooner, *For Love of Horses*, 34.

9. Spooner, *For Love of Horses*, 25.

10. S. Searight, *Oasis*, 16.

11. Spooner, *For Love of Horses*, 30–31.

12. *Western Morning News and Daily Gazette* (Plymouth UK), March 10, 1932, 8, and May 25, 1931, 2.

13. *Western Daily Press and Bristol Mirror*, February 11, 1932, 4.

14. Ashorne Hill quote from "Ashorne Hill—One Thousand Years of History," Ashorne Hill, https://www.ashornehill.co.uk/about-us/history-of-ashorne-hill (accessed September 5, 2016).

15. Capt. J. A. Durham and Mrs. George Bryant, letter, *Royal Leamington Spa Courier* (UK), November 24, 1931.

16. Durham and Bryant, letter.

17. Bruce, *Last Crusade*, 1.

18. Gen. Sir George de Symons Barrow, letter, *Bucks Herald* (Buckingham UK), March 4, 1932, 3.

19. Barrow, letter.

20. Spooner, *For Love of Horses*, 32.

21. *Illustrated London News*, Silver Jubilee ed., 52, and plate 12, May 1935.

22. Chris Hastings, "Churchill's Mission to Rescue the War Horses and How He Made Officials Bring Tens of Thousands Home," *Daily Mail* (London), December 31, 2011.

5. An End and a Beginning

1. Forrest, *If Wishes Were Horses*, 12.

2. Spooner, *For Love of Horses*, 32.

3. Spooner, *For Love of Horses*, 32.

4. Spooner, *For Love of Horses*, 24.

5. Spooner, *For Love of Horses*, 40–41.

6. Spooner, *For Love of Horses*, 37.

7. Spooner, *For Love of Horses*, 16.

8. Spooner, *For Love of Horses*, 36.

9. Spooner, *For Love of Horses*, 40.

10. Spooner, *For Love of Horses*, 64.

11. Spooner, *For Love of Horses*, 41.

12. Spooner, *For Love of Horses*, 41.

13. Spooner, *For Love of Horses*, 44.

14. Spooner, *For Love of Horses*, 44.

15. Spooner, *For Love of Horses*, 45–46.

16. Spooner, *For Love of Horses*, 45–46.

6. Street of the English Lady

1. Spooner, *For Love of Horses*, 52.

2. Spooner, *For Love of Horses*, 49–50.

3. Spooner, *For Love of Horses*, 51.

4. Spooner, *For Love of Horses*, 52–53.

5. Reynard, *Friends of God*, 203.

6. Kane, "Politics, Discontent and the Everyday," 121.

7. Spooner, *For Love of Horses*, 54.

8. The district even today is filled with butchers, though on the former site of one of these abattoirs, west of the Brooke Hospital, sits 57357 Hospital, one of the biggest and most modern children's cancer hospitals in the world. See 57357 Children's Cancer Hospital Foundation, http://www.57357.com/ (accessed September 5, 2016). At the time of Dorothy's visit the street was nicknamed *Sharia Sikkat al-Mazbah*, or "road to the slaughterhouse."

9. Petra Sidhom, email message to author, June 6, 2015; Richard Searight, email message to author, September 4, 2016.

10. S. Searight, *Oasis*, 19. Even today, according to Brooke veterinarian Dr. Mohammed Abd-Elhay, people still call the Brooke Hospital *El Sitt El Engleasyya*, or "place of the English lady," now shortened to simply "English lady."

11. Royal Air Force Command, RAF fatalities 1935, http://www.rafcommands.com /forum/showthread.php?17884-RAF-fatalities-1935 (accessed January 5, 2017).

12. Spooner, *For Love of Horses*, 82.

13. Spooner, *For Love of Horses*, 57.

14. S. Searight, *Oasis*, 18–19; 1961 pamphlet for Brooke Hospital for Animals, Cairo.

15. Spooner, *For Love of Horses*, 62.

16. Spooner, *For Love of Horses*, 62–63.

17. Spooner, *For Love of Horses*, 63. I'm grateful to Mohammed Abd-Elhay for sharing with me the story about Dorothy confiscating the whips of men in Bairam al-Tunsi Street.

18. Sarah Mourad, "The Stigma of Being Mentally Ill in Egypt's Abassiya Hospital," *Cairo Post*, June 2, 2014, http://egyptianstreets.com/2014/06/02/the-stigma-of-being -mentally-ill-in-egypts-abassiya-hospital/ (accessed September 5, 2016).

19. Petra Sidhom, email message to author, June 6, 2015.

20. Sidhom to author, June 6, 2015.

21. Spooner, *For Love of Horses*, 67.

22. Spooner, *For Love of Horses*, 67.

7. Going Home

1. Spooner, *For Love of Horses*, 58.

2. S. Searight, *Oasis*, 19.

3. Mohammed Abd-Elhay, email message to author, June 17, 2015. The euthanasia advertisement, "Killing animals humanely," produced by the American Humane Education Society in 1895, has been recently reproduced in an ebook reissue of Marshall Saunders's *Beautiful Joe* (275) based on the rescue and adventures of a Canadian dog. See Saunders, *Beautiful Joe*.

4. Spooner, *For Love of Horses*, 59–61.

5. S. Searight, *Oasis*, 19.

6. Spooner, *For Love of Horses*, 71–72.

7. van Emden, *Tommy's Ark*, 302.

8. *Yorkshire Evening Post* (UK), June 1, 1934, 10.

9. Spooner, *For Love of Horses*, 79.

10. *Citizen* (Gloucester UK), August 25, 1935, 7.

11. Wolseley Russell, *Yorkshire Evening Post* (Leeds UK), June 18, 1934, 6.

12. Russell, *Yorkshire Evening Post*, June 18, 1934, 6.

13. *Citizen*, August 25, 1935, 7.

14. Spooner, *For Love of Horses*, 80.

15. Spooner, *For Love of Horses*, 82.

16. Spooner, *For Love of Horses*, 73.

17. Gen. Sir John Theodosius Burnett-Stuart bio, King's College London, Liddell Hart Military Archives, http://www.kingscollections.org/catalogues/lhcma/collection/b/bu50-001 (accessed January 5, 2017).

18. Spooner, *For Love of Horses*, 73.

19. Spooner, *For Love of Horses*, 74–75.

20. Spooner, *For Love of Horses*, 74–75.

21. Brendon, *Decline and Fall*, 330–32.

22. *Northern Daily Mail* (Hartlepool UK), July 19, 1933, 6.

23. Clark, *Our Journey*, 384; Spooner, *For Love of Horses*, 83. Thanks to Dr. Mohammed Abd-Elhay and Atef Gad of Cairo for translation assistance.

24. Spooner, *For Love of Horses*, 77.

25. Richard Searight, email message to author, September 4, 2016.

26. Spooner, *For Love of Horses*, 109.

27. Spooner, *For Love of Horses*, 94–95.

28. Spooner, *For Love of Horses*, 95.

29. Spooner, *For Love of Horses*, 96.

30. Quran 17:33.

31. Spooner, *For Love of Horses*, 96.

8. World War

1. Dr. Mohammed Abd-Elhay, "Autumn," published in *One Side Life*, Higher Council of Culture—first book project, Egyptian Ministry of Culture, issue 1, 2010.

2. Gandhi, quoted in von Tunzelmann, *Indian Summer*, 16.

3. S. Searight, *Oasis*, 44.

4. Spooner, *For Love of Horses*, 86.

5. Hodgkins is listed as a lieutenant colonel on retired pay in *The Half-Yearly Army List* (July–December 1940), 877, London, January 1941.

6. S. Searight, *Oasis*, 22–23.

7. Spooner, *For Love of Horses*, 87.

8. S. Searight, *Oasis*, 23, 26.

9. S. Searight, *Oasis*, 23; Richard Searight, email message to author, September 4, 2016.

10. Mohammed Abd-Elhay, email message to author, April 3, 2015.

11. Abd-Elhay to author, April 3, 2015.

12. Yasmine El-Rashidi, "Brigadier Hassan Sami: An Equine Psychology," *Al-Ahram Weekly On-line*, no. 648 (July 24–30, 2003), http://weekly.ahram.org.eg/Archive/2003/648/profile.htm (accessed September 5, 2016); Nesbit, *Singing to Donkeys*, 18–19.

13. S. Searight, *Oasis*, 27. Note: the Transjordanian Frontier Force was formed in 1926 to guard the boarder of the Emirate of Transjordan. It was disbanded in 1948.

14. S. Searight, *Oasis*, 27.

15. S. Searight, *Oasis*, 27.

16. A. Cooper, *Cairo in the War*, 195.

17. A. Cooper, *Cairo in the War*, 201.

18. S. Searight, *Oasis*, 26.

19. Spooner, *For Love of Horses*, 90.

20. Spooner, *For Love of Horses*, 87.

21. S. Searight, *Oasis*, 27.

22. J. Cooper, *Animals in War*, 66.

23. J. Cooper, *Animals in War*, 68–69.

24. J. Cooper, *Animals in War*, 135.

25. J. Cooper, *Animals in War*, 139.

26. S. Searight, *Oasis*, 25.

27. Spooner, *For Love of Horses*, 93.

28. Spooner, *For Love of Horses*, 92–93.

29. Spooner, *For Love of Horses*, 93.

30. Spooner, *For Love of Horses*, 88, 97.

31. S. Searight, *Oasis*, 28–29.

32. Taylor Smith, *Speaking of Palm Trees*, 49.

33. Taylor Smith, *Speaking of Palm Trees*, 23.

34. Taylor Smith, *Speaking of Palm Trees*, 23.

35. Taylor Smith, *Speaking of Palm Trees*, 24.

36. Taylor Smith, *Speaking of Palm Trees*, 136.

37. Spooner, *For Love of Horses*, 99.

9. Their Portion Is Gardens

1. Taylor Smith, *Speaking of Palm Trees*, 15–16.

2. Taylor Smith, *Speaking of Palm Trees*, 15–16.

3. Taylor Smith, *Speaking of Palm Trees*, 15–16.

4. A. Cooper, *Cairo in the War*, 336.

5. A. Cooper, *Cairo in the War*, 343.

6. S. Searight, *Oasis*, 29.

7. Sayed Mahmoud, "Egypt's First President Mohamed Naguib: Homeless Forever," *Ahram Online*, October 13, 2012, http://english.ahram.org.eg/NewsContent/9/0/55309 /Heritage/Egypts-first-president-Mohamed-Naguib-Homeless-for.aspx (accessed September 5, 2016).

8. S. Searight, *Oasis*, 28, 29–30.

9. Spooner, *For Love of Horses*, 90–91.

10. Spooner, *For Love of Horses*, 90–91.

11. Spooner, *For Love of Horses*, 100.

12. Spooner, *For Love of Horses*, 100.

13. Spooner, *For Love of Horses*, 101–2. Kathleen Taylor Smith also served as vice-chairman for SPANA.

14. S. Searight, *Oasis*, 29.

15. Spooner, *For Love of Horses*, 102.

16. Spooner, *For Love of Horses*, 107.

17. Spooner, *For Love of Horses*, 103.

18. Spooner, *For Love of Horses*, 104.

19. S. Searight, *Oasis*, 29.

20. Spooner, *For Love of Horses*, 104.

21. Spooner, *For Love of Horses*, 106.

22. Spooner, *For Love of Horses*, 106.

23. Quran, 2:25.

24. Spooner, *For Love of Horses*, 111.

25. Spooner, *For Love of Horses*, 111.

26. Sam Webb, "Caught in the Crossfire: Tragic Plight of Terrified Animals at Gaza Zoo Left to Fend for Themselves amid the Shelling," *Daily Mail*, August 17, 2014, http:// www.dailymail.co.uk/news/article-2727169/Caught-crossfire-Hundreds-animals-trapped -dilapidated-Gaza-zoo-weeks-Israeli-shelling.html (accessed September 5, 2016); Louise Hastie, email message to author, January 16, 2016. This zoo, known as Khan Younis Zoo, is finally being shut down as of autumn 2016 and the animals taken to sanctuary, thanks to the efforts of Four Paws. See Alex Wheeler, "Gaza: 'Worst Zoo in the World' Closes after Charity Rescues Last 15 Animals," *International Business Times*, August 24, 2016, http://www.ibtimes.co.uk/gaza-worst-zoo-world-closes-after-charity-rescues-last -15-animals-1577839 (accessed September 5, 2016).

27. Jillian Kay Melchoir, "Ukraine's Animal Victims," *National Review* (New York), April 17, 2014, http://www.nationalreview.com/article/375933/ukraines-animal-victims -jillian-kay-melchior (accessed September 5, 2016).

28. "IS Threat to Syria's Northern Bald Ibis near Palmyra," BBC News, May 25, 2015, http://www.bbc.com/news/world-middle-east-32872350 (accessed September 5, 2016).

29. S. Searight, *Oasis*, 31.

30. Spooner, *For Love of Horses*, 108.

31. Ann Searight, email message to author, May 8, 2015. Ann Searight served as Brooke Trustee from 1979 to 2011 and as honorary vice-president in 2014.

32. S. Searight, *Oasis*, 29.

33. S. Searight, *Oasis*, 34–35.

34. Mohammed Abd-Elhay, email message to author, May 23, 2015.

35. S. Searight, *Oasis*, 34–35.

36. S. Searight, *Oasis*, 35.

37. Petra Sidhom, email message to author, June 6, 2015.

38. El-Rashidi, "Brigadier Hassan Sami."

39. S. Searight, *Oasis*, 38.

40. Richard Searight, email message to author, September 4, 2016.

41. Nesbit, *Singing to Donkeys*, 30; Richard Searight, email message to author, September 4, 2016. In 1986 Searight produced a film titled *The Street of the English Lady*, dealing with the Brooke Hospital for Animals and its history. The *40 Minutes* BBC 2 documentary was not a Brooke venture, but Searight's film did influence the BBC to take on what became "Cairo Vets."

42. R. Searight to author, September 4, 2016.

43. "Cairo Vets," *40 Minutes*, BBC TV, February 9, 1989; Fady Lahib, "The Brooke Hospital . . . A Brilliant History in Treating Sick Animals," *Watani* (Cairo), December 15, 2011, http://en.wataninet.com/archive-articles/the-brooke-hospital-a-brilliant-history-in-treating-sick-animals/8786/ (accessed September 5, 2016).

44. Dr. Graham Munroe, email message to author, August 20, 2016. Dr. Munroe qualified from Bristol Veterinary School (1979) and then took his Royal College of Veterinary Surgeons' certificates in equine orthopedics and equine stud medicine. He was in charge of the equine surgical and reproduction referral service at the University of Glasgow veterinary school, by which he was awarded a PhD (1994) for his research into equine neonatal ophthalmology, in which he also was awarded the RCVS fellowship.

45. R. Searight to author, September 4, 2016.

46. Loretz, "Animal Victims," 221–22.

47. S. Searight, *Oasis*, 40–41. In 2001 U.S.-led air bombings of Taliban bases in Afghanistan led to a refugee crisis for both animals and humans. BBC News reported in December that the refugee camps in Peshawar and Quetta were filled with as many suffering horses and donkeys as people, starved and galled with untreated wounds. Had it not been for Brooke's mobile clinics in the region, these animals would not have received treatment, many would have died, and their owners would have had no way to keep their families alive. Education for owners and veterinary help for the animals resulted in a win-win solution. As Richard Searight told reporter Ceri Jackson, "This is one of the most important ways of helping the people who have become victims of this war." See Jackson, "Equine Aid Agency's War Effort," BBC News, December 28, 2001, http://news.bbc.co.uk/2/hi/south_asia/1731789.stm (accessed September 5, 2016).

48. Haroon Siddique, Paul Owen, and Adam Gabbatt, "Protests in Egypt and Unrest in Middle East—As It Happened," *Guardian* News Blog, January 25, 2011, http://www.theguardian.com/global/blog/2011/jan/25/middleeast-tunisia#block-32 (accessed September 5, 2016).

49. "Mubarak Supporters Strike Back," Al Jazeera, February 2, 2011, http://www.aljazeera.com/news/middleeast/2011/02/20112315345153370.html (accessed September 5, 2016).

50. Andrea Sachs and Mackenzie Schmidt, "Cairo's Cats Forgotten as Its Humans Rebel," *Time*, February 12, 2011, http://content.time.com/time/world/article/0,8599,2048792,00.html (accessed September 5, 2016).

51. Soueif, *Cairo*, 108.

52. Fran Jurga, "Brooke Hospital Continues to Treat Horses in Cairo; Charity Appalled at Use of Horses in Riots," Jurga Report: Horse Health Headlines, February 3, 2011, http://equusmagazine.com/blog/brooke-hospital-continues-to-treat-horses-in-cairo-charity-appalled-at-use-of-horses-in-riots (accessed September 5, 2016).

53. Mohammed Abd-Elhay, email message to author, May 23, 2015.

54. Rick Dewsbury, "Innocent Casualties of Egypt's Riots: Harrowing Images of the Horses Starving to Death as Tourists Stay Away," *Daily Mail*, November 28, 2011, http://www.dailymail.co.uk/news/article-1354928/Egypt-protests-Horses-starve-death-tourism-troubled-region-dwindles.html (accessed September 5, 2016); Dr. Ammr Mahmoud, email message to author, October 8, 2015.

55. Abd-Elhay to author, May 23, 2015.

56. Evans, "Shadow of Equus."

57. Mohammed Abd-Elhay, email message to author, May 24, 2015. One free veterinary service, Egypt Equine Aid, founded by Jill and Warren Barton in 2014, is working at the pyramids to alleviate the suffering of equines there and educate their owners in improved care. See the EEA website, http://www.egyptequineaid.org/about/.

58. Dr. Ammr Mahmoud, email message to author, October 8, 2015; Evans, "Shadow of Equus."

59. Mahmoud to author, October 8, 2015; Petra Sidhom, email message to author, June 6, 2015.

60. Sidhom to author, June 6, 2015.

61. Sidhom to author, June 6, 2015.

62. Sidhom to author, June 6, 2015. As of 2016, Article 45 has added to the language around protection of the environment and endangered animals a sentence, at the end, that the state commits to "prevention of cruelty to animals." See Egypt's Constitution of 2014, https://www.constituteproject.org/constitution/Egypt_2014.pdf (accessed September 9, 2016).

63. Julien Toyer, Yara Bayoumy, and Kevin Liffey, "Egypt's Sisi Says Parliamentary Election to Be Held before Year-End: *El Mundo*," Reuters Canada, April 29, 2015, http://ca.reuters.com/article/topNews/idCAKBN0NK1B720150429 (accessed September 5, 2016). As reported by Alessandra Masi of the *International Business Times*, low turnout even among eligible Egyptian expats and a $60 fine for all eligible voters who did not cast a ballot made the much-anticipated election something of a nonstarter where reforms were concerned. See Masi, "Egyptian Election 2015: Low Turnout and Voter Indifference Makes Victory for President El-Sisi Inevitable," *International Business Times*, October 29, 2015, http://www.ibtimes.com/egyptian-election-2015-low-turnout-voter-indifference-makes-victory-president-el-sisi-2161872 (accessed September 5, 2016).

64. Sidhom to author, June 6, 2015.

65. Karenga, *Maat, the Moral Ideal*, 74–75.

66. Spooner, *For Love of Horses*, 111.

Epilogue

1. *Book of Poems for the Blue Cross Fund*, 8.

BIBLIOGRAPHY

Badsey, Stephen. *Doctrine and Reform in the British Cavalry, 1880–1918*. Aldershot, Hampshire, UK: Ashgate, 2008.

Barker, A. J. *The Neglected War: Mesopotamia, 1914–1918*. London: Faber and Faber, 1967.

Baynes, Ernest Harold. *Animal Heroes of the Great War*. New York: Macmillan, 1925.

Bekoff, Marc. *The Emotional Lives of Animals*. Novato CA: New World Library, 2007.

Bletchly, Henry. "The Cabs and Cabmen of Calcutta." *Saddlery & Harness* 2 (April 1893).

A Book of Poems for the Blue Cross Fund (to Help Horses in War Time). Blue Cross Fund, Lady Smith-Dorrien, president. London: Jarrolds, 1917.

Brendon, Piers. *The Decline and Fall of the British Empire, 1781–1997*. New York: Vintage Press, 2007.

Brooke, Geoffrey Francis Heremon. *Horse Lovers: Addressed to Those Who Are Thrilled by the Deep Note of a Hound, and Rejoice in the Feel of a Good Horse beneath Them*. London: Constable, 1928.

———. *Horse-Sense and Horsemanship of Today: Economy and Method in Training Hunters and Polo Ponies*. London: Constable, 1924.

Bruce, Anthony. *The Last Crusade: The Palestine Campaign in the First World War*. London: John Murray, 2002.

Chalcraft, John. *The Striking Cabbies of Cairo and Other Stories: Crafts and Guilds in Egypt, 1863–1914*. Albany: SUNY Press, 2004.

Chaney, Edward. "Egypt in England and America: The Cultural Memorials of Religion, Royalty and Revolution." In *Sites of Exchange: European Crossroads and Faultlines*, edited by Maurizo Ascari and Adriana Corrado. Amsterdam: Rodopi, 2006.

Chevenix-Trench, Charles. *A History of Horsemanship: The Story of Man's Ways and Means of Riding Horses from Ancient Times to the Present*. New York: Doubleday, 1970.

Christie, Agatha. *Death on the Nile*. Book 17 in Hercule Poirot Mysteries. New York: William Morrow, 2011.

Clark, Francis E. *Our Journey around the World*. Hartford CT: A. D. Worthington, 1894.

Cooper, Artemis. *Cairo in the War, 1939–1945*. London: John Murray, 2013.

Cooper, Jilly. *Animals in War*. London: Corgi Books, 2000.

David, Rhys. *Tell Mum Not to Worry: A Welsh Soldier's World War One in the Near East*. Cardiff, UK: Deffro, 2014.

Evans, Margaret. "Shadow of Equus: A Time of Turmoil for Equines in Egypt." *Canadian Horse Journal*, June 2011, https://www.horsejournals.com/shadow-equus-time -turmoil-equines-egypt/ (accessed September 5, 2016).

Fahmy, Dr. Salah Wahib. "The Health and Husbandry of Donkeys Used by the Zabbalin Rubbish Collectors in Cairo, Egypt." In *Donkeys, People and Development: A Resource Book of the Animal Traction Network for Eastern and Southern Africa (ATNESA)*, edited by Denis Fielding and Paul Starkey, 238–40. Wageningen, Netherlands: Technical Centre for Agricultural and Rural Cooperation (CTA), 2004.

Flaubert, Gustave. *Flaubert in Egypt: A Sensibility Tour*. Translated by Francis Steegmuller. New York: Little, Brown, 1972.

Forbis, Judith. *Authentic Arabian Bloodstock: A Reference Guide, Historical Articles, and Racing Records*. Mena AR: Ansata, 1990.

———. "Brief History of the Egyptian Arabian Horse." *Horse Times*, January 2004.

Forrest, Susanna. *If Wishes Were Horses: A Memoir of Equine Obsession*. London: Atlantic Books, 2012.

Goodall, Daphne Machin. *Horses of the World: An Illustrated Survey, with over 320 Photographs of Breeds of Horses and Ponies*. London: Country Life Books, 1965.

Graham, Col. Henry. *History of the Sixteenth, the Queen's Light Dragoons (Lancers), 1912 to 1925*. Devizes, Wiltshire, UK: George Simpson, 1926.

Grandin, Temple, and Catherine Johnson. *Animals Make Us Human: Creating the Best Life for Animals*. Boston: Mariner Books, 2010.

Hadaway, Stuart. *Pyramids and Fleshpots: The Egyptian, Senussi and Eastern Mediterranean Campaigns, 1914–1916*. Stroud, Gloucestershire, UK: History Press, 2014.

Hart, Liddell. *"T. E. Lawrence": In Arabia and After*. London: Jonathan Cape, 1937.

Jarvis, Maj. C. S. *The Back-Garden of Allah*. London: Butler and Tanner, 1941.

Kane, Patrick M. "Politics, Discontent and the Everyday in Egyptian Arts, 1938–1966." PhD diss., State University of New York at Binghamton, 2007.

Karenga, Maulana. *Maat, the Moral Ideal in Ancient Egypt: A Study in Classical African Ethics*. New York: Routledge, 2004.

Kennedy, Michael. *The Life of Elgar*. New York: Cambridge University Press, 2004.

Kirk-Greene, Anthony. *Britain's Imperial Administrators, 1858–1966*. London: Macmillan, 2000.

Lao She. *Rickshaw Boy*. Translation of *Camel Xiangsi* by Shi Xiaoqing. Beijing: Foreign Languages Press, 1981.

Laurie, Martin. *Cupid's War: The True Story of a Horse That Went to War*. Cirencester, Gloucestershire, UK: Mereo, 2014.

Lawrence, T. E. *Revolt in the Desert*. New York: George Doran, 1927.

Loretz, John. "The Animal Victims of the Great War." *Physicians for Social Responsibility Quarterly* 1, no. 4 (December 1991): 221–25, http://fn2.freenet.edmonton.ab.ca/~puppydog/gulfwar.htm (accessed September 5, 2016).

Lunt, James D. *The Scarlet Lancers: The Story of the 16th/5th, the Queen's Royal Lancers, 1689–1992*. Barnsley, Yorkshire, UK: Pen and Sword, 1992.

Mallett, Ross. "The Interplay between Technology, Tactics and Organisation in the First AIF." MA thesis, Australian Defence Force Academy, 1999.

Masefield, John. *The Poems and Plays of John Masefield*. Vol. 1, *Poems*. New York: Macmillan, 1920.

Massey, W. T. *How Jerusalem Was Won: Being the Record of Allenby's Campaign in Palestine*. London: Constable, 1919.

Masson, Jeffrey Moussaieff. *Altruistic Armadillos, Zenlike Zebras: A Menagerie of 100 Favorite Animals*. New York: Ballantine Books, 2006.

McKenna, Stephen. *While I Remember*. New York: George Doran, 1921.

Mikhail, Alan. *The Animal in Ottoman Egypt*. Oxford: Oxford University Press, 2014.

Murland, Jerry. *Retreat and Rearguard-Somme 1918: The Fifth Army Retreat*. Havertown PA: Pen and Sword, 2014.

Nesbit, Lynne. *Singing to Donkeys: A Life Working for the Brooke Hospital for Animals*. Laxey, Isle of Man, UK: dpdotcom, 2015.

Nicolson, Juliet. *The Great Silence: Britain from the Shadow of the First World War to the Dawn of the Jazz Age*. New York: Grove Press, 2009.

Paget, George Charles Henry Victor, Marquess of Anglesey. *A History of British Cavalry*. Vol. 8, *1816–1919, The Western Front, 1915*. Barnsley, Yorkshire, UK: Pen and Sword, 1994.

Payne, Robert. *The History of Islam*. New York: Dorset Press, 1987.

Peters, Margot. *Unquiet Soul: A Biography of Charlotte Brontë*. London: Hodder and Stoughton, 1987.

Reynard, John. *Friends of God: Islamic Images of Piety, Commitment, and Servanthood*. Berkeley: University of California Press, 2006.

Richard, Susan. *Chosen by a Horse: How a Broken Horse Fixed a Broken Heart*. New York: Harcourt, 2006.

Rodenbeck, Max. *Cairo: The City Victorious*. New York: Alfred A. Knopf, 1999.

Saunders, Marshall. *Beautiful Joe*. Edited by Keridiana Chez. Peterborough ON: Broadview Press, 2015.

Searight, Sarah. *Oasis: 60 Years of the Brooke Hospital for Animals*. Wiltshire, UK: Westernprint, 1993.

Soueif, Ahdaf. *Cairo*. London: Bloomsbury, 2012.

Spooner, Glenda. *For Love of Horses: Diaries of Dorothy Brooke*. London: Brooke Hospital for Animals, 2014.

Steele, Zelma. *Angel in Top Hat*. New York: Harper and Brothers, 1942.

Summerhays, R. S. *Encyclopaedia for Horsemen*. London: Frederick Warne, 1959.

Taylor Smith, Kathleen. *Speaking of Palm Trees: Letters from Egypt, 1946–1947*. Norwich, UK: Greenridges Press, 2007.

Tooley, Sarah A. *The Life of Florence Nightingale*. London: Cassell, 1904.

van Emden, Richard. *Tommy's Ark: Soldiers and Their Animals in the Great War*. London: Bloomsbury, 2010.

von Tunzelmann, Alex. *Indian Summer: The Secret History of the End of an Empire*. Toronto: McClelland & Stewart, 2007.

Wallach, Brett. *Understanding the Cultural Landscape*. New York: Guilford Press, 2005.

Woodward, David R. *Hell in the Holy Land: World War I in the Middle East*. Lexington: University Press of Kentucky, 2006.

INDEX

Grant Hayter-Menzies is the author of several books, including *From Stray Dog to World War I Hero: The Paris Terrier Who Joined the First Division* and *Shadow Woman: The Extraordinary Career of Pauline Benton*. He lives in Vancouver.

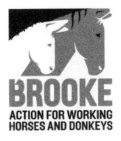

To find out more about Brooke | Action for Working Horses and Donkeys, please visit www.thebrooke.org